Good and Mad

Good and Mad

Mainline Protestant Churchwomen,
1920–1980

MARGARET BENDROTH

OXFORD
UNIVERSITY PRESS

OXFORD
UNIVERSITY PRESS

Oxford University Press is a department of the University of Oxford. It furthers
the University's objective of excellence in research, scholarship, and education
by publishing worldwide. Oxford is a registered trade mark of Oxford University
Press in the UK and certain other countries.

Published in the United States of America by Oxford University Press
198 Madison Avenue, New York, NY 10016, United States of America.

© Oxford University Press 2023

First issued as an Oxford University Press paperback, 2025

Library of Congress Cataloging-in-Publication Data
Names: Bendroth, Margaret, 1954– author.
Title: Good and mad : mainline protestant churchwomen, 1920–1980 /
Margaret Bendroth.
Description: New York, NY, United States of America :
Oxford University Press, [2023] |
Includes bibliographical references and index.
Identifiers: LCCN 2022027381 (print) | LCCN 2022027382 (ebook) |
ISBN 9780197654064 (hardback) | ISBN 9780197819753 (paperback) |
ISBN 9780197654088 (epub) | ISBN 9780197654095
Subjects: LCSH: Protestant women—History—20th century.
Classification: LCC BX4817 .B43 2023 (print) | LCC BX4817 (ebook) |
DDC 280/.4082—dc23/eng/20220815
LC record available at https://lccn.loc.gov/2022027381
LC ebook record available at https://lccn.loc.gov/2022027382

DOI: 10.1093/oso/9780197654064.001.0001

Paperback printed by Marquis Book Printing, Canada

For Éva

Contents

Acknowledgments

This book would not have been possible without a Project Grant from the Louisville Institute, which provided both financial support and generous encouragement. I am also indebted to the board and staff at the Congregational Library and Archives, who so often and so kindly gave me the time and space needed to research, write, and think about a whole other set of issues besides the ones on my desk. The Center for Global Christianity and Mission at Boston University also provided key assistance at a critical time, in the form of supportive colleagues and—so important to a nonaffiliated scholar—library privileges. Many, many thanks to Dana Robert and Daryl Ireland for their kind and thoughtful help.

I am also grateful to many friends and colleagues, including fellow Louisville Institute grantees, who listened to presentations and papers and simply let me talk about this project when I needed to. At the top of the list is David Hollinger, who provided both the initial inspiration for this project and a thoughtful and extremely helpful read of the manuscript, not to mention a much-needed arena for conversation, bringing together a stellar gathering of scholars for a workshop in mainline Protestantism in 2017. I am also grateful to my colleagues in the Boston Area Historians of Religion—Jon Roberts, Chris Beneke, Patricia Appelbaum, Maura Connolly, Chris Evans, and Cliff Putney. The Newberry Seminar on Culture and Religion in the Americas also provided a key opportunity to present a chapter draft. Many thanks also to Elizabeth Hambrick-Stowe and Davida Crabtree, who sent me personal files and told me some wonderful stories. As always, I am grateful to the archivists at the repositories I visited, especially Anne-Emmanuelle Tankam-Tene at the World Council of Churches in Geneva, who was consistently patient with all of my long-distance logistics.

And as always I depended on the good graces of my family, who learned long ago not to take a black mood too seriously, and to believe that despite everything I said, I would finish this book and perhaps even write another.

Fairly late into this project, I realized that it was as much an artistic challenge as a typical academic one. The stereotypical churchwoman, sporting a pillbox hat and big corsage and smiling gamely from the pages of her denominational magazine, had become interesting to me, but there was little reason to expect others to feel the same. How do you tell a compelling human story when most of the emotional valence is buried out of sight? I am grateful to Lauren Winner and my fellow attendees of the Kenyon Writers' Workshop for pushing me to transgress some academic conventions and discover the book I wanted to write.

I had two important people in mind while writing this book. The first is Ginny Brereton, who until her untimely death in 2004 was my best friend and closest colleague. She already knew much of what I discovered in researching this book, and even after all these years I deeply miss the opportunities I once took for granted, having a friend who could tell me what was of value in the roughest of rough drafts and then help me laugh it off over beer and Indian food. The other is a woman who is still in process, my sparkling granddaughter, Éva Sárosi, to whom I dedicate this book. She is a small miracle, so full of joy to be alive, and every day my hope for the future.

Abbreviations

ABHS   American Baptist Historical Society
CLA   Congregational Library and Archives
GETS   Garrett-Evangelical Theological School Archives
PHS   Presbyterian Historical Society
UMCA   United Methodist General Commission on Archives and History
WCC Archives   World Council of Churches Archives

Introduction

A Woman-Centered History of Mainline Protestantism

This is a story about women and mainline Protestantism, and like so many accounts of gender and religion, it is complicated. The main characters are socially progressive "churchwomen"—a word with all kinds of connotations today but very modern-sounding a century ago, and in fact a direct rebuke to the evangelical pieties of a previous generation. Predominantly white but also African American, coastal urbanites as well as salt-of-the-earth Southerners and Midwesterners, these thoughtful, educated laywomen campaigned for human rights and global peace, worked for interracial cooperation, and opened the path to ordination rights. They created a culture of good works that emboldened some of the most famous women of the twentieth and the twenty-first centuries, from Eleanor Roosevelt and Pauli Murray to that loyal Methodist churchwoman Hillary Clinton. And they chose to do so through Protestant churches that denied them equality.

For most of the twentieth century, women were barred from all official positions, even in the most liberal Protestant denominations. By law, custom, or a combination of both, they could not be ministers, elders, or deacons. Only a selected few were appointed to public roles on national boards and committees, and then mostly in stereotypically female areas like missionary work or religious education. What leadership churchwomen managed to achieve was in separate female-only organizations, but even those required constant vigilance against bureaucratic poaching. When changes finally came, they were late in the twentieth century, as barriers against women's ordination finally began to fall in the 1970s and 1980s, this after nearly two thousand years of prohibition and denial.

So what do we make of these progressive, subordinated churchwomen? Certainly they contradict what we would like to believe about gender equality in the twentieth century.[1] Though progress has been uneven and slow, women now possess important freedoms: they are no longer shunted into low-wage jobs advertised for "women only," prevented from voting, or

Good and Mad. Margaret Bendroth, Oxford University Press. © Oxford University Press 2023.
DOI: 10.1093/oso/9780197654064.003.0001

barred from higher education and professional schools. Though economic equality remains elusive and women are still vulnerable to violence and abuse, not to mention the frustrations of everyday sexism, opportunities have opened dramatically over the past century. The change in women's lives, as one historian writes, has been "so deep, so wide-ranging, so transformative" that we now have the privilege of taking it for granted.[2]

Protestant churchwomen were not, by their own insistence, feminists, or even proto-feminists. Their path was convoluted and uncertain, and far more episodic than that of their Jewish and secular peers, those rebellious women who founded and led the liberation movements of the 1960s.[3] Our subjects were highly accomplished, driven people, leaders like Mossie Wyker, Mildred McAfee Horton, Cynthia Wedel, and Georgia Harkness, who consulted with American presidents, achieved top posts in prestigious organizations like the National Council of Churches and in the world of academic theology. But they were not pioneers—they would not have taken that label, nor would the younger women coming of age in the 1960s and 1970s have granted it to them. While the outside world was getting used to "Ms.," Protestant church-women openly preferred to go by their husbands' first and last names, and recoiled at the idea of God as a "She" instead of a "He." (A *New York Times* obituary for "Mrs. Fred Bennett, A Church Worker," who died in 1950, did not even include her first name.[4]) Perhaps not surprisingly, a rising generation of Protestant feminists did not invoke them as predecessors, seeing themselves instead as a brand new force, a long-awaited challenge to thousands of years of male-dominated religion. In the wake of 1960s activism, with its distrust of institutions and assertive demands for change, the previous generation's faith in harmony, balance, and cooperation looked like compromise, a denial of women's right to be full-fledged individuals.

Yet their stories are important. They certainly contradict the assumption that "nothing happened" between 1920 and 1970, that American women slid into moral passivity once universal suffrage became law. These were in fact busy years, raising up remarkable figures like Frances Perkins and Eleanor Roosevelt, leaders like Fannie Lou Hamer and Rosa Parks, who were central to the cause of civil rights. And religion still mattered as well. Our Protestant churchwomen were deeply loyal to churches and denominations, and believed that Christian unity was essential to the social good. They remind us how easy it is for scholars to privilege secular narratives, to assume that, with the exception of civil rights, faith no longer motivated women's social activism. In doing so, however, we erase important achievements, even entire careers—thus, Thelma Stevens, who was a fervent Methodist and tireless leader of the denomination's Women's Division of Christian Service, ended up identified as a "social worker" in her brief 1990 obituary in the *New York Times*.[5]

The Female Majority

Complicated women are hard to place in history, and perhaps especially so when it comes to religion. We like stories of rebellious feminists contesting the status quo, insisting on the right to preach and challenging religious bigotry. And who doesn't enjoy a sensational outlier like Aimee Semple McPherson, Katherine Kuhlman, or Madalyn Murray O'Hair? These are all important, clearly, and the more the better. In the meantime, however, men are still carrying the main narrative, leading social reforms, writing and teaching theology, and directing denominational bureaucracies. The challenge is still out there, issued by historian Ann Braude years ago, to begin our stories about religion in the United States with the fact that the majority of believers are female. "We cannot expect to understand the history of religion in America," Braude said in 1997, "until we know at least as much about the women who have formed the majority of participants as we do about the male minority who have stood in the pulpit."[6]

There are plenty of good reasons for answering Braude's challenge. A woman-centered history does far more than complete what we already know about modern religion, as if the old "add women and stir" technique ever worked in the first place. It does more than simply complicate stock narratives and stale categories. Beginning rather than ending with women gives us a deeper, richer account of mainline Protestant religious life, beyond the world of denominational headquarters and seminary classrooms. Even more important, it helps us see, often in sharp relief, both the resilience of modern faith and the depth of its insecurities.

In particular, a woman-centered history helps us understand the churches that dominated so much of American cultural and religious life for, in the twentieth century, the so-called Protestant mainline.[7] A hundred years ago, they appeared to be comfortably elite, led by men who hobnobbed with diplomats and politicians, governed universities, and ran wealthy foundations. Today, after decades of disastrous decline, steady losses of money and membership, even the word itself, "mainline," seems painfully ironic. At the very least it is obtuse, presuming the centrality of white, Protestant churches and ignoring the fact of American racial and ethnic diversity.[8] Critics may well ask whether these mostly white, mostly northern denominations—Methodists, Presbyterians, Baptists, Congregationalists, Episcopalians, Lutherans, and Disciples of Christ—even deserve what scholarly attention they are beginning to receive. Moreover, some suggest that the mainline churches deserved their present-day decline, sitting at ease in Zion while scrappier, more evangelical sorts eked out hard-won success.

What would mainline Protestantism look like, if women were at the center? Many readers will recognize in this book some familiar landmarks: the struggle and decline of the foreign missionary enterprise, financial tightening during war and economic depression, theological innovation and drift, and the drive for Christian unity that culminated in the 1948 formation of the World Council of Churches. But the overall picture is one of resilience among lay Protestantism, more than the failures and successes of denominational leaders. Laywomen were persistently optimistic about the church's ability to change the world, and genuinely excited about the ecumenical movement and its momentous promise of global Christian unity. Removed as they were from decision-making power, they were able to take certain ecumenical risks, even crossing racial lines, aided in many cases by the hard-won wisdom of white Southerners. As this book demonstrates, a woman-centered mainline Protestantism was more interracial, less Northern, more international, and more resilient than all the analyses of decline and failure would lead us to think.

Under the lens of gender, the mainline churches also look less liberal. In fact, despite the present-day role of mainline denominations in progressive causes, they were never really equipped for life at the cultural cutting edge. They were essentially moderating institutions, many of them centuries old and deeply rooted in local communities. Even today, many Protestant congregations are still community centers, hosting Red Cross blood drives, town meetings, and until recently, the Boy Scouts.[9] The leftward turn of the 1970s, when mainline denominations took stands against the Vietnam War and attempted to embrace the counterculture, should not obscure another, perhaps even more difficult historical feat, negotiating the eternally shifting and increasingly elusive cultural middle ground of the United States.[10]

Behind it all was the threat of a female majority. Despite their cultural visibility and prestige, the mainline churches were aware of their vulnerabilities, the constant threat of irrelevance. Already in the 1930s and 1940s those churches found themselves shouting to be heard, talked over by experts in New Deal economics or Cold War foreign policy, sidelined by Freudian psychologists and secular sociologists. The true cost of that slippage would not become evident for many years, not until the 1980s and 1990s, when surging evangelicals pushed their older white Protestant cousins out of the cultural limelight. Yet certainly, early on, the churches that proudly called themselves the "mainline" knew they had weaknesses, and that certain topics had to be avoided at all costs.

They understood that the women could ruin everything.

The Twentieth-Century "Woman Problem"

By the early twentieth century, American Protestants were thoroughly, painfully familiar with the so-called woman problem. For a hundred years or more they had debated the rights of females to teach, to pray in mixed assemblies, to preach and to be ordained. Learned articles on Eve, Saint Paul, and Jesus provided regular fodder for scores of denominational magazines, no one seeming to notice that the combatants were plodding through the same old arguments, occasionally triumphing over a miniscule revision of a Greek verb or Hebrew syntax. This biblical back-and-forth operated as a kind of cultural white noise, rarely evoking indignation or surprise. Unlike the parallel debates about the Bible and slavery, the woman question did not demand a costly economic solution, much less a war; it did not erode faith in the Bible, at least at the time. It could simply persist.[11]

True, the Protestant churches periodically worried about the moral implications of women's right to vote, and endured a stream of public denunciations by spiritual iconoclasts like Victoria Woodhull and Elizabeth Cady Stanton. But in the late nineteenth century, they believed they had found a solution, one that would both silence secular critics and soothe worried conservatives. In the years after the Civil War, missionary societies run and funded by women formed in just about every Protestant denomination, white and African American, native born and immigrant, northern and southern. A source of enormous feminine pride, this effort proved tremendously effective, resulting in a network of orphanages and hospitals, as well as schools and colleges for women around the world and across the United States. "Woman's work for woman," as it was called, also galvanized American laywomen into a vast fundraising enterprise, raising millions of dollars to train, send, and support hundreds of female missionaries. Far from a threat, this demonstrated ability to generate enthusiasm—and money—for a task dear to nineteenth-century American Protestants proved immensely gratifying to all. For a time at least missionary work was the ideal solution for everyone concerned, fulfilling feminine desires for "usefulness" while also shoring up the bottom line of denominational budgets.[12]

As the nineteenth century came to a close, the "woman question" even seemed to be winding toward a consensus. By then the churches were generally reconciled to woman suffrage, if not enthusiastically in support. Prodded by the urgent promises of the Woman's Christian Temperance Union, the vast majority of Protestants recognized that there was little downside to sending the nation's most pious, teetotaling citizens to the ballot box. A few braver souls even recognized that the ideal Victorian Christian woman—kind, tactful, and morally upstanding—was better suited for the ministry than the average American male. "But if the purest should be called to the purest ministries," temperance reformer Frances Willard wrote in 1888, "then women, by men's own showing outrank them in actual fitness for the pulpit." The obvious fact of women's "holiness and wholesomeness of life, her clean hands and pure heart, specially authorize[d] her to be a minister of God."[13]

But the problem did not go away. In fact, as we will see, by 1920 the religious boundaries of "women's role" had become more problematic than ever. For one thing, the missionary societies that had once offered such a balanced, positive solution to feminine discontent had become alarmingly successful. The perceived threat went beyond the women's tendency to channel money into their own projects instead of boosting denominational budgets. The problem was one of perception: all that well-funded women's work was an ungainly weight, upsetting the equilibrium of denominational bureaucracies, racing to follow the models of order and efficiency set by the business world. In this sense, beyond the old-fashioned ideas about "woman's mission" and female virtue, women's missionary organizations were not truly modern.

The Feminization Dilemma

The offense to symmetry was not just the fetish of a few overzealous bureaucrats. The twentieth century brought back, with new force, the specter of feminization, that old, underlying anxiety about all those women in the church pews. Even sentimental Victorians had understood that too many females gave the outside world the wrong impression, tagging religion as an inconsequential pastime for ladies and children, not suited to red-blooded men. For a time, red-blooded Bull Moose rhetoric seemed the answer: perhaps men could be browbeaten into believing that Christianity was an essentially manly cause. In the World War I era and beyond the message went out from all quarters, from evangelists and fighting fundamentalists like Billy Sunday to liberal apostles of ecumenism like Bruce Barton. All of them insisted that Jesus was the paragon of whatever virtue they were promoting, doctrinal purity, moral fortitude, or business acumen. For their part, women learned to curb their restlessness, to avoid creating the impression that men were no longer needed. But the gender proportion in the church pews barely budged, and indeed, the problem threatened to become worse, as the twentieth century gave men even more reasons to find fulfillment in secular pursuits.

Should the mainline churches have worried about feminization? The question is worth asking, if only for the sake of clarification. As Ann Braude has pointed out, scholars have tended to use the term pejoratively, "to describe something like a contagious disease," when in fact the historic gender gap was never that dire. "Feminization" is a "misnomer," says Braude, expressing "a nostalgia for a religious landscape that never existed," a mythical time when there were equal numbers of men and women in the pews.[14] The demographic evidence is open to interpretation, mostly impressionistic until early in the twentieth century. Beginning in 1906 and continuing until 1936, the US Census Department provided extensive information on religion, including the relative numbers of male and female members. With some variation among denominations, the Protestant churches showed clear, though not overwhelming, female majorities, mostly in the neighborhood of 60 percent. Of course, census figures do not necessarily correspond to actual church attendance on any given Sunday, which anecdotally has been anywhere up to 90 percent female. Nor, of course, did those percentages reflect the strength of public perception.[15] Without a doubt the term is analytically fuzzy. "Even where there is evidence for some aspect of it," writes Sarah Imhoff, discussing the ongoing debate about Jewish synagogues, "feminization proves an unhelpful category of analysis because the concept is [so] ambiguous and shifting," ultimately, Imhoff argues, a "myth."[16]

But we cannot ignore it, especially as the idea has shaped so many perceptions of liberal religion. Ann Douglas was one of the first to introduce the idea to historians with her 1977 book *The Feminization of American Culture*, which described an alliance of convenience between liberal clergy and women writers in the Victorian era. Douglas argued that the flowery, empathetic sermonizing that replaced the solid certainties of Calvinism was nothing less than "sentimental sabotage," eroding religion's moral traction and ultimately benefiting an aggressive, amoral capitalism.[17] Some historians were skeptical of what seemed a sweeping and imprecise set of categorizations, but the central trope, the idea that liberal religion was intrinsically irrelevant and feckless, has been hard to eradicate.[18]

Feminization, put simply, assumes that femininity is a problem. The blaming is at times specific, naming women's participation as a key index, and perhaps a root cause, of religious decline. "[T]he keys to understanding secularisation in Britain," as sociologist Callum Brown has argued, "are the simultaneous de-pietisation of femininity and the de-feminisation of piety from the 1960s."[19] More mawkishly, religious conservatives have kept alive the old fundamentalist accusation that giving women too much scope— allowing them into the priesthood for example—will simply ruin the faith for everyone else. Masculine religion requires struggle, says conservative Catholic writer Rod Dreher, following a line of argument that muscular Christians carved out more than a century ago. "The current "trivialization of Christianity," Dreher warns, makes it "especially unappealing to men who want to spend their lives not on verbal games and pleasant rituals, but on the serious matters that can yield an insight into the meaning of existence."[20]

Yet even with all of the imprecision and moralizing, feminization, both real and imagined, is an essential tool for understanding mainline Protestant religion. It has operated as an invisible force that shaped everything from local church life to national decision-making, creating a reluctance among women to press for leadership, and empowering an outnumbered male hierarchy. Fears of feminization endowed a masculine minority with a symbolic role on behalf of all men, and cemented a perception of the church as essentially male, and relegated women to a permanent auxiliary role.

Good and Mad

In many ways, this is a story about limitations, perhaps even more than achievements. It revolves around people who did not pursue the spotlight, ladies who were comfortable in white gloves and pillbox hats, all too easily dismissed as uninteresting, even conformist. Those individual experiences demonstrate the complex calculus of "subordinated insiders," the "united but slighted" churchwomen described by Virginia Brereton.[21]

Character development matters, in other words—which is why this book includes four brief portraits of individual women, interspersed between the narrative chapters. By most outward indications, Helen Barrett Montgomery, Anna Canada Swain, Georgia Harkness, and Cynthia Wedel were powerful figures: the first two served as presidents of the American Baptist Churches, Harkness was a professor of theology, and Wedel the first woman elected a president in the National Council of Churches. But, as is so often the case for professional women, the road to success was messy and complicated, far from the single-track career building that measures masculine achievement. Much of this book therefore is an explanation of absence, the reasons why churchwomen have been so invisible, why it took mainline churches so long to embrace equality.

The fact is that wielding power in a feminized church was always difficult, especially in a white, middle-class Protestant culture that demanded attention to boundaries. Though a legion of scholars had long since set St. Paul in his historical place and the white noise thinned to a low hum, the mainline churches persisted in their prohibitions on female clergy, even to the point of embarrassment. Certainly mainliners knew that a secular world was watching, judging, and turning away. Instead of biblical back-and-forth they had to face an urgent practical concern, keeping the churches in step with the modern world's ethic of equality, yet not alienating the men they needed so badly.

Which leads to the final puzzle. Somewhere in the mix of uncertainty and ambivalence, churchwomen faced the possibility of anger. All women do, of course, and in the past decade especially, the rage has become public, even global, with the rise of the #Metoo movement, and mass protests from Washington, DC, to Mumbai to Saudi Arabia. Books and documentaries and movies have explored and explained what makes feminine anger so unique and so powerful, so potent a weapon against oppression.

We have only begun to understand, however, how this anger refracts through religious faith. What happens to women who carry special commitments to religious communities, to beliefs and practices that provide meaning and a sense of place? The women in this book had every reason to rebel, to throw crockery, tear the drapes, and upend the furniture. Though they held a degree of power they also knew the cost of their decisions; they were aware of hard bargains made with institutions that denied them equality.

They were, in fact, like countless other women across time and space who have lived with dual commitments and contradictory ideals, maintaining loyalties to institutions that have not responded in kind. They are, in other words, people who are terribly, delightfully worth knowing, whose lives may instruct, warn, and inspire our own.

1

And Yet

Christian Womanhood after Suffrage

"Is there such a thing as a woman?" Zephine Humphrey was asking an honest question. Well-educated, and moderately successful as a romance novelist, she was likely regretting the assignment she'd taken on, reviewing a book for *The Woman Citizen*, a progressive journal championing the recent passage of the Nineteenth Amendment. In retrospect, the name of the book, *Woman's Dilemma*, not to mention its author, should have given her pause. Alice Beal Parsons was a radical feminist with known communist sympathies, fiercely intelligent and impatient with sentimental nuance. Zephine Humphrey was an Episcopalian churchgoer and a writer with a popular following.

We can imagine her wonder and frustration in the spring of 1926, as she waded through argument after argument proving the equality of the sexes in every possible way, as Humphrey noted, in "endurance, variability, mental and physical efficiency, ingenuity, intelligence, [and] coordination"—all the traits "required by our modern life."[1]

The case for equality had found its moment. Scant years after the passage of the suffrage amendment, the scientific evidence was looking incontrovertible, proving, as Parsons wrote, that "woman is not handicapped except by tradition and habit." Her nature was all but "interchangeable with that of man." All of the old canards, that women's brains were smaller than men's, their lungs and hearts underdeveloped, were shown to be directly false by actual measurements to body proportions. Parsons even took on the ancient belief that menstruating women were more prone to violence, dismissing it with reams of scientific evidence—experiments requiring female subjects to hold a brass rod motionless within a hole (to detect "nervousness"), to name colors and opposites, and, for less than obvious reasons, to tap a metal plate with a rod 400 times in a row every day for four months. All the worries about women's bodies were folklore and

Good and Mad. Margaret Bendroth, Oxford University Press. © Oxford University Press 2023.
DOI: 10.1093/oso/9780197654064.003.0002

bunk, Parsons said, the kind "eagerly seized upon by girl students as an excuse for playing hookey."[2]

She certainly had a ready audience. Another book reviewer, writing in the *American Journal of Sociology*, expressed his relief that the literature on feminism was finally "passing out of the stage of emotional propaganda." "He who would write on the place and function of woman in the modern world," this academic expert intoned, "must take account of the very respectable body of scientific investigation being amassed" by a small army of trained investigators, both male and female.[3]

"And yet, and yet." All that evidence for equality made Mrs. Humphrey uncomfortable. Puzzling through page after inexorable page, she began to worry, as she said, "if Mrs. Parsons was going to leave to woman any peculiarly feminine attributes at all, save the physical function of bearing children." Were men and women truly interchangeable? The possibility left Zephine Humphrey, herself a modern woman, strangely deflated. Despite all the evidence to the contrary, she still wondered: "there is such a thing as a woman, isn't there?"[4]

That empty space is at the center of this book, and the focus of this opening chapter. Religion—in our case two centuries of Christian theologizing and institution building—had always answered questions like Mrs. Humphrey's, defined what it meant to be a man or a woman. Twentieth-century Americans were just a few years beyond an era that had defined the feminine sphere with absolute confidence, certain that domesticity was nothing short of God's eternal will. The Victorian ancestors had assumed, with all their hearts, that religion was women's business. "There seems to me," wrote Congregational theologian Horace Bushnell, "something sacred, or angelic" embedded in their very nature. "The morally grandest sight we see in this world is a real and ideally true woman."[5] The public confirmation of that belief was the evangelical "benevolent empire" of the early nineteenth century, a busy network of organizations run by women, for other women, everything from sewing societies to missionary fundraising to abolitionist rabble-rousing.

In the twentieth century, however, the old confidence eroded almost to the point of extinction. By the 1920s, paeans to "sainted womanhood" sounded antique, even a bit silly, the quaint obsessions of grandmothers in crinolines. "Am I the Christian gentlewoman my mother slaved to make me?" as one aspiring Bohemian writer asked, then answering her own question emphatically: "No indeed."[6] Now American society contemplated grand, rebellious examples like Isadora Duncan and Zora Neale Hurston, Crystal Eastman and Charlotte Perkins Gilman. They saw flappers in short skirts and short hair, languid starlets on movie screens—even the neighbor's daughter going off to college with boyfriend in tow and cigarette in hand. What did the moral passions of doughty temperance reformers even mean in such a world? Take, for example, Pauline Sabin, the leader of the movement to repeal the Prohibition amendment. Sitting in a Congressional hearing in 1928, listening to an official of the Women's Christian Temperance Union testify that she represented "the women of America," Sabin thought to herself "here's one woman you don't represent." Described by the au courant *Smart Set* as "slim, dynamic, yet utterly feminine," she was the quintessential counterpart to the solidly unfashionable generation who insisted that Americans would be better off drinking cold water instead of alcohol.[7]

Or take Zephine Humphrey herself: She was a professional writer, specializing in Christian romance novels. (Even in Alice Beal Parsons's world the genre remained durably popular.) Perhaps it was the dependable plot line, the wayward young suitors always brought to faith by the love of virtuous females. Though Humphrey's heroes and heroines were High Church Episcopalians, not known for erotic abandon, their love lives were still fraught with religious tension (a friend once entreated her to "write a whole book in which you didn't once mention God").[8]

Yet Mrs. Humphrey did not force her characters toward the standard outcome of her genre, spiritual union and true love. Their road was rockier, less certain, and strewn with modern temptations. Many chapters into *The Sword of the Spirit* (1920), the heroine is still stymied in her attempts to save Herbert, her crass alcoholic husband, a man who even after the untimely death of their only child remains boorishly impervious to her prayers and entreaties. In a standard Victorian novel, the saintly Isabel would have eventually prevailed, her sanctified womanhood impossible for any man to resist. But in Humphrey's twentieth-century plot, Isabel must first become a sinner, a fallen state she achieves in an unguarded moment with a handsome young curate. Only then is her husband drawn to faith. "You aren't a saint, then, are you?" he asks her, and then declares with joy, "You're just a human woman." In the end the oafish Herbert is almost effusive. "Perhaps—it sounds incredible, but everything is incredible today—perhaps, now that I've found saints and priests can get into scrapes, the whole business will seem more human to me, less priggish and impossible."[9]

Romance novels are not necessarily harbingers of secularization, but they are part of that complex, nonlinear, multileveled, discontinuous process, long debated by scholars of religion.[10] So much of what is written about religion in the modern world, what most of us imagine about the decline of belief, applies only tangentially to women. In fact, scholars have typically tracked the "spiritual crisis" of the Western world in social spaces that women rarely inhabited: seminary classrooms and university lecture halls, laboratories and debating stages, battlefields and voting booths. "Male absence," as Ann Braude has observed, has been the benchmark of secularization, not the ongoing reality of "female presence." Moreover, as feminist critics have pointed out, modernity itself has been defined and theorized around masculine norms, typified by the rebellious freedom of the turn-of-the-century male *flaneur*, and his pursuit of personal autonomy—freedoms would have marked women as sexually transgressive, even unhinged. Certainly the social and economic changes of the fin de siècle and the burgeoning twentieth century affected women, and no doubt influenced their beliefs about God and biblical truth; men did not have a corner on cultural awareness. But those standard narratives tell us little of women's experience of modernity, where it was both more costly and complicated. They do not explain what it meant for American women, for so long the rock solid foundation of religious belief, to begin to question God.[11]

Protestantism's gatekeepers had good reason to worry. Behind all the jokes about axe-wielding temperance crusaders and prudish missionaries was the unsettling possibility that the dependable bedrock of Protestant morality was developing seismic cracks. Not surprisingly, that reliable bellwether of mainstream Protestant opinion, the *Christian Century*, was worrying openly: "Can women be counted upon?" "It has always been carelessly assumed that the church give no attention to women," the editors fretted, "that it would hold them as a matter of course." But modern wives and daughters no longer believed "because they happen to be women. They pause and question here as in all things else."[12] And if women no longer believed, then men were in peril—as was the church itself.

The eroding double standard was as much a spiritual problem as a moral, sexual one. Turn-of-the-century doubt had been a white masculine prerogative, the métier of scientists and philosophers, theologians and poets. It had to be: Irreligion was thought to require a certain type of intellectual fortitude, an unflinching commitment to reason supposedly beyond the normal woman's capacities. Unbelief required a special degree of manly independence, a moral courage known only to the highly educated and daring, those determined to pursue the truth wherever it led. "By rejecting the easy consolations of religion," historian James Turner writes, "agnostics in their own eyes had climbed a moral Everest inaccessible to believers."[13] Yet men could not be unbelievers on their own. Masculine irreligion required feminine belief, an assurance that even in the face of withering scientific evidence, the church pews would never empty.

The threat to male autonomy and control was not just spiritual, however. It was also financial and administrative. When the suffrage amendment passed in 1920, most Protestant denominations were still depending on a division of labor that relegated women to a supportive fundraising role, segregated in separate missionary and benevolence societies and wielding influence rather than direct power. Men maintained a monopoly over all churches' offices, with few exceptions. In nearly every local congregation only they could take up the collection, distribute the bread and grape juice for Communion, baptize infants, or, of course preach from the pulpit. In many denominations women had limited say in national gatherings, which by law or tradition were run by ordained clergy for the benefit of same. A few theological seminaries admitted women, but generally steered them into separate gender-appropriate tracks, like religious education or preparation for missionary work.

Though rarely talked about, the inequality was hardly a secret. A Federal Council of Churches survey of 114 denomination, conducted in the late 1920s, documented the problem: though the governing bodies of 75 church bodies gave women "full status," 35 still denied them a say. When it came to ordination, more denominations prohibited than allowed it, with 61 against and 43 in favor. Among the holdouts were some of the largest mainline groups, including the Protestant Episcopal Church, and both northern and southern Presbyterians and Methodists.[14]

Many Protestant church leaders were aware of how all of this looked to secular outsiders, as the rest of the world was opening up, lurching its uncertain way toward equality. "A woman may be a physician, a lawyer, a dentist, and a legislator, provided she meets the necessary educational and legal conditions," observed Ella Boole, the president of the Woman's Christian Temperance Union. "They vote on the same terms as men, and every office in the electorate may be held by a woman if she can secure the necessary votes.

Practically every door is open to women," said Boole, "except in the work of the Church."[15]

Mrs. Boole was hardly one to lead a feminist exodus from orthodox Christianity. She was a loyal insider, the leader of Protestantism's most cherished social cause. Her exasperation might have been a warning to denominational officials, or at least an invitation to accept the inevitable, to open up church offices to women, remove restrictions on preaching, and embrace equality. As one frustrated Protestant admitted, "the old argument about the difference between men and women as a reason for assigning them an inferior place has been worn to a frazzle."[16] Certainly, as the following chapters show, many Protestant church leaders did try to introduce change, and they partially succeeded. But the inequalities festered. Prohibitions on ordination, restrictive quotas, and airy rhetoric about "women's role" lasted far longer, in some cases well past midcentury—many more years than, at least from our present-day perspective, seemed wise or necessary. The problem was not simply biblical literalism or misogynism, especially as mainline Protestants compared to their fundamentalist peers. Already in 1891 the question of female clergy was "past the theoretic stage," beyond the need "to present arguments *pro* or *con*," said Mila Frances Tupper, addressing the National Council of Women. No one should be held back, agreed Kate Woods, by a single "dyspeptic utterance" by St. Paul.[17]

Women themselves were the problem. Church leaders faced a conundrum: if they gave women too much direct say, they risked a loss of men and social prestige; if they gave them too little say, the women might well depart, taking their financial resources along with them. This was not, of course, something that church leaders could say aloud. As we will see, "feminization" would remain a problem that was both too important to ignore and impossible to acknowledge.

The Anatomy of Feminine Doubt

There were also historical burdens, worth taking a moment to consider in some depth. Even mainline Protestants, hardly fierce traditionalists, came to the twentieth century burdened by centuries of back and forth about the source and meaning of gender differences. By the time Zephine Humphrey posed her question, "is there such a thing as a woman?" thousands of theologians, philosophers, scientists, and other well-qualified professionals had weighed in on the problem. Was there such a thing as a feminine essence? Was there something irreducible, indestructible in women's inner nature that always inclined them toward God? In the centuries before Americans had access to scientific explanations about DNA and hormones—the biological mechanisms of sexual difference—that question had no final answer. It could be asked over and over, generation after generation—and thus this brief chronological digression.

A good deal of the fascination was the mystery of women's bodies themselves, a curiosity fueled by the potent combination of masculine attraction and disgust, and framed by dualistic notions of the material and the spiritual. "Medieval interpreters of the Bible," writes Carolyn Walker Bynum, "regularly taught that 'spirit is to flesh as male is to female'"—that is, that the male/female phenomenon stood for all others: strong/weak, rational/irrational, soul/body. Though Christian thinkers periodically flirted with dualistic notions, they could only go so far, restrained by Christianity's central teaching, that Christ was God incarnate, a divine being who saved the human race by taking on human form. To be sure, "the flesh" was the Pauline enemy of the spirit, the ally of the world and the Devil, but it also carried moral weight. To some commentators, the doctrine of the incarnation even affirmed the spiritual power of women's bodies. After all, the gospels taught that Christ received his bodily form without any masculine assistance: Jesus was born from a woman only.[18]

The question was how much bodies really mattered. Medieval theologians, like many people still today, pondered the problem with eternity in view. Would the glorified bodies of martyrs would still show their wounds? Would husbands recognize their wives, children their parents? Did earthly experiences carry eternal consequences? There was no easy answer. Christian thinkers had inherited the Greek understanding of gender differences, that male and female identities were more fluid than fixed, unstable points along a single continuum. "Woman" was not a single static category but an imperfect version of the primary male prototype. "In a public world that was overwhelmingly male," Thomas Laquer writes, this model explained "what was already massively evident in culture more generally: *man* is the measure of all things, and woman does not exist as an ontologically distinct category."[19]

The Western world invented sex in the eighteenth century. In the centuries before the invention of the microscope, it was easy to assume that women were mere passive receptacles in human reproduction, that the womb was a container for the tiny but fully formed human beings believed to be found in male semen. Now for the first time, scientific exploration of the reproductive organs demonstrated fundamental structural differences between men and women: the womb and vagina were not an inverted penis, and a woman's body was not an inert repository in the conception and development of a child. Women were clearly, bewilderingly different. They were a separate sex.[20]

The next question was how far the differences actually went. The ancients had believed that the soul had no sex, that it was an alien essence imprisoned in a body, longing for escape. The Enlightenment's discovery of sexual differences, in an age obsessed with the powers of the human mind, raised the possibility that gender differences were fundamental, that they affected every realm of human experience. Perhaps women's minds were also feminine, and perhaps their very nature, what nineteenth-century poets and philosophers would call the feminine soul, was utterly alien to the masculine norm. By the nineteenth century, this growing sense of the unity between women's inner and outer nature, the "eternal feminine," had both social and moral consequences. Instead of being an unstable, easily tempted, and fundamentally untrustworthy version of the perfect male, the "true woman" possessed an inherent aptitude for religion, an easy, natural sense of communion with God and knowledge of right and wrong.[21]

The nineteenth-century woman was "true" in the sense that metals are true, unalloyed and singular, without internal contradiction. She was what she appeared to be, inside and out; the true woman was essentially transparent, without contradiction in mind, body, or spirit. In an age of worry about "confidence men" and false claims, before the advent of tracking software and video recordings, this moral authenticity depended on absolute correspondence between outward and inward appearances. Being upright required looking upright.[22] But "true womanhood" mattered even more in the religious realm. As Boston pastor Justin Dewey Fulton wrote in 1869, God himself had placed "womanliness" within the feminine "heart and soul and nature, just as he gave a difference of nature, mould, and form, to the outward appearance of man and woman."[23] Congregational theologian Horace Bushnell opposed women's suffrage as a fundamental "reform against nature," an attempt to separate the mind and heart from the body, an impossible act. "The fiber of a woman's brain," wrote Bushnell, "is likely to be as much finer as the fiber of her skin."[24]

Women could not preach or be ordained, as Methodist James Buckley flatly declared, "because they are women." The problem was not religious tradition, the Bible, or the rules of denominational polity. The fairer sex had simply been "intrusted [sic] by God with a form of mental and spiritual influence, and a corresponding work different from that of man."[25] In one sense Buckley's argument was not earth-shattering. Over the course of Christian history, churches had barred women from priesthood and pulpit because they believed them weaker and more sinful than men. He was also, however, saying something new, that women were disqualified because they were in every way "not male." As Bushnell wrote, the two sexes were so different, in every respect and from the dawn of creation, that "they are a great deal more like two species, than two varieties." Men and women were "different classes of being," two opposite sides of the "whole" of humanity.[26]

An irreligious woman was by definition an unnatural one. "A fallen woman is an abomination," declared Fulton. "She is the foe of the home, and the enemy of all that is pure. Hence she is thrown out upon the rocks, and left there to die, unpitied and unbefriended, without God and without hope in the world."[27] Even the nineteenth-century's iconoclastic freethinkers (who were predominantly male) could not imagine a female atheist. One of the great problems with religion, in fact the source of their contempt, was the fact that it attracted women, "who are naturally more credulous, and more disposed to believe what is told them than men are."[28]

The investment in feminine religiosity was not just religious cant, the province of a few cranky conservatives. As many historians have demonstrated, the true woman ideal was elastic and powerful enough to serve a range of social purposes, defining moral and religious boundaries as well as racial ones. By the early twentieth century, as Maureen Fitzgerald has argued, white Protestant women represented a non-sectarian ideal for social reform, undergirding the creation of a welfare state that relegated all others— "Catholics, Jews, conservative evangelical Protestants, and African American Protestants"—as outsiders, too explicitly religious to be considered progressive.[29] At the same time, it almost goes without saying that white Protestant womanhood operated as a powerful racial foil, whether memorializing the "lost cause" of the defeated Confederacy or fueling cultural anxieties about manliness and Western civilization.[30]

By the turn of the century, female religiosity was important enough to become a scientific fact, documented in laboratory experiments conducted by qualified professionals, men with an unparalleled ability to combine praise with condescension. Psychologist of religion George A. Coe concluded that "women respond to religion more feelingly, and in some respects more continuously" than men. Male conversion typically involved turbulent emotions and agonizing doubt. "Men display more friction against surroundings, more difficulty with points of belief," said Coe. Their questions "go deeper—more deeply, that is, into the region of clear self-consciousness, decision, initiative." In contrast, women went "more easily with the tide," with no need to wrestle through to faith. Religion was "a sort of atmosphere in the life of women—something all-pervasive and easily taken for granted."[31] Edwin Starbuck likewise found that men came to faith in pursuit of a moral ideal or "conviction for sin," while women responded to social expectations, or merely the power of suggestion. "The inference seems to be," he wrote, "that *males are controlled more from within, while the females are controlled more from without.*" In his magisterial study of belief and unbelief among university professors and students, James Leuba explained the far higher levels of female religiosity as a residue of domesticity—in short, intellectual and personal immaturity.[32]

The Case against "True Womanhood"

The first hint of dissent came from fundamentalists. To modern ears their overwrought denunciations of flappers and film stars sound fearful and cranky, perhaps even laughable. Yet in the post–World War I era, those criticisms were oddly, subtly modern, a rebuke to the sentimental maxims of the previous century. Fundamentalists harbored a visceral dislike of Victorian piety, particularly the notion of sainted womanhood. Look at the evidence, they said. "The average girl today no longer looks forward to motherhood as the crowning glory of womanhood," the evangelist Billy Sunday complained. "She is turning her home into a gambling shop and a social beer-and-champagne-drinking joint," full of "jilted jades and slander-mongers. She is becoming a matinee-gadder and fudge-eater."[33] No one should be surprised: the Bible itself declared that all have sinned and fallen short of the glory of God—not just one sex, but both.

Women were in fact the shock troops of pending moral chaos, their revolt a sign of the "last days." "We have heard much of the emancipation of the female part of the race," one Bible scholar warned in 1921. "It forebodes nothing but evil." Indeed, Christians should not be surprised at the "world movement among women," the *Moody Bible Institute Monthly* advised. Feminine "rebellion" simply verified the Apostle Paul's prediction that in the last days "silly women" would pervert the gospel, chasing after every "wind of doctrine."[34] Fundamentalism's distinctive theological system, known as dispensational premillennialism, offered no hope for social progress toward equality: women were inferior and subservient by divine decree, a rule dating back to the opening chapters of Genesis. All of the promises of social reformers, including the claim that female voters would usher in a new age of sobriety and civic order, amounted to empty rhetoric. As one fundamentalist commented tersely, "there are vicious and incompetent women as well as vicious and incompetent men."[35]

The deepest scorn was reserved for Protestantism's most loyal and active churchwomen. They were the ones naïve enough to take money from John D. Rockefeller and give it away to wishy-washy missionaries, to listen to the treacly sermons of "little infidel preacherettes," as Baptist William Bell Riley so memorably described them. Female churchgoers did not—could not—understand the theological principles at stake in the battle for orthodoxy, nor how their own presence undermined the manly, independent quest for purity and truth.[36]

Fundamentalists were not the only ones entertaining cynical notions about feminine sanctity, but at least they were offering answers. Similar doubts resonated in the upper echelons of educated American society, among the most progressive and most rebellious. The psychologists and left-leaning journalists who contributed to a sleek symposium on "Our Changing Morality" in 1924 were surprisingly frank about their bewilderment and confusion. Freda Kirchwey, editor of *The Nation*, spoke for all. Never before, she said, "have human beings so floundered about outside the ropes of social and religious sanctions." The "old rules fail to work," she said. The new woman confronted "bewildering inconsistencies," as "things that were sure become unsure." Slowly, often clumsily, those young women were trying to construct a framework of certainty, "something to take the place of the burden of solemn ideals and reverential attitudes that rolled off her shoulders when she emerged." But in the meantime, confusion reigned. "Obscenity hawks its old wares at one end of the road," said Kirchwey, "and dogmatic piety shouts warnings at the other—while between is chaos."[37]

Meanwhile, people in the cultural middle ground had to wonder: perhaps the fundamentalists were on to something. In the election of 1924, women did not vote as a righteous bloc, nor in convincing numbers. During an era of generally low voter turnout (from 80% in the late nineteenth century to 50% in the 1920s), only a third of eligible women went to the polls, a figure that would stand until fairly recently. Even worse, it appeared that feminine morality was all too easily neutralized by political party insiders, who easily subsumed and then marginalized a potential female voting bloc. "Once in the organization, we could be controlled," a Republican woman lamented. "Our nuisance value was gone."[38]

Perhaps women themselves had changed. "There used to be a good deal of talk, most of it by men," a female social scientist wrote in 1929, "about women purifying politics. Purification was looked for through the exercise—no, not the exercise—the mere possession of some superior and usually unnamed virtues." Now, the future of American politics would be determined by each women's different "experiences" and "interests," virtuous or otherwise. The moral voting bloc that nineteenth century suffragists had promised had turned out to be an unstable mixture of individual women, representing the full human spectrum of beliefs and behaviors. To fundamentalists this was a disaster that they could at least take comfort in predicting.[39]

No one should have been surprised. The opportunity to question, to be a fluid, malleable self with infinite possibility, had its own deep roots in women's protest. "Let them be sea captains," as Margaret Fuller had declared in her ground-breaking study of *Woman in the Nineteenth Century* (1845). Writing on "The Solitude of Self" in 1892, suffragist Elizabeth Cady Stanton was bold to insist that not all women were alike. "We come into the world alone, unlike all who have gone before us, we leave it alone, under circumstances peculiar to ourselves," she declared. "No mortal ever has been, no mortal ever will be like the soul just launched on the sea of life." As "nature never repeats herself," said Stanton, "the possibilities of one human soul will never be found in another."[40] Virginia Woolf repeated the ethic in her famous essay on *A Room of One's Own:* "Women have served all these centuries as looking-glasses possessing the magic and delicious power of reflecting the figure of man at twice its natural size." She appealed to young women that "it is more important to be oneself than anything else. Do not dream of influencing other people. . . . Think of things in themselves."[41]

Yet, in the early twentieth century, the freedom to construct a self, to transcend limitations of gendered conventions was both intoxicating and frightening, even for women who had already parted ways with conventional religiosity. This much is clear from a series of seventeen biographical essays on "The Modern Woman," published in *The Nation* in 1926 and 1927. The essays represented a range of age and experience, all geared toward explaining the sources of feminist rebellion, and the feminist experience. (*The Nation* had three psychologists, two males and one female, write concluding pieces.) Phyllis Blanchard, a distinguished child psychologist, wrote that she had had little difficulty losing her religion, "slough[ing] off what little superstition I had acquired without any sense of discomfort." Yet "readjusting" her ideas "to a world which had suddenly lost its feminine integrity . . . was a serious matter." "Always I had repressed questionings because they led to criticism of the fundamentals of society," wrote Mary Alden Hopkins, a feminist advocate for working women. "The brain cannot function if it is not allowed to question, and my intelligence was as weak as that of a new-born babe." "Curiosity" became the "driving emotion" of her life. Writer Ruth Pickering exulted in the freedom "to do what interests me—inside my home and outside as well. My deficiencies and my capacities are my own," she said, "—not those of my sex." In other words, "I have grown up."[42]

Elusive Middle Ground

The mainline Protestant churches occupied a place somewhere in between frightened fundamentalists and baffled moderns, hoping that at some point the talk would die down. On the one hand, all that conservative fervor about sex and sin seemed, well, unnecessarily vulgar: more centrist Protestants not only disliked conversations about sex, they chose to believe in the new generation's practical, clear-headed approach to faith. "The modern girl looks at both men and life in a more objective way than did her mother," Congregationalist John Scotford wrote in 1922. "She does not ask the minister to coddle her infirmities, but to give her frank counsel. Religion is less of an emotional indulgence and more a normal aspect of wholesome living."[43]

Yet the modern woman was unpredictable. This much was painfully clear to the Methodists who gathered in Springfield, Massachusetts, in 1924, hoping for a brief, straightforward discussion of women's ordination. "Rushing to the platform and shaking her first in the face of Bishop Frank M. Bristol of Chattanooga, Tenn.," the *New York Times* reported, "Miss M. Madeleine Southard of Winfield, Kan., an advocate of making women fully ordained clergymen, added to the excitement which gripped the Quadrennial General Conference." When Southard made her "spectacular dash" to the podium, ten delegates were already "shouting for the floor in unison," and Methodist dreams of harmony were visibly dwindling.[44]

The times called for honesty and clarity, for clearing out the sentimental cant that threatened the future of religious belief in the modern age. It meant, in other words, finding a place in Protestant churches for women to assume the male privilege of questioning, doubt, and choosing to believe. The years after World War I would have been an opportune moment, a time when many Americans, religious or otherwise, were rethinking the old and ready to embrace the new. A study of "The War and the Woman Point of View," conducted by the Federal Council of Churches, warned Protestants that change was inevitable. The "modern women" wanted challenging work to do, not yet more "dilettante effort" that required neither expertise nor "emotional idealism." "Everyone seems to be more or less conscious that we are on our way to a new social order," the report concluded, and at its heart was a new woman, "searching, often unconsciously, for a God who will bring human life to its fartherest [sic] goal of self-fulfillment."[45]

Few of these optimistic visions came to pass, however. To be sure, in the post–World War I era, the mainline churches did engage in extensive housecleaning—but the introspection was not directed at gender inequality. The quest for honesty turned out to be administrative, cleansing church structures of unwieldy, inefficient Victorian vestiges, and creating rational structures with clear lines of accountability and measures of effectiveness. It proved easier to overhaul denominational bureaucracies than to change beliefs and practices about gender roles. In fact, as the following chapter demonstrates, women ended up a problem to be dealt with, an impediment to progress, not a force for transformation.

And so, church leaders worried. The truth is in the paperwork. From the 1920s onward, mainline Protestants regularly—even obsessively—measured, compared, examined, and reported on their female members, reassuring themselves, over and over, that they were remaining loyal.[46] The answers, as the following chapters demonstrate, were not necessarily reassuring: "woman's dilemma" would demand far more than institutional window-dressing. It required both women and men to imagine "the church" itself in an entirely new way.

Helen Barrett Montgomery, Courtesy of the American Baptist Historical Society, Atlanta, GA.

PORTRAIT

Helen Barrett Montgomery's Bittersweet Missionary Jubilee

Helen Barrett Montgomery likely knew when the trouble started. A prominent Baptist laywoman, highly regarded biblical scholar, and president of the Woman's American Baptist Foreign Missionary Society—she would be elected the first female president of the Northern Baptist Convention in 1921—Montgomery could recognize a problem when she saw it.[1]

Perhaps she even marked one moment in particular, April 26, 1900, the conclusion of "woman's day" at the Ecumenical Missionary Conference, an international gathering held in New York City. The conference itself was groundbreaking, a dramatic display of Christian unity, declaring the end of one "missionary century" and the beginning of another, full of promise. For eleven eventful days, scores of veteran missionaries, international Protestant icons, and Christian converts from around the world celebrated the pioneers of the past century and watched as a new generation of young people laid plans for the "evangelization of the world in this generation."

Women sat proudly at the center of it all, "hundreds of the best and most able of the Christian sisterhood of all lands," as one admiring observer put it. No longer shy and apologetic outsiders, they had stepped into their "true and rightful sphere of influence." Finally the Protestant churches were witnessing the "epiphany of women." And clearly the female delegates knew they had, in some sense, arrived. "The manner in which they bore themselves," said the enthusiastic reporter, was "more than justified" by their achievements.[2]

The celebration showcased the particular genius of women's work, a blend of hard-headed practicality and high-minded idealism. The delegates received tips about fundraising and hints about running "well-organized" meetings, but also thrilled to remarkable stories about lives they had transformed, from India, the little girl who converted her entire village to

Christianity with just the gospel of Mark, and Corinna Shattuck, the "heroine of Oorfa," who had rescued Armenian women from marauding Turks.

And like any good conference, there was a sense of homecoming, a chance to savor the past and plan for the future. The delegates got to see legendary figures from the founding generation—Methodist educator Isabella Thoburn and missionary founder Clementina Butler—as well as contemporary stars like Montgomery and Lucy Waterbury Peabody. The mood was celebratory, and for good reason. "While there are still women who do not know a telegram from a telephone, and who think a zenana must be a new embroidery stitch," said Waterbury, "a million and a half women have been enlisted in this work." In 1898 alone, she pointed out, they had raised over $2.5 million for the cause of foreign missions.[3]

The celebration concluded with more fanfare: 412 missionaries on the stage, American, British, and European, a stunning display of "women's work" in its full geographic span. One awestruck participant was compelled to list them all: "From Africa, India, and Ceylon," she wrote, "from Assam, Laos and Burman, from Korea and Japan, from Persia and Oceania, from Turkey and Mexico, from Spain and South America, from Madagascar and China they came, the veterans of well-nigh threescore years of service." The evening ended the only way it could have, with the delegates singing as one, "Blest Be the Tie That Binds."[4]

Helen Montgomery must have viewed it all with mixed feelings: she knew what the men had been talking about. In the past few days she had heard plenty of back-and-forth about efficiency and business management, words that fired the imaginations of every forward-thinking churchman of the day—and threatened everything she and thousands of other Protestant women had labored over for nearly half a century. During the New York gathering she had sat through strategy meetings, and listened to charges that "women's work" was divisive and selfish, that it funneled money away from more important denominational projects. Of course, women had been hearing this masculine grousing for years, complaints that "the opulence of the women's treasuries is gained at the expense of the general boards." But this time was different: the problem was more basic, a palpable dislike of women in large groups. As Montgomery restated the argument: " 'We have enough,' they tell us, 'of women's clubs, women's papers, women's charities; let us not have *woman* in religion.' " The men were now claiming the high ground of Christian unity—which, translated into financial terms meant no more separate fundraising, no more separate budgets, just "one great missionary reservoir," joining together "all the streams of beneficence now turning the wheels of many societies."[5]

The worst criticism, however, was a new one, the charge that "women's work" was inefficient. This was an especially bitter pill, given that women's organizations prided themselves on their cost-saving instincts, a talent they believed was uniquely feminine. Montgomery in fact had to point out the obvious, that women's work was essentially free, carried out by an "army of unpaid officers and helpers." "How short-sighted, how wickedly wasteful it would be," she said, "if the Church of Christ should leave unutilized such resources."[6]

She was right, of course. The women's organizations were miles ahead of everyone else when it came to cooperation and streamlining. In the early twentieth century, both the home and foreign wings created national federations, with the Council of Women for Home Missions (CWHM), formed in 1903, and the Federation of Women's Boards for Foreign Missions (FWBFM), formed in 1912. "By the 1920s," one reported stated, "cooperation [was] definitely the watchword."[7] These efforts would bring even higher levels of success, resulting in millions for interdenominational women's colleges in India, China, and Japan, and a line of highly successful missionary education books, which would sell some two million copies by 1921.[8] Women's cooperative work also attended to the spiritual: in 1917 the World Day of Prayer, organized by missionary leaders in the late nineteenth century, was being observed in some 16,000 American communities and more than 70 countries.[9]

Women's organizations were also a financial gift to denominational budgets. To take just one example, the three Congregational Woman's Boards, headquartered in Boston, Chicago, and San Francisco, accounted for hundreds of laywomen directly administering the work at home and abroad, handling hundreds of thousands of dollars every year. They decided policies, recruited and trained hundreds of missionaries as well as "native teachers and nurses and evangelists." The women's national boards also directed more than fifty state and local organizations, each with its plethora of committees and subcommittees, accounting for another thousand active volunteers. "Except for a small number of paid secretaries," one of the board presidents reminded the denomination, "all this is done as lay service."[10]

The men saw things differently, of course. In their view, the fabled efficiency of women's work led to all kinds of "odious comparisons," making the denominational boards look fat and lazy. Bureaucrats could grumble that the low overhead was possible only because the men were subsidizing it—the women's boards supported only single and celibate female missionaries while the men's boards carried the full cost of missionary families—but the grousing mattered little to the thousands of enthusiastic supporters in the hinterlands.[11]

Still, the headwinds were growing stronger, the shift in the weather confirmed by the next ecumenical missionary conference, held in Edinburgh in 1910. That year marked the silver jubilee of the women's missionary movement, and groups all across the country were rising up to celebrate five decades of achievement. The gatherings began in October 1910 in Oakland, California, and continued for the next forty days, a series of two-day sessions in forty-eight cities. By the time the jubilee reached Cleveland, the luncheon meetings were attracting 2,200 women in a single day; Buffalo sold out tickets a week in advance, and Pittsburgh's numbers topped 4,800. And everywhere the women were filling offering plates, reaching over a million dollars in spontaneous donations.[12]

Everyone wanted to see Helen Barrett Montgomery. They packed into halls too crowded to allow tables, balancing luncheon plates on their laps, and lined up for mass meetings, rallies, and social gatherings. Over the course of two months, Montgomery herself gave over two hundred speeches, an "avalanche of meetings" supplemented by a celebrity contingent of missionaries giving testimonials. When the jubilee reached Washington, DC, she and her friend Lucy Peabody were entertained by President and Mrs. William Howard Taft, and squired by the city's leading socialites. The final event, in New York City, filled Carnegie Hall. A "pageant of missions" at the Metropolitan Opera House included 1,000 actors, a chorus, and a sixty-piece orchestra featuring musicians from the Philharmonic Society and the New York Symphony—all of it convincing one awe-struck Congregationalist that "we seem to have passed the day when women cannot be heard."[13]

And, as no jubilee is complete without a chronicle, that task also fell to Montgomery. Her enormously popular book, *Western Women in Eastern Lands*, was a compendium of success upon success, selling some fifty thousand copies in six weeks. "We began in weakness, we stand in power," she declared, backing up her claim with an entire page of statistics, hard numbers testifying to innovative, gritty, and astonishing achievement.[14]

Yet Montgomery knew that all the good intentions in the world did not guarantee success. That truth was personal, in fact: all the while she was touring and celebrating, her husband's business back in Rochester, New York, was foundering. The financial situation was so dire that the couple was forced to downsize, selling their home and taking up residence in a cramped apartment. Even through those hardships, which proved to be temporary, Helen and William Montgomery remained loyal Baptists, never flagging in their financial support for denominational projects.[15]

As she wrote away in that Rochester apartment, Montgomery's own money worries were no doubt resonating with larger anxieties about the future of the women's missionary cause. The final chapter of *Western Women in Eastern Lands* was an extended plea for the survival of all the work her book had chronicled. "The opportunity for self-expression and the development that comes through responsibility are as necessary to women as to men," she insisted. The "modern educated woman" would not stand for denominational bureaucrats deciding how and where to spend the money raised for missions. And after all, why tamper with success when the need was so apparent? "So long as our national bill for chewing gum exceeds our gifts to foreign missions," Montgomery noted acidly, "and our ostrich feather and candy outputs could float the missionary benevolences like skiffs on a river, we need not fear impoverishing the churches by too much importunity."[16]

The men were not listening, however. Just a few months before, in June 1910, the world's missionary forces had met in Edinburgh, Scotland, a follow up to the New York Conference, the single largest gathering in the movement's history, and the most consequential. Historian Andrew Walls has declared it "a landmark in the history of mission; the starting point of the modern theology of mission; the high point of the modern Western missionary movement and the high point from which it declined; the launch-pad of the modern ecumenical movement; the point at which Christians first began to glimpse something of what a world church would be like."[17] Helen Barrett Montgomery, however, was only a minor figure. In part, the press of jubilee celebrations prevented her from attending most of the relevant conversations, but Montgomery had to have been aware that her marginal role was deliberate. The meeting planners had decided not to appoint a separate Commission on "women's work"; they would instead solicit their "help" in a general way, as to "not draw a line between work for men and work for women." As a result, only two of the nine Commissions reporting to the Edinburgh meeting had any female members at all, three out of twenty on Commission III and four out of twenty-four on Commission V.[18]

Montgomery was one of three women appointed to the twenty-person Commission VI, tasked with considering the "home base" of foreign missions. The published report devoted twelve pages to women's boards, under the heading, "Problems of Administration." While not affirming the "radical step" of eliminating them, the Commission did urge action to "avoid the impression of divided interest or even rivalry," with the ultimate goal of "closer organic unity."[19]

Montgomery was incensed. Writing to Commission VI chairman James Levi Barton, she charged that the report was based more on male opinion than fact. "[N]o attempt," she said, "had been made to get the facts from the Woman's Boards." But her anger might not have mattered at that point. The Methodist Episcopal Church, South, was already busy consolidating all of its women's boards into a single national one, and in the years to follow, as we will see in the next chapter, the trend would continue.

The jubilee celebrations of 1910 would prove both the high point of an enormously successful, historically influential movement of women—and the beginning of its ending. The "prudent silence" of the Edinburgh meeting, as one woman described it, was perhaps the most damning aspect of all.[20] Historian Brian Stanley puts it more flatly: "Edinburgh 1910 . . . undoubtedly contributed to the decline of the women's missionary societies as an autonomous movement in the course of the twentieth century."[21]

2

The Gender of Efficiency

"Woman's Mission" in a Modernizing Church

In retrospect, the question is obvious: why did the Protestant churches set out to dismantle a network of flourishing, enduringly popular organizations, all squarely in line with their hopes for world evangelization? By any measure the decision was disastrous. By the end of World War II, as historian Dana Robert writes, the women's missionary movement had "virtually ceased to exist," with only a handful of organizations surviving, in vastly truncated form. Robert's conclusion is apt: the systematic dismantling that took place 1910s and 1920s, "makes for depressing reading."[1]

Male jealousy and a certain pragmatic cruelty clearly played a role in the reorganizations, but they were hardly the only reasons. As this chapter argues, the dissolutions attempted to solve a nineteenth-century gender problem in a twentieth-century way. The age-old question of "woman's place" would become an administrative issue, not an ideological one. It is not surprising, moreover, that missionary organizations became the target. In the postsuffrage era, mainline Protestant uneasiness about gender melded with larger doubts about the missionary enterprise, and even more important, bureaucratic arguments about efficiency and control. In the truly modern church, an institution taking shape in the World War I era, gender differences were no longer supposed to matter.

Modern Missionaries

To a degree, the women's missionary project suffered from the general malaise facing foreign missions in the early twentieth century. By that time, doubts first voiced in nineteenth-century seminary classrooms about the superiority of Christianity and the eternal destiny of the heathen were being voiced in public and filtering through pews and pulpits. All but the most conservative church people recoiled at the triumphalism of the previous

Good and Mad. Margaret Bendroth, Oxford University Press. © Oxford University Press 2023.
DOI: 10.1093/oso/9780197654064.003.0003

generations, the effrontery of Christians "presum[ing] always to teach, yet never to be taught; presum]ing] always to give, yet never to acknowledge that other religions also had something to bring to the 'common store.' " Forward-looking missionary theorists took that lesson even further, acknowledging that other faiths were not only "stepping stones" to Christianity, but genuine paths to God, perhaps even endowed with superior spiritual insights.[2] World War I crushed even that limited confidence, the carnage on European battlefields visibly undermining presumptions to Western superiority. Missionary theorists struggled to define their cause, to provide any reasons why Asian and African converts should look to Christians who had so thoroughly demonstrated their moral ineffectiveness.

But the enterprise was far from over. In many respects, the missionary cause flourished well into the twentieth century, maintaining a global network of hospitals, schools, and churches employing hundreds of talented, well-educated men and women. Moreover, once theological visions had been readjusted and Western preconceptions pared to more modest dimensions, Protestant missionaries and their children played a more influential role than ever, well beyond their immediate church circles. As historian David Hollinger has shown, a genuinely astonishing number of foreign policy experts, novelists, anthropologists, and larger-than-life Americans were raised on the mission field, from newspaper statesman Henry Luce and novelist John Hersey to actresses Jayne and Audrey Meadows. Growing up as a minority in foreign countries, this generation learned cultural tolerance, and went on to shape not only American racial attitudes, but also wide swaths of post–World War II foreign policy.[3]

Yet, surprisingly, their progressive social vision did not include feminism. "Missionary-connected advocacy of women's rights was modest," Hollinger writes. Nearly all of those larger-than-life missionaries were men, and as he notes, even the most progressive paid little attention to women's rights. They were, in many ways, heirs of a church culture that had tried, often earnestly, to proceed as if gender differences were irrelevant.[4]

This lack of influence reflects, at least in part, the specific toll of modern global realities on the women's missionary cause, and its particularly heavy investment in assumptions of Western superiority. Since the Civil War, these organizations had defended their right to exist by insisting on their unique mission, in their view, to bring the liberating word of Christianity to women living under the oppressive regimes of non-Christian faiths. This message was the driving force behind "woman's work for women," the hundreds of schools and hospitals built to uplift oppressed and benighted sisters in foreign lands. World War I was a "major blow" to the entire enterprise, requiring a far longer retreat from the moral high ground, and a far more extensive reformulation of the cause itself.[5]

After the war, scrutiny of women's work intensified. One of the first orders of business for the International Missionary Council, an ecumenical coalition formed in 1921, was a full study of women's missionary organizations in the United States, Great Britain, and on the European Continent. Some of the issues were familiar—waste and duplication, competition for funding—but others were new, brought on by the changing political and social conditions in the former colonies of Western powers. It was becoming clear that many of the so-called benighted and oppressed women of nineteenth-century missionary literature were more liberated than their American and European counterparts. Indian and Chinese women were organizing for suffrage and female doctors and teachers were heading hospitals and schools across Asia. "Hereditary prejudices are disappearing," the American report declared; "social customs, hoary with age, are breaking up; the spirit of conservatism is giving way to the spirit of progress. It is an hour of golden opportunity as it is an hour of great responsibility for the Christian Church."[6] In fact, a follow-up study in 1927 reported, "inherited ideas from the West" often presented more of an obstacle than local customs. "Unless we create it," said Jane Shaw Ward, reporting from China, "we shall not need to overcome local prejudice."[7]

The famous "Hocking Report," a study published in 1932, took the criticism even further. *Re-Thinking Missions* is best known for the theological controversies that swirled around it, about the uniqueness of Christianity and the ethics of evangelizing non-Western people. But it also mounted a thorough often biting critique of the women's missionary enterprise, not just the American women whose "mental picture of eastern women" was "heavy with shadows of the depressed, illiterate masses, almost unrelieved by high lights of progress." It also decried the "possessive" attitudes and "maternalistic" motives of the female missionaries themselves. Sequestering and westernizing young girls—protecting them like "hot-house plants in the 'purdah' atmosphere of the boarding school"—did little to equip them for a rapidly modernizing world. What those women really needed was up-to-date, forward-looking programs, including coeducation, technical training, and leadership development. Missionaries needed to teach young women how to navigate a "changing environment, enjoying the privileges of a new freedom."[8]

The masculine critique of "women's work" was comprehensive and devastating. Now female missionaries and their supporters were not just inefficient and expensive, they were socially backward. They were easy to dismiss as sentimental Victorian holdovers, not worth the serious attention of modern clergy, even in the local parish. The meetings are "exceedingly dull," a Presbyterian seminary professor advised his students in 1927. "They read a letter from a missionary in the foreign field, make no comments on it, read several more in a matter-of-fact way, and then the cup of tea."[9]

Some of the sharpest and perhaps most damaging criticisms came from insiders, from women themselves. None was more controversial than novelist Pearl Buck and her high-profile rebuke, delivered to two thousand Presbyterian women in 1932. Though raised in a missionary compound in China, Buck had already lost faith in the missionary enterprise, and her disillusionment was evident. Her much-anticipated talk "Is There a Case for Foreign Missions?" ended with a qualified "yes," but hardly a resounding one. The audience was apparently so confused that they received her message with stunned silence, forcing Buck to leave the room abruptly. Conservatives pounced, decrying the novelist's "ruthless, heartless, insane, bigoted, intelligentsiacal cynicism," and demanding her resignation—which she provided, sailing back to China and gaining even more fame as a writer and publicly drifting from Protestant Christianity. If there was a winner in the controversy, it was clearly Pearl Buck, who became the "most influential interpreter of China to the West since Marco Polo," and an internationally beloved novelist with impeccable "anti-imperialist, antiracist, and even feminist credentials."[10]

For a variety of reasons, and then in short order, a key nineteenth-century legacy, a vast network of organizations founded and funded by laywomen, was systematically downsized, crippled, or eliminated. "Ironically, a movement that had sought empowerment for Christian women around the world," writes Dana Robert, "found itself disempowered by patriarchal forces within the Western churches themselves."[11]

The retrenchment affected women's work across the Protestant spectrum, including two of the leading African American denominations. Between 1900 and 1932, every meeting of the African Methodist Episcopal Church's General Conference entertained a motion to merge the women's organizations. Matters came to a head in 1932, when the meeting erupted into a "sustained uproar," a direct confrontation between laywomen and the bishops and clergy attempting to gain control.[12] National Baptists engaged in a protracted tug-of-war over ownership of the National Training School for Women and Girls in Washington, DC, the signal achievement of the incomparable Nannie Helen Burroughs. The Training School's "hybrid pedagogy" offered an academic curriculum that included courses in English, Latin, music, and "Negro History" as well as vocational instruction designed to "professionalize" domestic work. Burroughs battled to retain control of the school until 1938, when the denomination ordered the Women's Convention to stop all funding, a move she denounced as "undemocratic and reactionary," and "manifestly unfair." Under Burrough's successor Willie Layten, the Training School and the Women's Convention became auxiliaries, without an independent funding base or decision-making power.[13]

Ironically perhaps, Protestant women's best ally was social conservatism, buttressed by some shrewd organizational planning. The major exception to the merger trend was the Woman's Missionary Union (WMU) of the Southern Baptist Convention, an organization that remains independent to this day. To a degree, the near-mythic aura of WMU leaders and founders—women like Lottie Moon and Annie Armstrong—made it a difficult target for denominational takeover. Pragmatism also helped: in the 1920s, when Southern Baptist mission boards were plagued by financial scandal and diminishing receipts, the WMU raised all the revenues that went to missionaries rather than creditors. Denominational officials did not fail to notice that, by 1931, the women's organization accounted for nearly 70 percent of the Foreign Mission Board's budget.[14]

A New Quest for Order

The modern church was to be gender neutral, modeled on the efficiency standards of the early twentieth-century business world. By the turn of the century, most captains of industry understood that unbridled competition was more often than not wasteful and ineffective. They had also learned to be wary of family connections: a sentimental businessman might soon be a penniless one. The modern tycoon understood that all the mergers and monopolies in the world meant nothing without a business plan, carried out in a coordinated, efficient manner. Successful businesses were "integrated enterprises," managed by trained, salaried middle managers. Long-term profits, as well as a business with the staying power for the swashbuckling founder to hand down to his children and grandchildren, required a steady eye on the long game and consistent attention to detail. It was not enough for a business to be big; real growth meant a complex, coordinated network of administrators running all the separate parts of a business—sales, production, and the like—toward the same goal.[15]

The Protestant denominations were quick to understand the advantages. Over time, the institutions that had once ordered American church life had become prime examples of disorder, jury-built amalgams of worthy causes. Denominations had become an array of competing fiefdoms—women's missionary societies (home and foreign), student movements and young persons' organizations like Christian Endeavor and the Epworth League, Sunday schools and denominational colleges—all making separate appeals to the people in the pews.[16]

Of course, not everything changed at once. Personal piety and dedication to moral causes, those old hallmarks of nineteenth-century religiosity, lived on, as they do today. Mainline Protestants would continue to stress the immediacy and urgency of the Christian gospel, variously defined. But in the aftermath of World War I the evidence was inescapable: all the moral fervor in the world was not enough to save humanity from itself. To achieve any kind of social traction, twentieth-century churches would need to build efficient, coordinated institutional structures. They would need the right kind of people, not just clergy but smart and well-educated laypeople who understood how modern organizations worked, and who possessed the training, abilities, and understanding to manage the books and keep the doors open day after day.[17]

This kind of ordering and centralizing made sense for Protestant denominations, for reasons both idealistic and practical. A well-oiled organization was, after all, fundamental to any possibility of a united Christendom. Even the simplest denominational merger involved years of complex back and forth, amalgamating centuries of accumulated tradition, money, and organizational structures, from pension funds and missionary hospitals to Sunday school curricula and the credentialing of clergy. Logical and streamlined institutions were simply an ecumenical necessity.

Yet, pragmatism was not all. For managerial Protestants, the twentieth-century search for order was also a spiritual aspiration. Even today many secular-minded Americans have yet to shake the belief that corporations have the ability to do good, or at the very least, that all it takes to bring people together is the right kind of organization.[18] A century ago, that belief was far more immediate and specific: efficient meant ethical. The "efficient

Christian," as a Baptist author described him, "brings worthy things to pass," and "gets results." More than that, he brought in not just new but repeat customers, adding important support for the denominational bottom line. "The application of this logic to the church," our Baptist friend noted simply, "is too obvious to require elaboration."[19]

Even Congregationalists, whose decentralized polity had always required a certain tolerance for organizational chaos, came enthusiastically on board. When they began paring down and centralizing their sprawling infrastructure in 1913, it included eleven denominational agencies, all soliciting local churches for support. They touted their results, a neatly symmetrical set of national boards, as a gain for Christians everywhere, doing away with "the emphasis on mechanism," and "humanizing and spiritualizing" the task of world evangelization.[20]

Women and Bureaucracy

What was to be "woman's role" in the modern denomination? The Sunday schools might have provided a clue. Since the early nineteenth century, men had always run the national organizations and denominational departments; just as in the public school system, the local superintendents were male and the teaching staff was female. The one difference was in the Sunday school primary department, which everyone acknowledged was women's special expertise. "A man though ever so earnest, can only make a well-meant bungle in the infant class," the New York Sunday School Teachers' Association agreed in 1872. Better a "bull in a china shop," another expert declared, than a "blundering man" in a room of small children.[21] Women not only taught small children, however; they also wrote specialized curriculum that incorporated cutting-edge educational theory from the kindergarten movement, and organized their own professional societies. The National Primary Union, formed in 1884 with Sarah Timanus Crafts as its first president, reflected the proud conviction that motherhood was a "science," requiring careful study and standardized information.

Yet, as Helen Barrett Montgomery pointed out, when the Religious Education Association was formed in 1903, as the center of expertise and training, not a single woman was asked to speak, and none were appointed as officers. Clearly, men were not ready for equality, not yet "emancipated from the caste of sex so that they can work easily with women, unless they be head and women clearly subordinate." The churches had a "long stretch of unexplored country to be traversed," said Montgomery, "before the perfect democracy of Jesus is reached."[22]

Bureaucracy did have its benefits, though. Modern denominations offered career opportunities for women as secretaries and typists, as well as a few instant—though clearly tokenized—promotions. There were also new occasions for competition between women, eroding the gender solidarity that Victorians took for granted. A small but select group of women entered denominational bureaucracies at the top. To compensate for the loss of their independent societies, the women's boards received a set number of seats, usually one-third, on national mission boards and committees. The move was hardly fair, of course, as it rendered women a permanent minority in a male-dominated bureaucracy. Baptist Lucy Peabody was deeply skeptical of the arrangement. "On the whole," she said, "women work rather better with women. While they can hold their own fairly well with individual man on most questions, collective man on a Board is another and a modern problem."[23]

Yet other women directly affected by mergers—the soon-to-be-institutional insiders—were mildly intrigued at the possibility of working on denominational boards with men. A Congregational insider admitted that while "we do not want to be merged," we still "want to play the game and we have faith in Congregational gentlemen."[24] One of her colleagues agreed that she felt a "thrill" about "history in the making." She worried about having "stage fright" and that her "brain [would] not function in the presence of this conservative, august body," but she also had a plan. She aimed to win their confidence by being "as quiet and humble and receptive, as I can be on occasions." That, she said, "always makes a hit with men!!!"[25]

These changes at the top should not obscure the fact that in its own neat, efficient way, the modern denominational bureaucracy offered a solution to the churches' persisting "woman problem," cutting through centuries of wrangling about complicated biblical texts and specious theological arguments. From the local church to the national headquarters, pastors and bureaucrats needed secretaries and office administrators, work that in the early twentieth century was not yet coded female, but soon would be. Mimeograph machines and typewriters required no heavy lifting, and in fact seemed naturally suited to agile feminine fingers. During the Great Depression, a female workforce was also economical: in 1932 Methodists reported a solid increase of full-time women employees, from nearly 8,000 in

1928 to 9,100—this in comparison to 15,000 male clergymen. The number, which included secretaries and pastors' assistants but not the 4,000 nurses in Methodists hospitals, was particularly noteworthy given decreases in the number of female missionaries and deaconesses.[26]

Best of all, the church administrator's status was ambiguous enough to keep at bay nagging questions about women exercising "authority" in the churches, allowing them an insider status without risking a run-in with St. Paul. The church secretary was often the literal gatekeeper to the pastor's study; even the office worker typing memos for a denominational bureaucrat knew something of the internal mysteries of the institution's structure and procedures. But administration was not the same as actual leadership. No one revered the church secretary: she typed sermons and mimeographed the Sunday bulletins, a spiritual intermediary at best.[27]

In the short run, everyone looked to benefit. The Protestant churches found ways to keep women busy, shoring up the whole instead of spinning off separate organizations. Women had an opportunity to learn not just routine office skills, but to gain an insider's organizational knowledge—where to send a particular memo, or how to reign in a wandering committee, assemble an invitation list for a difficult meeting, or assess the qualifications of a recruit for a key position. These are valuable skills, all too easily maligned as soul-destroying and "bureaucratic," and would prove immensely useful in years ahead.

If there was a victim in all the upgrading and reshuffling, it was the minister's wife, saddled with the most traditional of all church roles. " 'Unaccountably,' " a puzzled clergyman confessed, " 'my wife eventually came to resent the presence of this woman on my staff. Why, I do not know.' " True, he had confided in his secretary, but for good reason. " 'Naturally, she was conversant with what was going on in the deliberations of the church council, in the family and personal affairs of the people around us. How could it be otherwise when she handled all my correspondence?' " In the end, the beleaguered minister decided to "placate a jealous wife," and let the secretary go, with considerable guilt and reluctance. " 'I know, in my own heart,' " he confessed, " 'that there is more than one way of wronging a woman, and I have wronged this one to humor another's prejudice and baseless jealousy.' " Even that move did not rectify the situation, however, as the clergyman's home life descended into "hell" and his work life became a morass of inefficiency—and all, he was convinced, for no good reason. " 'I do not believe that there is more than one man in a hundred thousand to whom his secretary means anything more than a business associate.' " All the whispering and innuendo was a " 'slander on an educated, competent, hard-working body of women.' "[28]

From there the stereotypes abounded further, including sexual competition between the worldly-wise secretary and the jealous, frumpy minister's wife, insulated from the pressures of the modern workplace. "We secretaries are the butts of more jokes and suspicions than we deserve," said one exasperated correspondent to *Church Management*, "and all because we spend more waking hours with our bosses than any other individual." As a professional woman she understood, and did not object, when her superior treated her as a "machine to carry out specific wants and demands." Of course, the church secretary was a step above the masses in the corporate typing pool; she worked "for the love of the task." "[I]f a minister has confidence in his secretary and makes her a co-worker in a great task is he not doing as Jesus would do in using personalities?" An intelligent pastor's wife would be "grateful that another does the petty details and leaves her free to share the honors of his profession."[29]

One solution was to upgrade the role of the clergy spouse to a semiprofessional status. By the 1930s, many church periodicals had set apart a special page of cheery stories, reading lists, recipes, and hospitality tips. The editors at *Church Management*, the mid-twentieth-century bible of Christian efficiency, created a separate department for ministers' wives, a place to share "positive suggestions" and womanly advice.[30] But the message was not lost: times had changed, and no woman, not even the pastor's wife, could expect to wield power just because she was female.

In the 1920 and 1930s it appeared that the pain of bureaucratic reorganization was worth enduring. Beyond all those sexist bureaucrats and messy office relationships were genuine opportunities for to stake out new, ambitious, modern goals. In contrast to their mothers and grandmothers, who had carved out and defended a single space of sex-segregated turf, the rising generation began to believe that equality was possible. Perhaps, finally, the American Protestant churches were finally ready for the twentieth-century world.

Historic legacies are not easily discarded, however. It was one thing to incorporate the latest business methods and corporate structures, something else entirely to accommodate the "new woman," competent, ambitious, and unambiguously equal. How would modernizing churches deal with the modern women in the pews, now free from the spiritual and social constraints their Victorian mothers and grandmothers had endured? In the postsuffrage era, no group came to understand the hard reality of unintended consequences more than northern Presbyterians. Their story is worth considering in some detail.

At What Price Inclusion? The Presbyterian Dilemma

Margaret Hodge and Katherine Bennett were not cynical people. They were smart, dedicated, and competent women making their way in a man's world, presidents of the Presbyterian women's home and foreign missionary societies, respectively. They were used to being listened to, and for good reason. Beneath that polite exterior was serious potential for disruption.

That much is evident in a photograph from 1925, a group portrait of a Presbyterian delegation to Calvin Coolidge's White House. The two women are standing together in the front row. Though three other female faces are half-visible in the second, peering out between masculine shoulders,

Margaret Hodge, Katherine Bennett, and Presbyterians visiting the White House, 1926, Courtesy Presbyterian Historical Society, Philadelphia, PA.

Hodge and Bennett are clearly the two that mattered. Dressed in dark hues like the men, they are conspicuous in their very large, flowery hats. Hodge nearly towers over the rest; she is a full head taller than Bennett, a small, somewhat rumpled figure, defiantly clutching the long strap of her pocketbook.

No one looks relaxed or comfortable. And understandably so: William Jennings Bryan occupies front and center, displacing even President Coolidge, who is standing off to one side. Later that year, Bryan would make headlines prosecuting John Scopes at a courthouse in Tennessee, a sad and controversial end to a distinguished career as a statesman. Yet well before he took on the Darwinists at Dayton, he had thoroughly roiled Presbyterian waters. Bryan was a central figure in the General Assembly in 1923, where after narrowly losing his bid for moderator, he turned his energies to bringing down Harry Emerson Fosdick. The New York pastor's sermon "Shall the Fundamentalists Win?," resounding as a taunt to the denomination's conservatives, had made him an easy target. Bryan also pressed Presbyterians to take a stand against evolution, and pushed for stringent doctrinal standards. By the time of his death in the summer of 1925 he had stoked enough controversy to last the denomination for years. In 1929, Presbyterians ousted one of Princeton's leading New Testament scholars, J. Gresham Machen, and precipitated a full-out schism, with the founding of a separate Orthodox Presbyterian Church in 1936.

In the long run, however, Bryan would be less of a problem for Presbyterians than the two women standing to his left. Margaret Hodge and Katherine Bennett represented a much more intractable, complicated challenge to male Presbyterian leadership—and in 1925 they were just getting started.

Northern Presbyterians had entered the modern managerial business world with the zeal of recent converts. Some of the love for order was inborn: the historic Presbyterian system operated as a kind of judicial hierarchy, with local presbyteries and regional synods channeling all major decisions and doctrinal questions to a national body, the General Assembly. Yet even a well-oiled, functioning chain of command was no match for organizational sprawl. By 1919 twenty different boards as well as a fluctuating number of independent committees were attempting to administer the work of Sunday schools, missionaries, and ministerial pensions. The denomination provided what oversight it could through the office of the Stated Clerk, at best a stop-gap position. When William Henry Roberts filled that role, from 1884 to 1920, it was only part-time, and consisted mostly of routine office-work, taking minutes at the General Assembly, receiving requests for rulings from presbyteries and synods, and keeping track of church statistics.

The reorganization plan, finalized in 1923, promoted the Stated Clerk to a busy top executive, overseeing four large departments dealing with administration, publicity, statistics, and local church oversight. A twenty-seven-member General Council acted as his board of directors, tending to the work of the denomination between meetings of the General Assembly. The newly created Office of the General Assembly functioned as "a sophisticated executive department, centrally organized and compromising multiple layers of management." Further restructuring trimmed and straightened even further, consolidating ten boards—everything from missions and Sunday schools to temperance and "sabbath observance"—to four departments: National Missions, Foreign Missions, Christian Education, and "Ministerial Relief and Sustentation."[31]

As we have seen, efficiency spelled trouble for the women's boards, and Presbyterians were no exception. The reorganization ended their semi-independent status in one move, merging both the home and foreign boards into their respective departments. In return, women received seats on each of the four national boards, amounting to one-third of the total. It had seemed a simple, common-sense approach, thoroughly discussed by various committees and commissions. Their Congregational cousins had weathered a similar unification with minimal disruption, amicably and effectively.

But unlike those Congregationalists, Presbyterians' polity gave women no say in the matter. Only elders and ordained clergy had a vote in the General Assembly, and by rule both categories were exclusively male. As a result, as one scathing review put it, the women's organizations "were taken from them without their consent, and in some cases in opposition to their wishes, by a purely masculine vote." The "majority of church members" were a legal "minority," denied "the right of separate expression."[32]

The move was both high-handed and confusing. It allowed local women's groups (some 6,000 in regional synods and local presbyteries) to continue raising money for their own projects, schools or hospitals that had long depended on them for support. But the reorganization plan also included an open-ended codicil, that the women's boards could allocate funds *unless otherwise determined by the General Assembly.* Even more unsettling, savvy denominational bureaucrats in other departments were starting to hover, aware that the new rules put in play funds once earmarked for missionary work. The Board of Christian Education was first off the starting block, reasoning that since one-third of its members were now female, they were entitled to make a direct appeal to the women of the denomination—that is, to receive a share of the money raised by local missionary groups.[33]

Still, denominational leaders had reason to believe that the women were in a conciliatory mood. After all, in 1919 the General Assembly had considered removing barriers from the office of church elder, even ordination to the ministry. A specially appointed committee had conducted an exploratory survey of 100 clergy and leaders of women's organizations, and discovered little taste for controversy. Only a tepid majority supported the measure, amid worries that ordination "would afford an excuse for men to shirk *their* duties," and hinder a reunion with the denomination's southern branch, the Presbyterian Church in the U.S.A. Even the women who supported ordination insisted that they were only claiming "the right for their sisters," and "disclaimed any wish to occupy the office themselves." Perhaps all the more telling in 1920, the denomination's energetic conservative wing failed to muster much indignation: a scholarly article by Princeton Seminary theologian B. B. Warfield generated some back-and-forth about Greek verbs and ecclesiastical practices of first-century Corinthians, but also irritation that the ordination question was "going to crowd itself upon us in the church," when more serious matters loomed. When an ordination overture went out to vote in 1920, it quietly failed. Presbyterian officials no doubt exhaled in unison.[34]

Within a few years, however, they had an angry constituency on their hands, far larger and more organized than any fundamentalist faction. In a variety of ways, the two insurgent groups were similar, both perceiving themselves—rightly or wrongly—as loyal, jilted insiders forced to endure a rank injustice. As an Illinois woman declared, "it comes as a distinct and disappointing shock that after so many years of faithful cooperation in the upbuilding of the organization to the point of its great efficiency, it should be 'swallowed whole' without even Fletcherizing" (referring to a popular digestive regiment requiring rigorous chewing).[35]

In the ensuing controversy, Margaret Hodge and Katherine Bennett occupied the same position as they had in their 1925 group portrait, front and center, but somewhat awkwardly off to one side. Denominational officials enlisted them as mediators, and tasked them with investigating "The Causes of Unrest among the Women of the Church," likely reasoning that once the grievances had been aired, safe middle ground would be in sight.

Instead, church leaders received a stark warning of more trouble ahead. In their opening statement, Hodge and Bennett took pains to let Presbyterian officials knew that though some churchwomen were content with the "status quo," others were prepared to bring the walls down. Many were deeply angry, insisting that "everything is wrong in the church," especially the high-handed mistreatment of its female membership.[36]

Clearly, Presbyterian women were as roiled as fundamentalists; however, the similarity only went so far. In contrast to conservatives, who bemoaned the drift from Calvinist orthodoxy, churchwomen criticized the Presbyterian church for being insufficiently modern. The truth, as Hodge and Bennett stated over and over, was that the denomination was retrograde. In terms of women's rights it was one of the most backward in the country. And there was actual proof: a survey conducted by the Federal Council of Churches found northern Presbyterians the "most consistently negative of any large denomination," bringing up the rear with Southern Baptists, Plymouth Brethren, and Defenseless Mennonites.[37]

More fundamentally, the supposedly modernized church was out of step with its own laywomen—and it was in danger of losing them. The "thinking church woman of today," Hodge and Bennett warned, is well aware of "the larger opportunities for service that are now open to her in practically any field." In "business and professional life," women were "rapidly taking their place side by side with men, with full freedom to serve in any position for which they had the qualifications." What an irony that the church, an institution affirming modern democratic values and proclaiming the spiritual equality of all, was becoming more autocratic by the day. This "illogical and difficult situation," they declared, was unjust and unsustainable.[38]

What was the answer? Hodge and Bennett were quick to deny that the right to ordination would solve anything; it was at best a narrow and symbolic solution to a much more pervasive problem. "Few wish any specific opportunity," they wrote. "What they do wish is the removal of inhibitions which constantly remind them that they are not considered intellectually or spiritually equal to responsibilities within the church." If Presbyterians truly wished to be modern, in other words, they had to embrace the true spirit of the twentieth century, and treat women "in the light of [their] ability, and not of [their] sex."[39]

The upshot was that Presbyterians had a "woman problem" that was, to a large degree, the result of their own bureaucratic bungling. "It seems unthinkable," the report warned, that a church "which has thought it best to destroy woman's Boards of Missions, to arbitrarily keep women in a minority on the new Boards," and to siphon off any money they raised, "is nevertheless not only allowing, but often encouraging the drifting into another situation as to the activities of women in the church without making any plans."[40]

This much male Presbyterian leaders understood. In 1928, the General Assembly convened an influential gathering of "fifteen representative women" with top denominational officials, including Lewis Mudge, Robert Speer, and Henry Swearingen. The discussion was lengthy, honest, and wide-ranging, and exposed a curious but understandable disagreement between the men and women present. It was the men, not the women, who ended up the outspoken advocates of equality. The times called for a "rather bold and challenging statement," declared Rochester, New York, pastor W. R. Taylor, decrying the church's "illogical and indefensible" prohibitions. "I stand for the ordination of women not only to the diaconate but to the eldership," William Chambers Covert agreed. He was in fact ready to go "the whole length as far as that is concerned." "The women have a right to what Christ has given them," seconded Tennessee pastor, S. T. Wilson, "the right of equality with those who happen to have been born as men."[41]

The women were skeptical. Instead of rushing toward a simplistic solution, as Emma Speer explained, the men needed slow down and understand the scope of the problem. Far too often, she said, well-intentioned "Christian men" try "to do things for women, rather than let women do things for themselves and the Church." Everyone needed to stop and take stock of how much had changed just in the last fifty years, almost more than in the entire history of Christendom. Men and women both were facing a genuinely new world, one they yet understood "only in the most dim way."[42]

The men did not appear to listen. The tumultuous 1920s came to an end with a genuinely unusual situation: male church leaders pushing for women's ordination without the support of a female constituency. A "Council of One Hundred Women," convened in St. Paul in 1929, was explicit: "The women of the church as a whole," they said, "have not been concerned with their ecclesiastical status: they have been anxious as to the future of their separate and peculiar services to the church through the organizations they have formed and fostered."[43]

Not to be discouraged, the General Assembly issued overtures approving women elders and ministers. Yet when the denomination-wide vote took place, neither the approval of the first nor the failure of the second raised much of a stir. One contributor to the *Presbyterian Banner* likely spoke for many when he poo-poohed the entire episode. Even the worry that female pastors and elders would "feminize" the church was not worth the energy—that had already happened long ago. At worst, the overtures might encourage "unfit" women into the ministry, but then again, it might introduce a much needed feminine spiritual tone.[44]

Presbyterians were in the midst of a classic twentieth-century conundrum, caught between the ideal of gender equality and women's practical need for a separate institutional power base. Add money to the mix and the contradictions deepen further. That much is clearly evident in a debate over women's control of funds they had raised for foreign missions, chronicled in a questionnaire sent to women's groups and local pastors. Asked whether they favored allowing the Board of Christian Education a share of their proceeds, the women narrowly voted no (182 to 163). Their responses show them confused, incensed, and cynical about "coercion from the 'higher-ups,'" willing to cooperate but feeling a "great and growing weariness" with out-of-touch bureaucrats and overly ambitious projects. "Are you taking away their work by placing it on the level with that of the men?" a Nebraska pastor's wife asked. "Or are you giving them more work?" Presbyterian clergy were equally cynical about women's organizations. "Enthusiastic Missionary women are often the uninformed dead weight on advance in educational programs," said one pastor. "[L]et the women do what they please—they will anyway," counseled another.[45]

Everyone agreed that the women needed to reorganize, to take on bigger tasks rather than smaller. Well, almost everyone. "By all things holy," said one minister, "do not start another women's organization in the church." But he was a minority. "As church women were are vitally interested in the entire program of our denominations," a Kanas group declared. "We form 60 per cent of the church membership and contribute 58 per cent of the benevolence gifts of the church and 59 per cent of the local expense budget." Kansas women were teachers in Sunday schools and Vacation Bible Schools and summer conferences; they supported student pastors and raised money for tuition costs. And they supported foreign missions. "All the women should support all the causes," a clergyman agreed; "The era of divisions by sex is passing," said another.[46]

Certainly some kind of change was needed. The old institutional base in domestic and foreign missions would steadily erode, until, as Dana Robert writes, those organizations "virtually ceased to exist" by the time of the Second World War. It was time, as the next chapter shows, for mainline

Protestant women to write a new story, to take modernization into their own hands. This required a new religious persona, no longer tied to particular denominations or single issue, free from the whims of bureaucrats and the burdens of old Victorian stereotypes. The "churchwoman" would finally bring her church into the twentieth century.[47]

3

Liberating the Ladies' Aid

Protestant Churchwomen in the 1930s

"My earliest recollections of a Ladies' Aid," said Alma Newell Atkins, a Midwestern preacher's wife writing in 1939, "was at a village church, where a small, but aggressive group of women quilted and sewed carpet rags on Thursdays to pay for the twice-a-month preaching." The tiny congregation was hanging on by its fingernails, worshiping in a threadbare building with "holes in the carpet, falling plaster, squeaking pews, [and] sticking keys on the old reed organ." Nevertheless, Mrs. Atkins recalled, "the women ran the church—definitely. They paid the bills and formed its policies. The men neither prayed nor paid."[1]

The situation was not ideal, an unstable mix of power outside of formal constraints—with good reason an Iowa laywoman described Ladies' Aid groups as "potential TNT."[2] To Mrs. Atkins they were nothing more than a "vast commercial project—one of the largest organizations for unlicensed peddling in America." The women sold "pot cleaners, extracts, jelly powders," and "cookbooks, mops, dust cloths, scouring pads, calendars, greeting cards, tidy tacks, knives, toilet articles, and what not." They sponsored "rummage sales, bazaars, country fairs, hobby shows, fishponds, white elephant sales, food sales, saving wrappers and coupons and a restaurant business on a grand scale." At some point, it all felt a bit sordid: the fundraising ploys became the goal of the congregation's life together, rather than the means toward it. "These women," Mrs. Atkins wrote, "have all but divorced themselves from, at least have lost sight of, *the actual program of the church.*"[3]

What's most notable about this joyously incriminating portrayal is that it appeared in *Church Management,* a Protestant magazine devoted to the gospel of good business. Readers received regular diatribes against "selling rackets" that limited congregational budgets to the haphazard proceeds of cake raffles and yard sales. Smart churches had long-term financial plans built on the solid ground of annual member pledges. The advice came with ardent testimonials of success—"we have come through the depression with flying

Good and Mad. Margaret Bendroth, Oxford University Press. © Oxford University Press 2023.
DOI: 10.1093/oso/9780197654064.003.0004

colors, an Illinois pastor declared—and insistent, upbeat calls for "functional organization." Churches needed to create programs and carry them out by a "step by step plan," mirroring the methods employed by modern business. Our fathers never dreamed that such a "set-up" might be necessary, the editor William Leach explained in 1936. But new times demanded new strategies, a dedication to pragmatic problem-solving that would have been unimaginable to the church deacon of earlier, simpler days.[4]

Efficiency experts were not the only ones to declare the Ladies' Aid the enemy of progress: the more devastating critique came from within, from a new generation demanding more meaningful church involvement, and coming to the fore in the 1930s and 1940s. The "churchwoman," as the *Christian Century* described her in 1930, was tired of endless fundraising for choir robes and parlor cushions, endless lantern slide lectures about missionary schools in faraway countries. The modern woman was frankly appalled by the "sordidness in the Ladies' Aid," said the *Century*, and bored by the "aloofness in the missionary society." The capable modern woman wanted to assert her "full influence" in the church and beyond that, in the wider world itself.[5]

Though a word like "churchwoman" may sound antique, even a bit stuffy to twenty-first-century ears, it had an exciting ring in the postsuffrage era. The neologism represented a progressive alternative to traditional forms of belief and belonging, a rejuvenated grassroots Protestantism equal to the challenges of modern times. "The problem of woman's relation to the church," the *Christian Century* opined, is only one part of a larger conundrum, finding ways to invest "church membership itself—that of men as well as women, the old and the young—with significance."[6]

As this chapter shows, gaining organizational traction would take time and some creative thinking beyond old, well-trod paths. No one wanted to go back to the Victorian division of labor, and the churches knew that women needed some kind of formal recognition. But the solution was far from clear. Presbyterians, in fact, even mulled the possibility of a "third category" of delegates to their General Assemblies, giving unordained women the "same power as to participation and discussion and as to voting" as ministers and ruling elders.[7]

Most church people, men and women both, knew that ordination was not the solution. Historians are often tempted, in analyzing restless moments like these, to assume that this was the goal everyone looked to, that the culmination of all women's religious activism was the pulpit. It is important to remember, however, that the ministry was not an attractive career path in the postsuffrage era. Too many Americans associated a female ministers with splashy evangelists like Aimee Semple McPherson or holiness preachers like the Salvation Army's Evangeline Booth. The woman in the pulpit was often a theological entrepreneur, like Alma White, founder of the Pillar of Fire Church, a holiness denomination, and Ellen G. White of the Seventh Day Adventists. Respectability, therefore, was a perennial problem. The International Association of Woman Ministers (IAWM) was organized in 1919, in large part to emphasize the professionalism of female clergy, promoting a "more refined, middle-class, mainline" persona, and, not incidentally, policing boundaries of race and class.[8] As an association for "'high minded cultured educated consecrated evangelical Christian women," the IAWM carefully distinguished itself from "Pentecostal preaching women on the one hand and feminist 'cranks' on the other."[9] They were fighting an uphill battle, however. Applying for Congregational credentials in 1930, Margaret Blair Johnstone was gently turned down. "Think of the sensationalism of women evangelists," the credentialing committee advised. "No matter how earnest you would be, no one would believe you."[10]

Ordination was just too narrow and specific; the churchwoman's answer was to take on the whole of Christendom. This chapter describes how this happened, through the stories of two organizations, the Woman's Division of the Methodist Church and United Church Women (UCW), formed in 1939 and 1941, respectively. More than just "another women's group," they reflected the spirit of their age, particularly the idealism of a Protestant ecumenical movement that was enjoying peak success and support. Yet they were also more than an auxiliary to a movement dominated by male theologians and church officials. In the 1930s and 1940s churchwomen created something new and distinct, a feminine form of Protestant ecumenism that blurred the traditional boundaries of the white, mostly northern mainline churches.

The result was a new and stronger mainline Protestantism, fueled by a new type of ecumenical outreach, from the "bottom up" rather than from the "top down." In that sense it reflected the myriad concerns of Protestant women suddenly released from a single focus on missionary work. The world beckoned, with a nearly unlimited set of challenges, everything from the prevention of war to "smut" in movie theaters.

The unspoken subject was gender: churchwomen's ecumenical organizations took extraordinary care not to be female. In part this was because "woman only" groups were starting to feel old-fashioned, a vestige of a generation who had courted in parlors and front porches, and unimaginable to a younger set going out on dates in the family automobile. The most flourishing Protestant organizations were coeducational, groups like the World Student Christian Federation, Christian Endeavor, and Epworth Leagues offering both men and women opportunities for informal camaraderie and shared leadership.[11]

Yet in the postsuffrage era, all women's organizations, both church-based and secular, were problematic. Instead of emphasizing feminine solidarity, the New Deal–era model downplayed gender differences, touting the virtues of competence and collegiality. Eleanor Roosevelt's feminism, writes Mary Ann Glendon, was "ardent but pragmatic and subordinate to her broader social concerns." "If women want equal consideration," Roosevelt declared, "they must prepare themselves to adjust to other people and make no appeals on the ground of sex." Certainly biological differences mattered, and deeply so, especially the bond between mother and child. Homemaking was women's "first field of activity," she said, "and it will always remain our most important one." Yet instinct was no substitute for expertise. "A woman who cannot engage in an occupation and hold it because of her own ability had much better get out of that particular occupation, and do something where her ability will count."[12]

The League of Women Voters is another good example, a nonpartisan organization formed six months after the passage of the suffrage amendment, and described by historian Kristin Goss as "both a woman's organization and not a women's organization." Though the League's membership was entirely female, it presented itself as a "citizen organization whose work is carried on by women simply because they happen to be able to organize their time and energies in a convenient working pattern." More subtle rhetorical messages established the League's gender identity, denying gender differences while "simultaneously signaling" that women were naturally better than men when it came to organizing, "more conscientious, less brazenly political, and more public-interest oriented."[13] In the New Deal era, the ambiguities extended to details of dress: Molly Dewson, a brilliant political strategist who headed the Women's Division of the Democratic Party, adopted the persona of a "nice Boston aunt." As "men are at their best with their mothers and favorite aunts," said Dewson, her wardrobe consisted of silk prints and matching jackets, low-heeled shoes and suits with pockets, presenting her as neither a dowager nor a "befuddled old lady."[14]

Churchwomen carried an additional burden. They understood that their success would be problematic, not only resurrecting old fears of feminization, but even the prospect of a completely parallel set of female-dominated institutions. The *Christian Century* called the question in 1948: "Will Women Launch Their Own Church?" The point at issue was the UCW's resistance to affiliating within the National Council of Churches, and the new charge was "sectarianism," a damning and ironic criticism of a women's ecumenical organization. In a deeper sense, however, the accusation revealed the true worries of male church leaders, briefly recognizing their precarious position as a small masculine contingent attempting to lead a majority feminine institution. As this chapter shows, they had reason to worry.[15]

First Off, the Loyalty Question

For a short while, it looked as if the mergers of women's missionary organizations had ended successfully, a troublesome obstacle removed with minimal uproar. "You were a little afraid of us at first," a Baptist woman told the men of her denomination in 1922. "You didn't feel quite sure that we could be depended upon to play the game, and to tell the truth, we, too, suffered some of the same qualms about you."[16] Yet at the same time, the denomination was sponsoring "Loyalty Luncheons" for churchwomen, to ensure that they would not bow out of "the whole great task of the denomination." Though actually an occasion for collecting the money raised by women's groups, Baptist officials hoped the gatherings would "send a thrill of loyalty to Christ and His work through all the churches."[17]

Congregationalists were also beginning to worry. Already in the mid-1920s they were congratulating themselves, confident that what had looked like a divisive process had created more unity than before. Who could argue that a smoothly functioning, simplified American Board was a genuine step forward, "humanizing and spiritualizing this whole matter of missions"? For their part, the women seemed ready to cooperate, to all appearances excited about the prospect of joining denominational boards and committees—albeit under a quota system allowing them only one-third of the available seats. Perhaps, they declared, the day has come to retire the old slogan, "Woman's Work for Woman," a catchphrase "which has rallied the women of the churches to their banner for more than fifty years." The new call was for "men and women to work together for better understanding and support of a common task."[18]

The truth of the matter, as Congregationalists were to discover, was much messier. Beyond the handful of women elevated to national male-run boards were thousands of others, suddenly cast adrift from a cause they had long cherished. "Certain missionaries and institutions on the mission field are to the women like their own children," a churchwoman explained. Relinquishing the work to a "large and necessarily unwieldy board" is "like asking a mother to give up the control of her own child."[19]

The question was genuine: if women no longer had control of separate space, would they remain faithful? The implications were definitely worrisome: Congregationalists stood to lose the unpaid service, the regular donations, and the loyalty of thousands of active laywomen. And clearly, many state and local organizations, which had been left intact after the merger, were foundering under male leadership. "'I see now where I am going to have a vacation,'" one laywoman reportedly said, after hearing news of the merger. "'That great new American Board will not need me.'" Not surprisingly, by the early 1930s, Congregationalists were backtracking rapidly, looking for a new "secretary of woman's work," whose primary job was to cultivate "loyalty to this unified program." Armed with a "discerning and loving personality," she was to rebuild a lost "sense of responsibility and sacrificial devotion" among the denomination's drifting women.[20]

By then, however, the effort was too late. Congregational missionary executives were already aware that the merger had "relieved the women of a sense of definite responsibility," and soon realized that this loss of interest inflicted a wound on the cause itself. Local churches were simply used to seeing missionary work as female territory; once the women lost interest, support dwindled and disappeared. Income was already falling by 1929, and in the cash-strapped years ahead, the momentum never fully recovered.[21]

In the meantime, Congregational women filtered back together, with the older state fellowships joining under a combination of words the denomination had once hoped to discard, a new department of "Women's Work." Led by its own national secretary, the department raised money for the "Woman's Gift," an annual donation to denominational projects, and forcefully guarded it from bureaucratic poaching. The efforts formalized with the founding of the National Fellowship of Congregational Christian Women in 1953.[22]

Their Episcopalian colleagues could have warned them that the "parallel church" was difficult, if not impossible to dislodge, even with promises of power and formal office. Though many Episcopalian women had received the right to vote in parish meetings by 1920, they chose not to. Instead, as historian Joan Gunderson explains, they "redefined parish life" to create their own separate base of power. The typical local congregation "contained two structures," she writes, "the 'official' parish controlled by the male vestry and clergy, and the 'women's church' controlled by women's organizations." By the early twentieth century, the local parallel church had grown horizontally, with national women's organizations corresponding to the male-centered hierarchy. Of course, power was asymmetrical: men would hold a lock on ordained positions and important decision-making until (at least) the 1970s, with the opening of the priesthood. But in local parishes, the changes at the top were less consequential than the work—and the money—women already controlled, in altar guilds and missionary societies.[23]

What the Survey Said

To varying degrees, top Protestant officials realized they had a problem, one that went beyond particular tensions in parishes and denominations. Frustration was fast becoming the dominant emotion among women appointed to national and denominational boards, those who had been instantly promoted by the new quota systems. Take, for example, the Federal Council of Churches' effort in 1936 to convene a high-level discussion of "woman's sphere today."[24] The hand-picked members of its Women's Committee were no rag-tag band of rebels; they were accomplished and influential, most married to wealthy and prominent men, including Mary Woolley; the president of Mount Holyoke College, Dorothy (Mrs. Henry Sloan) Coffin; and Charlotte Niven of the National YWCA.[25] Used to social deference, they did not enjoy being treated as inferiors by male denominational executives. Reports that the men viewed their female colleagues as "timid—Afraid to speak up" must have rankled, even when male executives were willing to admit that "Men are condescending to women." "Underlying the 'disability feeling' of women on Boards," the group concluded, "is the *secondary place of women* in the entire church administrative set-up. We should be working for more equality and definite training should accompany our efforts."[26]

Many influential laywomen were ready to write off the FCC entirely, including its earnest fact-finding on the "status of women." A San Francisco woman wrote to Anna Caldwell, the Commission secretary, turning down an invitation to participate. "I think if the Federal Council is going to do nothing about women and the church excepting to tabulate a lot of data concerning church organizations, it will be another eighteen-hundred years before the church has any real message about women in the church, and then only, I fear, will women rebel."[27]

The survey, conducted by the FCC's Department of Research and Education in 1938 and 1939, attempted to be exhaustive. Queries and questionnaires went everywhere, to leading laywomen and executives in all the major denominations, even to female pastors out in the hinterlands. Yet amid the reams of evidence coming into New York offices, the most telling finding was not about women, but about the men who sent in responses. The vast majority of denominational officials had little concrete information to offer—or, it appeared, any interest in generating it. Even efficiency-minded Presbyterians kept no statistical count of women elected as Ruling Elders, or as delegates to the General Assembly. Lewis Mudge resorted to a bit of bluster. "We have never assembled statistics in this connection," he said, "because from the beginning we have felt it highly important that men and women alike should be elected to this office on the basis of their competency to serve." The lack of information was in fact a denominational policy, Mudge insisted, a commitment to "to consider men and women from the standpoint of personality and endowments and not from the standpoint of sex."[28]

The final FCC report, published in 1940, provided other reasons why the mainline denominations were slow to address their "woman problem": they were not sure what it was. "Probably the most important reason for objecting to women on the governing boards," the report stated, is that "tradition is against it." Yet depending on the denomination, "tradition" could mean almost anything, a literal interpretation of the Bible's prohibitions on women speaking, allegiance to hierarchical church governments, or even nostalgia for mythical bygone days when everyone knew their place and stayed there. And behind all that was another welter of uncertainties, not about restless women on the march, but about men left sitting on the proverbial couch. A Methodist clergyman, for example, who deplored "the lack of man-power" in churches, warned that the "corollary of success" by women would be "a further loss of male leadership." The strongest doubts, however, came from women themselves, worried that any advances would leave their fathers, sons, and husbands beyond the pale of organized religion—or drifting toward secular Sundays of golf and morning papers. "Sometimes I wonder," a

Congregational woman admitted, "if our Christian life would be more vital and vigorous if our men would . . . take over *all* the offices of the church."[29]

Grassroots Ecumenism: United Church Women

The truth was that the average woman in the pews cared little about male-run church boards. The real energy, and the important opportunities, were in new organizations dedicated to ecumenical cooperation. The first half of the twentieth century was a heyday for visionaries, devoted to stream-lining and unifying the vast sprawl of American denominationalism. Some of the achievements were historic, as when Methodists reunited in 1939 after nearly a century of separation over slavery. Other times enthusiasm outran historical realities. In 1919 Congregationalists were exploring a plan to allow Episcopal bishops to ordain their clergy until the effort fizzled in 1923, denounced by critics as "completely fatuous." Certainly the vision was astonishingly ambitious: The American Council on Organic Union of the Churches of Christ was a plan created in 1919 (and abandoned by 1925) to bring together twenty-three Protestant denominations.[30]

Below the headlines, however, was a thriving grassroots movement of local church federations. Though small and sparsely funded, these groups took on the full agenda of the Federal Council of Churches, everything from evangelism and social service to international relations, juvenile delinquency, alcohol, and poverty, aiming to create an "inclusive, more cooperative religious culture throughout the nation." By the World War I era, church federations in towns and cities were on the adventurous edge, in many cases overcoming not just Protestant differences but interreligious ones.[31]

Where would women fit in? Like the ministry and most national church boards, the new ecumenical organizations were dominated by men. When sociologist Paul Douglass conducted a study of twenty-one local federations in 1930, he found only three women in leadership positions. Nearly all of the committee work was run by men as well: even in a traditionally feminine area like "social service" only 18% of the participants were female. Women predominated only as staff members in local federation offices (53%), and then in lower clerical positions, as secretaries and typists, earning significantly less than their male counterparts. Though worlds beyond the gender-segregated Victorian church organization, the federation movement offered only limited opportunities for women to participate, let alone lead.[32]

A women's organization looked inevitable. Though Douglass found the prospect dubious—the veteran sociologist fretted that the federation movement did not have a strong enough "overhead organization" to constrain the "woman separatist tendency"—ecumenically minded women had already begun to meet together, though initially with the explicit guidance of the men in charge of the local federations.[33]

The first women's gathering was held in Pittsburgh in 1924, a meeting marked by a polite but gathering restlessness. Florence Quinlan, representing the Council of Women for Home Missions, was genuinely irritated that the agenda consisted of three addresses by male clergy, which the churchwomen were invited to discuss. The clergy, moreover, appeared willfully uninformed about work already underway, and did not hesitate to "indicate the lines of procedure that they thought the women should take." The female audience "rustled" at each slight, according to Quinlan, until they were "nearly bursting."[34]

Within two years the churchwomen were considering an "all inclusive program for local interdenominational groups," without the benefit of male clergy. By 1927, when they met in St. Louis, they had achieved separate momentum, largely independent of the male-run federations. The Boston meeting in 1928 announced that the women had "perfected an organization they will call for the coming year at least, 'The National Conference of Church Women'"—marking the first time the new terminology defined an organization with an agenda and a following.[35]

The new group's rhetoric and goals echoed the unifying vision of the ecumenical movement. As one of the keynote speakers declared, "The church, like the rest of the world, has passed through a period of specialization, and is now faced by the necessity for more cooperation." Their organization was to be "a new power released for the uplift of the world," the "power of united womanhood." As an example of unity to the churches, "it means the dawn of a new day in the forward march of Christian women, under the invincible leadership of the Master."[36]

The vested interests were skeptical. Meeting in joint session in 1929, leaders of the women's interdenominational home and foreign missionary federations compiled a litany of criticisms, as if they sensed an old order passing. The Boston meeting was, they said, neither "well balanced" nor efficient—hardly an auspicious beginning for a new women's organization. In fact, the home and foreign missionary leaders were not even sure what to call the upstart effort. The most reassuring conclusion was that it was "a quest for a unified program and a unified approach," or perhaps simply a "method of procedure," or "an experiment"—or possibly even a "high adventure in fellowship in service."[37] The more alarming possibility was that the churchwomen would further damage the already eroding women's missionary enterprise. *"The Real Question,"* the interdenominational leaders agreed, was how to "best conserve and increase the missionary interests of these local groups," and keep "their interest focused on the needs to which the Federation and the Council minister."[38]

The concern was justified. The new organization's announced goal was to unify "the efforts of church women in the task of establishing a Christian social order in which all areas of life shall be brought into harmony with the life and teaching of Jesus Christ." Questionnaires sent to local church women found missionary work only one interest among many, alongside such challenging topics as "International Relations and World Peace, Legislation and Law Observance, Christian Race Relations, Christian Citizenship, Christian Social Service, Marriage and the Home, the Deepening of Spiritual Life, [and] the Motion Picture and the Drama."[39] Leaders of this new movement understood that traditional appeals to "woman's mission to woman" had gone the way of hoop skirts and corsets. The modern Protestant laywoman expected a range of choices: "the ultimate *consumer*," they declared, "is the woman in the local church."[40]

She did not choose foreign missions. In 1941, after a decade of sometimes prickly negotiation, the three interest groups—home missions, foreign missions, and churchwomen—merged to form a new organization. The goal of United Church Women (UCW) was "the closer integration of women into the total life and work of the church" and "the building of a world Christian community."[41] Organized barely a week after the attack on Pearl Harbor, the UCW immediately took up "war-time problems of families, the spiritual implications of racial problems, and sacrificial living."[42]

Outside observers saw the UCW as a distinct, down-to-earth church organization—the *Christian Century* praised its "pronounced allergy to stuffed shirts" and "male dowagers."[43] In contrast to the FCC and other interdenominational efforts, the new women's organization was not composed of delegates chosen by their respective denominations. UCW was a grassroots organization composed of local church members who supported its vision. Its "Plan for Organizing Councils of Church Women" included all kinds of practical advice: how to enlist a local minister or host a gathering of women from different denominational backgrounds, how to make "abundant living possible for all people in the community."[44] The UCW was also genuinely interdenominational, including Unitarians and Universalists, denominations barred from the FCC for being insufficiently Christian. In 1949, the UCW included women from eighty-four church backgrounds, "representing all shades of theological beliefs, from conservative to liberal," according to an official pamphlet. "We are simply Christian women, united by a great Christian Concern, and rejoicing in the constantly widening avenues of service we make as we walk together."[45] Even more significantly, as we will see, UCW was interracial, and would make race relations, if not the consistent inclusion of Black women, a major concern.

UCW was also astonishingly successful. With 420 local councils at its inception, in 1948 the number had more than tripled to 1,432, with an estimated 10 million members.[46] By the 1950s, it was the largest women's religious organization of its time, with a robust social agenda that included antiracism, opposition to Japanese internment, pacifism, and human rights. The leaders of the UCW lobbied Congress, talked with atomic scientists, and championed the United Nations and the Charter of Human Rights.[47]

Expanding the Mainline: The Women's Division of Christian Service of The Methodist Church

The "woman-centered" mainline Protestantism that was developing in the 1930s and 1940s transcended many boundaries, including regional ones. In fact, the Methodist story testifies to the surprising energy generated by northern and southern churchwomen, brought together in ecumenical alliances.

When three Methodist bodies—the northern and southern wings as well as the smaller Methodist Protestant Church—came together in 1939, many hoped, as the *Christian Century* put it, that "the unified church may turn out to be more liberal than the sum of its parts."[48] In regard to both gender and race, however, the reunion was a setback: Mary McLeod Bethune, who had become a Methodist in 1923, denounced it as "hypocritical and racist," as it clearly was. To prevent the possibility of African American bishops governing white churches, The Methodist Church placed all black congregations in a segregated Central Jurisdiction, a moral blot on the reunion that would take decades to rectify.[49]

The merger also reversed gains by women, requiring the Methodist Protestants to rescind their long-standing support for women's ordination.[50] At the same time the reunion granted southern women, who had no clerical status whatsoever, a small step forward, awarding them the ambiguous rights eked out by their northern counterparts. In the new Methodist Church women could be deacons and elders and ordained as ministers, but they were denied conference membership, which meant in practical terms that they were barred from appointments to any local pulpit. .[51]

This was not surprising. Women did not, in fact, have a voice in the merger negotiations, in spite of their demand for inclusion. "It is literally true," the editors of *Zion's Herald*, admitted, that no woman—not a single one—had any part in formulating the "Plan of Union." The Uniting Conference in 1939 included 900 delegates, only 77 of whom were women. As one worried editor put it, Methodists were in "peril of creating a man's church."[52]

In fact Methodist women had already taken matters into their own hands. In 1938, twenty-seven churchwomen from all three of the Methodist denominations met to plan a new women's organization, with its own Constitution and bylaws, guaranteeing "the right to form plans and policies," and to control and perpetuate women's work already underway. The plan was for "one autonomous organization" with the power to raise funds and to select and support workers. It was to be "the greatest organization of which any Methodist woman can be a member," as one supporter declared. "It combines Christian citizenship, international outlook, social service, genuine Americanism, and a spiritual idealism incomparable." Indeed, every one of the denomination's women "ought to feel like a woman who has suddenly been notified that she had been remembered in the will of a rich relative, so greatly has her heritage been enriched by unification."[53]

Some of the organizers worried that about the "inconsistency" of making plans "to separate ourselves so completely from the whole" during an ecumenical reunion, of "advocating a divided church," as some male church leaders charged. The women were unmoved. "A woman's church forsooth!" one of the planners wrote to a colleague. "Who is responsible for the fact that today we actually have a man's church? Have not the men created conditions that leave us—the 60% of the membership—entirely out of the real church councils? What would they have? Put us back where we would serve as the money collectors for the Boards while the men do the administering? *I am not a feminist, but*," she said, "I am a great believer in the development of woman kind [sic] and know that the years when we have been free to do our own planning and administering have been the years when women have made their largest contribution to the Kingdom."[54] Ultimately, Methodists, the women did not trust male bureaucrats. "[B]ishops and ministers are trained in the art of oratory," one committee member warned, "and can outtalk women from the start."[55]

The Woman's Division of The Methodist Church was a formidable progressive force. Combining six women's organizations, north and south, its purview included home and foreign missions, the Wesleyan Service Guild (an organization for business and professional women), and even the Ladies' Aid Society. The new organization instantly united 20,000 local groups. As Southern Methodist churchwoman Thelma Stevens wrote, "nearly two million women became charter members of the new organization and started down the road together, seeking to become one in spirit and in mission."[56] Significantly, the Woman's Division also maintained financial control, a legacy of the autonomy forged by the missionary societies in the nineteenth century. The budget was considerable—$3.5 million in 1941. Bucking the tide in other denominations, Methodist women "maintained the tradition of separate funding" and a modicum of power.[57]

Redefining Mainline Protestantism

One of the most enduring themes in the history of American religion is the problem of decline, a storyline dating back to the seventeenth-century Puritan divines who bemoaned New England's deteriorating godliness. Though historians of American religion have generally flattened out the narrative, the idea persists, particularly in regard to mainline Protestantism, where by some accounts the entire twentieth century was mostly prelude to collapsing numbers in the 1980s and 1990s. Yet as Ann Braude has pointed out, declension is a thoroughly gendered concept, resting on "the assumption that the public influence of the Protestant clergy is the most important measure of the role of religion in American society." If historians took the persistent female majority into account, she argues, they would recognize the paradigm as little more than "narrative fiction."[58]

Certainly when women occupy the center, twentieth-century mainline Protestantism looks far more resilient than the standard tropes would have it. The churchwomen's movement drew from and generated vigorous energy at the grassroots, a constituency largely removed from the travail of the Ivy League "establishment" so memorably described by historian William Hutchison. The issues that matter to historians—whether the Social Gospel was an outdated concept or biblical criticism a challenge to scriptural authority—mattered relatively little to female activists. Busy, ambitious churchwomen simply did not have the time for the endless debates that so preoccupied their male counterparts, and proudly so. "The battle of Fundamentalism versus Liberalism might rage in the pulpits," wrote Gladys Gilkey Calkins in her history of women's ecumenism, " . . . but these would not throw the women off course. There was too much that needed to be done."[59]

As we will see in the next chapter, the women's mainline also crossed the racial lines that separated white and black Methodists, Baptists, and Presbyterians. As Calkins explained, " 'interdenominational' unquestionably meant 'interracial.' " Local councils desegregated, another observer agreed, "when they realized they could not really be ecumenical if Negro women were not included."[60] This was not easy to do, of course: even with all the good will in the world, an interracial meeting was a logistical nightmare in the Jim Crow era, with African American women forced to negotiate a humiliating maze of segregated hotels and restaurants. Yet every encounter with white women was a teachable moment, a chance to refute negative stereotypes and to begin honest, sometimes even painful, conversations across yawning social divides.

Much was left unsaid, however. The next chapter also considers the limitations of female ecumenism in the 1930s and 1940s, how it strengthened invisible social conventions even as it challenged public ones. Churchwomen's progressive faith came with provisos, built on and fortifying the parameters of class and social status that defined midcentury mainline Protestantism.

4

Race and Class, but Not Gender

Ambitions, Limitations, and Realities

Of all the social causes that churchwomen took on, race relations was the most challenging and the most telling. In many ways, the strength and independence of women's organizations allowed them to be adventurous, to achieve what denominations, bound by old traditions and competing regional interests, could not. In a time when few American Protestants crossed color lines, white and African American churchwomen were doing some of the hard work necessary for racial understanding. Yet, we can still ask what it all meant, within the larger history of women's interracial efforts—and for the African American women who participated.

The story begins in the 1920s, from not one but several sources. One of the most important was the Young Women's Christian Association (YWCA). By then it was the nation's second-largest female organization, with 600,000 members, behind only the American Federation of Women's Clubs, at 1 million. The YWCA was also, as one nervous observer described it, an association of women "with no denominational brakes."[1]

Certainly the twentieth-century YWCA had moved well beyond its pietistic evangelical roots, a trajectory markedly different from its male counterpart, the YMCA. Into the early twentieth century the men's group maintained its religious identity, largely in the form of "muscular Christianity," a heady mixture of masculine spirituality designed for a business-oriented middle-class. The YMCA's fourfold program for the "whole man" provided for spiritual, intellectual, spiritual, and most notably, physical growth. It did not include a social consciousness: according to YMCA policy, "when questions of moral reform become political party questions, our association, *as such*, can have no relation with them."[2]

In contrast, the YWCA took progressively more controversial stands on religion, race, and international politics, even when it meant shedding formal ties with the Protestant churches. Beginning in 1920, when the Y removed a church membership requirement for campus groups; voting members had

Good and Mad. Margaret Bendroth, Oxford University Press. © Oxford University Press 2023.
DOI: 10.1093/oso/9780197654064.003.0005

only to be "true follower[s] of Jesus Christ," thus, as a conservative critic charged, "deliberately open[ing] the doors of its active membership to those who do not believe in the New Testament's teachings." Conservative board member Helen Gould Shepard resigned in protest, "in loyalty to my Lord and Saviour," while angry fundamentalists charged the Y-WMCA with betraying its pious founders, "substituting organization for regeneration, and social service for the fruit of the Spirit."[3]

As a "quasi-religious" group, the YWCA flouted not only doctrinal standards but also conventions on race. From the 1920s onward, the Y was intentionally interracial, protesting Jim Crow regulations that hampered African American members from attending national conventions, and refusing to allow racial segregation in local groups. In contrast to the men's organization, YWCA bylaws allowed only one branch organization in a community, which meant that, especially in urban areas, they were automatically racially integrated.

The YWCA's organizing principle was the power of friendship, a belief that healthy human interactions would break down barriers of race, ethnicity, and class. Though perhaps not revolutionary in retrospect, the idea was daring enough in the 1920s: as historian Nancy Marie Robertson writes, the YWCA was one of the nation's first to make race relations a national priority. By the 1940s, the women were even further out in front of American social mores: its "Interracial Charter," passed in 1946, committed the organization to desegregation, declaring women as the key force in bringing about world peace and harmony. As Robertson aptly notes, "social righteousness had shifted from being a consequence of women's religiosity to being proof of it."[4]

Interracial Friendships

If the YWCA was nimble, the Protestant establishment was not. In the post–World War I era, in the wake of deadly race riots, a resurgence of lynching, and the rebirth of the Ku Klux Klan, the Federal Council of Churches (FCC) did in fact arise and demonstrate alarm, issuing a statement on the "Race Crisis" and creating a Department on Race Relations. Yet historian James Findlay sums up these efforts as "determinedly conventional and unspectacular," noting that the Department of Race Relations was without a full-time executive secretary until 1934. The FCC's best-known effort was "Race Relations Sunday," which was instituted in the 1920s. According to Findlay, it was popular largely because "it required so little of local churches—a once-a-year reminder, usually in February, that problems of race still existed in the country."[5]

The situation would not improve in the 1950s. Amid the rising drama of the civil rights movement the National Council of Churches (NCC) followed a "cautious, evolutionary, go-slow approach." As Findlay writes, decisions about the pace of change remained "in the hands of whites, which usually meant little or no change," and little commitment to the long-term strategies that racial inequality required. A statement condemning the murder of Emmett Till in 1956 languished for months in subcommittee; even in the wake of the 1954 school desegregation decision, the NCC did little more than encourage further study. The mainline churches, says Findlay, were simply "unprepared" to affect "in any lasting way the course of the racial struggle in the late 1950s and 1960s." Change was in the offing, of course, but it would arrive painfully and suddenly—and from the outside.[6]

Meanwhile, churchwomen were meeting in person. The first encounter took place in 1920 at the Tuskegee Institute in Nashville, at a meeting of the National Association of Colored Women. Two white Southern Methodists, Sara Estelle Haskins and Carrie Parks Johnson, came not as organizers but as guests, invited by Lugenia Burns Hope. The two white women were quickly astonished by the caliber of the 800 Black churchwomen in attendance, "orators, writers, poets, artists, business women, teachers, secretaries, lawyers, [and] bankers." "I had a new world opened to me," said Johnson, "a world I had never conceived before."[7]

Despite plans for a follow-up meeting in Memphis, African American churchwomen were skeptical, suspecting that the white women's enthusiasm for "Negro Betterment" was a ruse for finding domestic help. It did not help matters when Johnson went out of her way to downplay lynching and racial violence, and appeared tone deaf to the daily injustices that Black churchwomen faced. All the same, however, the Memphis meeting was incredibly challenging for its time, an opportunity for white women to hear presentations about "What It Means to Be a Negro" and a pointed challenge from Charlotte Hawkins Brown: "All Negro women feel that you can control your men," she said. "So far as lynching is concerned, if the white women would take hold of the situation, lynching would be stopped, mob violence stamped out," and "justice meted out in due course."[8]

Yet even in the face of these bald realities, churchwomen trusted in the power of friendship. The first Interracial Conference of Church Women met in Eagles Mere, Pennsylvania, in 1926. The conferences dealt with housing segregation, inferior schools, lynching, and unequal employment, but the methodology was interpersonal, aimed at building empathy across racial lines. A meeting in 1928, for example, introduced white women to the works of African American writers and artists, and laid out the daily handicaps—and dangers—of travel under segregation restrictions. Addie Dickerson, a Philadelphia lawyer, "urged that white women try being a Negro for a day."[9]

African American women knew the risks of this approach, and they counted its costs. They were not, as historian Judith Weisenfeld reminds us, simply mirroring white women's work "in some 'black' way."[10] They knew full well that they would have to generate most of the honesty in whatever interracial dialogue took place. "It is easy for inter-racial gatherings to deliquesce into sentimental experience meetings or love feasts," said poet and political activist Alice Dunbar-Nelson. Sticking to the "cold, hard, unsentimental facts" required "real courage"—and the persistence of Black women "who kept the discussion on a frank and open plane," insisting that "all is not right and perfect in this country of ours, and that there is a great deal to be done by the right thinking church women of both races."[11]

African American women did have an incentive for persisting. Leadership roles on national boards and ecumenical projects meant that they did not have to deal with the fraught gender dynamics of male-dominated Black denominations. Clergy held tight control over missionary work in both the African Methodist Episcopal (AME) and National Baptist churches, forcing women to fight continuously for control over budgets and programs. The AME was in a sustained uproar during much of the 1920s and 1930s, with laymen and women facing off against powerful bishops and clergy. National Baptist leaders did everything possible to wrest control of women's work, even the flagship work of Nannie Helen Burroughs, founder of the National Training School for Women and Girls.

Interracial Ecumenism

All of this toil and effort was rewarded in 1941, when United Church Women (UCW) made racial awareness a top priority. Its first set of officers encompassed all the major Protestant denominations, including the AME, and the constitution required that all UCW meetings "be held under conditions in which there shall be no racial discrimination."[12] In 1945, at the urging of the Committee on Race Relations urging, UCW recognized only those state councils open to all races, one of the first women's organizations to do so.

The Methodist Woman's Division of Christian Service also prioritized race relations, and justly so, given the denomination's segregated Central Jurisdiction. The Woman's Division not only protested this racist policy but proceeded adamantly in the opposite direction. One participant described the "spirit of excitement" at the first national gathering, as all the delegates—"a scattering of black deaconesses and missionaries, episcopal and ministerial leaders, and white women . . . all felt the thrill: the women were commencing a larger program."[13]

The merger had made this possible. The southern wing of the denomination, coming in with firsthand experience with Jim Crow laws and the atrocities they permitted, brought seasoned leadership and moral conviction. As a young schoolteacher in Mississippi, Thelma Stevens had witnessed a lynching, the murder of an innocent Black man by members of her own community. "[T]here were hundreds, literally hundreds, of people on the hillside," she told an interviewer in 1972. "And there was a man hanging from a limb. And men standing all around him with guns in their hands, shooting at him. See, they . . . . It was a lynching. And you can't conceive it, and I'm not trying to tell you what it was like, but if you can imagine anything any more devastating than that, then you're very good, you're very imaginative."[14]

Before the 1939 merger the Woman's Missionary Council of the Methodist Episcopal Church, South had been the denomination's voice of conscience, making common cause with the National Association for the Advancement of Colored People (NAACP) and its efforts to establish interracial committees across the South, some 800 by 1926. They worked to build day nurseries, parks, and playgrounds, and pressed for better housing, schools, and sanitation; Southern Methodist women also helped launch the Association of Southern Women for the Prevention of Lynching, under the leadership of Jessie Daniel Ames. The denomination's southern wing, therefore, came into the merger with experience in interracial cooperation—and in firsthand knowledge of injustices perpetrated by their own denominational leadership.[15]

Ultimately, interracial programs did cross over into the civil rights movement. In 1948, for example, Thelma Stevens hired a struggling young lawyer, Pauli Murray, to research segregation laws in the South, a way of helping local women's groups avoid legal challenges to their desegregation efforts.

Stevens realized she did not even know whether the segregation policies at her Methodist alma mater Scarritt College were legal. In fact, no had yet untangled the confusing mix of custom and statute that made up Jim Crow in the South, including the NAACP and American Civil Liberties Union (ACLU). The project not only put Murray back on her feet financially, it gave her the encouragement and visibility she needed to pursue her scholarly and political career.[16]

Still, it would be an overstatement to depict the churchwomen's movement as radical. Even the clear interracial directives of UCW leadership were more a goal than marching orders in the South. By the late 1950s, not one of the South Carolina state councils had taken up race relations; most were not integrated. In 1958, the president of UCW in Mississippi resigned her post in protest, angry that the national organization had made integration too much of an "absorbing interest."[17]

Moreover, many interracial programs were, as Bettye Collier-Thomas writes, actually biracial, that is, parallel efforts, not partnerships of equals. "Interracial" could mean that a conference or committee was simply focusing on racial problems, not necessarily practicing—even favoring—racial integration. Moreover, women's interracial efforts were particularly limited by narrow boundaries of social class, even more than the similar gatherings of white and Black churchmen. African American churchwomen were keenly aware of the burden of racial suspicion, the assumption that they were somehow less "respectable" than their white counterparts. In order to counter prevailing stereotypes of Black women as sexually promiscuous and untrustworthy, they had to "reframe respectability," insisting that theirs was a moral voice, equal to that of white churchwomen.[18]

It is also important to note that interracial "friendship" filled a space once occupied by "sisterhood." In a larger sense, social class filled a space once occupied by gender, a substitution that limited moral traction. After they were alerted to the "shocking" conditions of farmworkers in their community, the Southern California chapter of UCW set earnestly to work improving the lives of "our migrants." "We joined in the fight against various evils or potential evils in public life," as one member reminisced in 1959, "and threw the weight of our dignity into our protest."[19] This is not to discount the activism and genuine courage clearly evident in the history of UCW and the Methodist Woman's Division, not to mention all of the African American and white laywomen who ventured across color lines to eat dinner in each other's homes or meet together in public hotels and restaurants. It is simply that the inability to declare female solidarity, the relative silence about the meaning and implications of gender, made social class all the more salient.

What Was Lost

Indeed, pursuing "woman's mission" in a modern era was a far more subtle, complex enterprise than it had been in the nineteenth century. Though the achievements of twentieth-century churchwomen are certainly worth celebrating, they have yet to make the history books as did those of the previous generation. Susan B. Anthony and Frances Willard are household names, or nearly so; Thelma Stevens and Nannie Helen Burroughs are not. Beneath the dogged success of UCW, the YWCA, and the Methodist Woman's Division is the stubborn fact of their relative invisibility, even among historians today. And so we may well wonder what happened to that powerful combination of feminine grievance and moral superiority which had led an earlier generation of missionaries and suffragists, abolitionists and temperance reformers far beyond the traditional boundaries of woman's sphere.

The problem was not a lack of Protestant moral fervor. Despite the evangelical stereotype of mainline churches as a feckless, self-satisfied "establishment," a strong social gospel radicalism survived, even thrived, through the Great Depression and into the 1940s. The bilingual, bicultural children of missionaries, as David Hollinger has described, were great advocates for international understanding, playing leading roles as ambassadors and analysts, scholars and journalists. After World War II, religious groups, writes historian Samuel Moyn, were some of the most idealistic and active advocates of a "just and durable peace," and including the framing of the United Nations Universal Declaration of Human Rights.[20]

Yet translating this broad social agenda into a discrete women's movement was no easy task. The goals and the structure of missionary and temperance societies had always been achingly clear: convert the world to Christianity and rid the country of alcohol. Twentieth-century churchwomen's groups, however, undertook a wide range of causes, everything from foreign missions to Christian citizenship, from pacifism to the evils of movies and comic books. Their membership structure was equally diffuse, no longer a select vanguard of women lining up behind a particular cause. The Northern Baptist National Committee on Women's Work claimed to include "*all* members of the local church." Yet as one study observed, "realistically there is often wide discrepancy between the number of women who are members of a local church and the number who are listed in the active membership of a local woman's society." In the mid-1940s, according to denominational statistics, only 10 percent of Baptist women fell in the latter category.[21]

The organizational problem, however, rested on a larger social and cultural one. The earlier wave of women's activism had depended on a certain kind of female solidarity, built on the moral imperatives of motherhood. Thus, Frances Willard mobilized the Woman's Christian Temperance Union's (WCTU) rank and file in support of "Home Protection," a slogan that persuaded thousands of conservative Protestants to demand the right to vote. Progressive-era activists called it "social housekeeping," justifying legislative campaigns against grift and corruption with the homey image of a woman wielding a broom. Twentieth-century churchwomen did not—and perhaps could not—make that argument. In the first place, an overt call to female solidarity undermined the new identity they sought, as members of the entire church, not just a single, narrow cause.

Nor could they appeal to their role as mothers. The twentieth-century "Christian family" was relational and consensus driven. It was monitored and motivated by professionally trained experts, Christian educators who urged parents to nurture their children's faith through silent example rather than dogmatic declaration. The inward turn mirrored the sociology of the 1920s and 1930s, which was shifting away from a primary focus on the family's outward social function, that is, the ways that neighborhoods and communities shaped individual households. The new fascination was with its interior processes, how parents and children and spouses related to each other. To the experts who studied it, the modern family was "less a thing or a structure" and more of a "process that changed over time as the individuals within it changed." Families were "islands of adjustment, floating on an impersonal social sea."[22]

The point is not to glorify the Victorian middle-class family, obsessed as it was with roles and respectability, nor to deny the benefits of the modern one, at least in terms of human thriving. It is the historical fact of what Jane Addams called "the family claim" on women's lives, the practical realities of motherhood. At times, women have used their private role to justify a public voice, to gain moral traction and even a certain amount of free expression by virtue of their responsibility to children and households. Hardly a perfect tool, of course, but an extraordinarily effective one in its time. The relative absence of appeals to motherhood in the twentieth century are therefore an important sign of historical change, measuring out the distance between the WCTU and UCW, between a Frances Willard and a Thelma Stevens.

Equally diffuse, however, was the twentieth-century religious impulse itself, driven by a desire to find meaning through experience. That yearning took many different forms. For evangelicals and Pentecostals, authentic belief required a conversion from sinner to saved, going forward at a Billy Graham crusade or receiving the baptism of the Holy Spirit. The key was the individual's assent, his or her lone encounter with God. Mainline Protestant spirituality was less literal and less atomized, but no less geared toward experience. God became real through action, in work with like-minded other people. This is perhaps why, of course, evangelical critics tagged it as theologically empty, even insincere. In fact, mainline Protestant religiosity was difficult to put into words, hard to summarize in a simple story of sin and salvation. It was "second-degree" spirituality, a faith that was not directly personal, at least as evangelicals and fundamentalists defined it. Mainline piety did not require constant internal monitoring and adjustment, listening for divine direction at every traffic light; the true test was what many Protestants simply called "churchmanship," the careful, loyal stewardship of religious institutions.

Churchwomen in particular struggled to articulate a Protestant faith that was forceful and direct about social realities, including gender. Speaking about a "spiritual new day" to Presbyterian women in 1929, Bertha Condé admitted that "We have become free, but are not yet sure of our direction." More than ever, she said, modern women needed to be "more spiritually minded," to "reach out for those spiritual realities we can't see, and don't understand in the scientific realm." True purpose required a "second touch of Christ on ourselves, where we cease to see men as important as we now think they are."[23] Baptist women were encouraged to support the denomination's evangelistic outreach by creating "*the atmosphere* in which God can work." Their role was to be, as one woman put it, " 'mood-makers' for Christ in our homes, and in our churches."[24]

Piety also found expression in programs—a Day of Prayer or in devotional poems and liturgies—and in activities that required cooperation and good behavior. "Keep us, O God, from pettiness," a Methodist "Women's Collect" petitioned. "Let us be done with faultfinding and leave off self-seeking . . . [and] make us grow calm, serene, and gentle."[25]

Second-degree spirituality was easiest to articulate in ritual. Even Baptist women, heirs of a historic aversion to rote formality, devoted a great deal of time, effort, and creativity to visual display. A historical retrospective of missionary work in 1937 featured bugle calls and scroll readings, leis and crosses, with each district proudly displaying its own color and flower. One of the most elaborate rituals surrounded the "Love Gift," a fundraising program instituted in 1932 to make up a denominational deficit of half a million dollars. Silver boxes—a color scheme chosen to dispel figurative dark clouds—went out to individual homes, where they were placed on dining room tables, silently entreating family members to drop in a daily coin. All of the boxes remained unopened until they were brought forward in a public ceremony, elaborately staged according to detailed instructions from organizational headquarters—everything from costuming and casting to set design and background organ music. The message was, if non-literal, hardly subtle. One pageant featured a running confrontation between an "Evil Spirit," abetted by "Discouragement," "Moral Failure," "Disease," "Ridicule," and "War," and an angelic host, flanked by seven female "Gift Bearers" and a Heavenly Choir.[26]

Whether or not the Victorian ancestors would have recognized these activities as "religious" is a legitimate question. Churchwomen were less likely to invoke the name of Jesus or seek conversions, much less declare the superiority of Christianity to other faiths. They were more apt to declare loyalty to denominational institutions than proclaim a personal relationship with Christ. By some measures, that apparent absence of certainty is an indication of secularization, a shift toward a "post-Protestant" sensibility. Yet there were continuities with the past, a fundamental pragmatism and an abiding faith in the power of Christian example. The missing piece was the ability to name gender differences, to assert female solidarity without claiming it as a moral prerogative. It was a difficult position at best in religious institutions that were ambivalent about their presence, especially in moments of conflict.

The Man Problem

Not surprisingly, UCW's most challenging ecumenical partnership was with male ecumenists, specifically the leadership of the FCC and its successor, the NCC.[27] The women's group agreed to cooperate with the NCC early on, in 1946, when that organization was still in the planning stages—provided the UCW would retain control over its program, structure, and financing. But UCW members were wary of becoming the NCC's "women's department," which meant, as one woman described it, "landlady detail," relegated to the "humdrum tasks in the church which 'belong' to women."[28]

When the women relented in October 1949, they were promised "a place on all policy-making and programming committees and commissions of the new agency." Of the four vice-chairmen of the board of governors, "at least one" was to be female. The UCW also maintained the power to appoint its own board, subject to "confirmation" by the board of managers of the NCC, a step not perceived as a problem. "The women are certain," journalist Margaret Frakes wrote in the *Christian Century*, "that such confirmation will in every case be forthcoming."[29]

And of course, problems began almost immediately. At the first meeting of the General Board of the NCC in December 1950, Luther Fry, president of the Lutheran Church in America and chairman of the NCC's Policy Committee, raised an objection based on the "Evangelical Principle" the NCC's bylaws (Article XI Section 4). The UCW included Unitarians and Universalists, groups that the ecumenical movement had deemed beyond the Protestant pale. " 'What are they doing to us?' " Mossie Wyker muttered. "'They promised to leave our constituency free,'" UCW president Dorothy McLeod objected. Though NCC officers agreed to "study the matter," the women heard nothing until Wyker and McLeod were informed by NCC president Lewis Sherrill that "a committee will not be necessary." He was ruling in favor of Fry's interpretation of the bylaws. "'Then you'll have to tell the women,'" McLeod shot back. This ended up her task, however, and ultimately the UCW was forced to remove the four Unitarian and Universalist women from its Board of Managers.[30]

Another issue was financial. After becoming part of the NCC, UCW created an Ecumenical Register of Church Women, with each member donating a dollar "as a token of her interest in the ecumenical movement." The program was highly successful, providing UCW with an all-important source of separate funding, and a measure of independence from other NCC departments.[31]

Most telling, perhaps, is the growing awareness that work with the NCC was going to require a highly professional, ladylike demeanor. Misfits and rebels need not apply. That much is clear from the careful list of qualifications compiled by UCW leaders in the search for a female Associate Secretary in 1952. Twila Cavert, whose husband Samuel Cavert was then NCC president, led the effort, well aware that the ideal candidate was able to "work happily with men and women without being unaware of or unhappy about the differences between them." She should be "attractive," "outgoing," and tire-lessly competent, "experienced enough to command confidence and young enough to *attend endless committee meetings, write innumerable speeches, travel countless miles, dictate and sign letters galore, read, write, digest, criticize incessant reports.*" Perhaps most important of all this mythical individual was to "*keep her temper and her judgment under constant control.*"[32]

In many ways these requirements were no different from the poised per-fection expected of the female professionals of this era, the ability to achieve without appearing competitive. But churchwomen knew, as did male church leaders, that religion was not necessarily a "man's world," certainly not on the same level as business and government, medicine and law. As we will see in chapter 5, Protestantism's best hedge against feminization was recruiting more men, a problematic campaign at best, but an urgent one. The times required, more than ever, a revitalized religious masculine persona, a new model of the Protestant layman.

Anna Canada Swain, Courtesy of the American Baptist Historical Society, Atlanta, GA.

PORTRAIT

Anna Swain and the Fundamentalists

"Minnesota was *some* experience," Anna Swain wrote to her husband in 1944. She was just a few months into her two-year tenure as president of the Northern Baptist Convention, and the fundamentalists were already hard on her heels. This time it was Richard Clearwaters, the pastor of Fourth Baptist Church in Minneapolis, and the occasion was a banquet given in her honor by the Minnesota Baptist Convention. After Swain's remarks, Clearwaters had come up to the podium and delivered an "unforgivably rude" put-down, as Swain confided. It was all there on full display, fundamentalist contempt for liberals, and liberal women in particular.[1]

There were limits, though. It was one thing to "stand for the faith once delivered to the saints," as the fundamentalists liked to say; it was something else to violate the platform etiquette of a Baptist banquet. Even some of Clearwaters's own parishioners were appalled, to the point of absolute mortification. As one woman moaned to a friend, "What *can* we do to let Mrs. Swain know we don't all think as Dr. Clearwaters does? Oh we are so humiliated that our pastor spoke thus to our president."[2]

Swain knew better than to get angry, though. "At first as he talked," she told her husband Leslie back in Rhode Island, "I thought I would answer him but the more he said the more I realized that he wanted to draw me into a controversy—a procedure that would have gotten us nowhere." When she returned to the podium for some final words, I "simply ignored all the nasty things he said and put it all on a very high spiritual plane." Anna Swain was not just being polite: she knew full well that her display of Christian virtue had left the man "very much in the dog house." There were rules, after all, and Reverend Clearwaters had broken them. "I think the whole state was very sore with him," she wrote, gloating just a little, "and proud that I had not descended to his level." The spiritual high ground was a good place to be, and Swain stayed there, declaring her concern for the truculent minister's soul to another apologetic correspondent (whose husband, Earl V. Pierce, was a leading Minnesota fundamentalist). "I feel only sorrow for Mr. Clearwaters," said Swain, "that a Christian minister has allowed himself to foster so much bitterness in his heart. Such a spirit continued for too long will harm him terribly."[3]

Anna Swain was no fool. Raised as a Baptist in Providence, Rhode Island, the denomination's heartland, she had fully earned her way to the presidency. Her first job after graduation from Brown University's Pembroke College for women in 1911, was superintendent of a Baptist Sunday school Junior Department. Propelled by an early passion for missionary work, she rose from leader of a state girls' group to become president of the Rhode Island Baptist women's missionary society, and then in the 1930s, Swain became known as an author of books and plays about foreign missions. In 1938 she was appointed a delegate to the Madras Conference of the International Missionary Council, the most significant ecumenical gathering of the decade. She became president of the Woman's American Baptist Foreign Missionary Society in 1942, a post she held until 1950 and then in perpetuity as an honorary post. In 1949 she would be the first woman selected for the Brown University Board of Trustees.[4]

Anna Swain arrived in Minnesota knowing full well that it was enemy territory, home to some of the nation's most aggressive fundamentalists. Minnesota Baptists were a notoriously conservative group, securely under the thumb of the legendary William Bell Riley. The imperious Minneapolis pastor had made a name in the 1920s as leader of the World Christian Fundamentals Association, and led the charge against Clarence Darrow and the theory of evolution in the 1925 Scopes Trial. Northern Baptists knew him as a dogged instigator, heading the conservative shock troops in the Fundamentalist Fellowship. He was not a man to accept failure either: after the liberals eked out victory in the national denomination, Riley turned to grassroots organizing. In the 1930s and 1940s, his "boys," graduates of his Northwestern Bible Training School, infiltrated and gradually dominated Minnesota Baptist pulpits. Liberals could do little more than gnash their teeth. Riley was the undisputed "boss" of the state churches, as a safely anonymous critic described him, a "shrewd and aggressive manipulator" with all the "cunning and resourcefulness" of a secular politician. His election as state president in 1944 only formalized the iron control he had been building for more than a decade.[5]

Richard Clearwaters was an able lieutenant, balding and bespectacled, as smooth-faced and righteous as a banker. What he lacked in charisma he made up for with solid fundamentalist credentials. After attending Moody Bible Institute, Clearwaters went on to Northern Baptist Theological Seminary, a school formed to protest the denomination's liberal leanings. After graduating in 1928, he kept adding to his conservative portfolio, with a BA from Kalamazoo College and an MA in New Testament Greek from the University of Chicago, where he ended up just shy of a PhD. When he arrived in Minneapolis in 1939, Clearwaters was a veteran denominational infighter, a loyal member of the Riley's Fundamentalist Fellowship and president of the Iowa State Baptist Convention. In 1942, he helped Riley engineer the Minnesota Baptist Convention's departure from that "Modernist incubus," the Federal Council of Churches. By the time of his encounter with Swain, Clearwaters was riding high, the leader of a fundamentalist faction, what would become the Conservative Baptist Association of America.[6]

The rest of the Northern Baptist Convention, even the conservatives, had hoped to manage doctrinal differences with company-best manners. When Swain was elected president, William Bradbury, the editor of the fundamentalist-learning *Watchman-Examiner*, did not denounce her in public. Instead he notified Swain of his disapproval in a personal letter, declaring that he was "fundamentally opposed to the election of a woman to preside over and direct the affairs of any organization which men predominate." Just as quickly, however, Bradbury assured Swain that he would keep his views to himself. Their disagreement was, he said, "something for you to endure and me to control," and from there Bradbury affirmed his "loyalty and good wishes . . . and sincere devotion to the best." "Knowing you as I do," he said, "I am sure that all will receive indiscriminate treatment." Swain was equally committed to keeping her feelings private. The carbon copy of her exceedingly polite return letter to Bradbury includes only a brief handwritten note to posterity: "*His* letter to me when I was elected was the only letter regretting a 'woman' president."[7]

Most Northern Baptists disagreed with Bradbury anyway. After years of fundamentalist acrimony, said the *Baptist News*, a woman president was just what the embattled denomination needed. Anna Swain would be a "symbol of our unity and our desire to accomplish the will of God in modern life."[8] Far from divisive, polarizing figures, Baptist laywomen were safely above the fray—or perceived that way. Many saw a parallel with Helen Barrett Montgomery's irenic role during the fundamentalist uprisings of the 1920s.

"It seemed to me," a denominational executive wrote to Swain, "when Mrs. Montgomery presided over the meetings of the Northern Convention that the boys behaved a little better. I am quite sure," he said, "that you will be able to restrain some of the naughty chaps that insist on making trouble."[9] A young Texas sailor, writing to Swain as a "total stranger," was even more explicit about her maternal role. In his letter of congratulations he confided to her, that though his parents had died, "I know they would like for me to write to a kind lady." He encouraged her to "go forth in the strength of your duty and in your nobility of ladyhood."[10]

Women were far more reluctant to acknowledge that Swain had a gender. In an effusive letter of congratulations, Ruth Worrell, executive secretary of United Church Women, was particularly thrilled that Baptists had "recognized your worth as one of the greatest leaders that they have regardless of sex—and that makes us proud and happy." Certainly Swain's presidency "has lifted the status of women in every church in America," but "we have passed the day when we talk about women's rights," recognizing as we do the "sacredness of personality and the individual worth of people be they men or women."[11] Just a few months before Swain's election in June, some Northern Baptists—women, not men—were insisting that they did not even care about theology. They just want "more real religion," said Alice Brimson, the executive secretary of the Woman's American Baptist Home Mission Society. Fundamentalists were outraged at the "inane pronouncement"—in their view, theology *was* real religion—but everyone else saw the remark for what it was, a signal to denominational leaders that women were and would remain neutral in any battle over doctrine.[12]

Swain knew her constituents, and courted them with a shrewd combination of feminine charm and organizational skill, radiating "cheerful energy and enthusiasm," as an admirer enthused, and using her "pertly tilted chin and nose" to considerable effect.[13] While never denying her femininity she used it carefully, just enough to put the fundamentalists in their place. All those unruly "boys" just needed a mother to keep the peace. "As you would expect," she told the *Baptist News*, "I have a reason—a sort of woman's reason—for accepting this great responsibility and high honor." My reason, she said, *is our family,*" all those Baptists "*related to each other by loving family ties which bind them together very closely even though they be separated by many thousands of miles.*"[14]

Though she had spent her life building her career and had no children, Swain titled her 1946 presidential address "The State of the Family." Her message was simple: there was nothing wrong with a little conflict, as long as everyone behaved themselves. "No normal family is a continuous picnic," she said, "for there are always differences of opinion when two or more people, even brothers, get together. Often they are sincere and honest disagreements. It is only when they are disputed angrily and not in the spirit of Christian love that harm comes to the whole family." Modern, forward-looking Northern Baptists did not need a Victorian patriarch, a "dictator" who made all the decisions for the rest to obey. "Those who are wise tell us that the only way to make of the family a happy, loving community is to have all decisions reached cooperatively by those who are responsible members of the family."[15]

As Swain stood on the platform, "smiling and poised" but with a "steel-like quality," according to the Baptist press, she won—though for what cause they could not exactly say. "No one could tell from her actions which side she was on," a Baptist leader marveled, "but because she was entirely fair, the majority won the day." "I can think of no man who could have carried us so well through that trying time," said another. "She has been the target of unkind criticism and calumny, much of it anonymous, but she took it all philosophically and with understanding."[16]

Despite their reluctance to proclaim Anna Swain a female role model, Baptist women saw her as one of their own, an older sister perhaps. After her election, instead of exulting over a woman in charge, they joshed about Mr. Swain "eat[ing] his mince pies alone this year" ("ha ha"), and one kind soul even offered to help pay for a "trousseau." "I know that your travels will require much in the way of clothes and that there is no allowance for such," she wrote. "I am earning a little money substituting as my husband's secretary and am having so much fun using it for special things. I hope you will be one of my 'specials,' though I realize it won't go far in the purchase of clothes today."[17]

Most of all, however, Swain was Queen Esther, a reluctant heroine, called by God to service at a time of dire need. "I know you will be equal to the task," a West Virginia woman wrote, "and I shall be remembering you in my prayers day by day. Esther came to the Kingdom for such a time as this, and I feel that you have a definite mission in bringing peace and harmony among the ranks of our Northern Baptist Convention."[18] The comparison was apt. If anyone was equal to the task, it was Swain, who had already achieved some of the denomination's top honors and was on her way to worldwide fame as the only woman (and only Baptist) in the executive committee of the World Council of Churches.

But of course, like any good metaphor, the Old Testament story worked on multiple levels. If Anna Swain was Queen Esther, then who were Richard Clearwaters and William Bell Riley, and all of the misbehavers in the Northern Baptist Convention? They were enemies that she could not defeat on her own. Queen Esther preserved the nation of Israel from annihilation, not through bold action but through misdirection. She was certainly brave: she risked the wrath of her husband King Ahasuerus by entering his court, a masculine inner sanctum if there ever was one. But she won the day by subtler skills, manipulating him into destroying Israel's enemies by appealing to his manly pride. She was not Deborah, who led an army into battle, nor Jael, who murdered the evil Sisera by pounding a tent stake through his head as he slept. Anna Swain, like Queen Esther, was a powerful woman because she understood the rules of her situation. She knew exactly how far she could go, and went there resolutely—but no further.

5

Is the Church Male or Female?

The Problem of Mainline Masculinity

Protestant churches needed men. They always had. Sometimes the empty pews went unremarked, like the color of the sky or the wetness of water, just another social fact. At other times, the missing men signaled peril, fueling a popular perception that churchgoing was a harmless pastime for ladies and children—and a waste of time for red-blooded males.

The churches' best response, up through the early twentieth century, was proclaiming the opposite. All kinds of American Protestants, conservative, liberal, and in between, promoted "muscular Christianity," the claim that real religion—not the tea-sipping, pinky-raised feminine type—required mental and physical toughness. In the years of Teddy Roosevelt, high stakes prizefighting, and football, that assertion made its own kind of cultural sense. After all, this was an era of political bluster, of "big" business, and over-the-top yellow journalism, of Billy Sunday and Rough Riders and John L. Sullivan, the Irish pugilist.[1]

In the long run, however, muscular Christianity was not a workable solution. The Protestant churches did not, by any stretch, "remasculinize" themselves by the 1920s. Instead, as this chapter outlines—in a brief but important digression back to the late nineteenth century and into the mid-twentieth—they tried to set a different course, recognizing that they could not bully or bluster men back into church any more than they could impose strictures against feminism. These were fundamentalist tactics that spoke more than anything else of intolerance and desperation. The more practical course was to redefine the "layman," transforming a historically generic term into a shorthand for a new masculine ideal. The great need of the churches was not just "more men," but a specific kind of man, one instilled with the pragmatic values and managerial expertise of the surrounding business world.[2]

That plan introduced its own set of problems, of course. As efforts to mobilize men gathered steam in the midcentury decades, they appeared to stem the perception of a feminized church; yet in the long run the layman proved

Good and Mad. Margaret Bendroth, Oxford University Press. © Oxford University Press 2023.
DOI: 10.1093/oso/9780197654064.003.0006

an unreliable ally, his energies sporadic and often unsolicited—a clear sign that the mainline churches no longer defined a masculine role any more than they imposed a feminine one.

All of this made for a touchy situation. Many churchwomen were well aware that they could not afford to alienate Protestantism's masculine minority, whom they viewed as untrustworthy, even timid allies at best. An Episcopalian woman spoke for many when she observed that "the men are 'far too ready to let the women shoulder the burden of the church work anyhow.'" If women gained more power, then "the men will just shrug their shoulders as if to say, 'let them take it and run it,'" an outcome that, everyone knew, would have created more problems than it appeared to solve.[3]

Are Women Laymen?

A brief chronological detour illustrates the depth of obfuscation. For centuries, the word "layman," like the generic "man," has been an ambiguous term, at the same time grammatically gender-neutral and specifically male. In everyday conversation it refers to a nonexpert, the amateur bird-watcher or cake-baker or historian, who can be either male or female. Within the Western Christian tradition, however, the word took on a specific liturgical meaning, signifying all nonclergy, that is, anyone not formally ordained into the church hierarchy and thus bestowed with the authority to administer the sacraments. The Protestant Reformation expanded the layman's spiritual standing: God has deputized all believers, said Martin Luther, and has set aside just a few for the professional clergy, charged with preaching the Word and administering the sacraments. Protestant churches also gave the layman formal power, though some traditions more than others. In "free churches," meaning all non-Episcopalian or Anglican, the laity had a direct voice in church decisions, from the congregational level on up to the regional and national.

But did that include women? They were church members, of course, but of a special sort, denied a role in corporate decision-making. Even those that proclaimed the spiritual equality of clergy and laity—Congregationalists and Baptists, for example—assumed this did not really mean everyone. "It is generally thought desirable that the female members of a church should be present at the transaction of all ordinary business, for their satisfaction and instruction," a Congregational authority wrote in 1840, "but, it is utterly inconsistent with established usage for females to take any part in business transactions." Citing the list of prohibitions by the apostle Paul, he said, "Their views and wishes are to be expressed privately to their pastor or their brethren."[4] Yet in every respect besides voting, women were by definition laypeople, and therefore every bit as responsible as their male counterparts to attend worship, live an upright life, and support the church financially.

The ambiguity persisted through the late nineteenth century. In 1870, the Congregational churches of northern Ohio had to act quickly when two women appeared as delegates to a conference meeting, arguing that "they were as much lay members of the church as were the male members." After the chair ruled against them, a "very spirited discussion ensued" about the "ecclesiastical meaning of the world layman." Though the conference upheld the chair's ruling by a vote of 188 to 65, the ladies voted in favor of their own admission, "thus contravening all known precedents in voting on a question touching their own qualifications to sit as delegates."[5]

Northern Methodists went through a longer, more public battle over the gender of laity rights, beginning in the 1880s. The issue actually went back further than that, with a general push in the 1860s to democratize the denomination's hierarchical structure; according to Methodist rules, only bishops and ordained clergy had the right to vote at national General Conference meetings. Though few realized it at the time, demanding a voice for laypeople opened a new set of knotty questions about women's rights. That reality hit home in 1880, when several regional conferences elected female delegates to the upcoming 1888 General Conference meeting—five women, including the Woman's Christian Temperance Union (WCTU) president Frances Willard. This was no empty gesture. Willard was Methodism's most famous female, a leading figure in the temperance movement and the suffrage campaign. She was also in the thick of debates over women's ordination, a measure which the denomination had made a special point of voting down in 1880. Willard was hard at work on her rejoinder, a set of essays on *Woman in the Pulpit*, which was published in 1889.[6]

Perhaps it was best that Willard was called away to attend her ailing mother: the 1888 General Conference was no place for a woman with a sensitive soul. Conservatives objected at the start to seating any female delegates. Led by James Buckley, who edited the denominational paper, the *Christian Advocate*, they argued that church rules—what was known as the Methodist Discipline—had always defined the laymen as male, and rightly so. Women were ill-equipped, they warned, for the boisterous give-and-take of a General

Conference meeting. God had bestowed them with quieter gifts, an ability to serve out of the public eye. But even that argument did not really matter: a female layman was a literal impossibility. "All objections to the admission of women into the General Conference come at last to this," Buckley declared, "that they are *women* and not men."[7]

More quietly, however, he named his real concern. "What kind of a General Conference would 'natural rights' give us?" said Buckley. If delegates were elected proportionately according to sex, the gathering would be two-thirds female; if the male minority also included clergy, the proportion of lay men would be reduced even further. "A General Conference of 600 would thus contain 400 women, 196 laymen, and 4 ministers," said Buckley. It would be, in other words, a dull, namby-pamby affair, far from the raucous brawl the denomination had come to expect, Lacking a "peculiar knowledge of parliamentary law," as well as the "rapid physical movements" and "piercing voice" apparently required by Methodist polity, women would be "utterly lost." Clearly, Buckley warned, "a plan was afoot to " '*feminize*' " the body."[8]

Not surprisingly, Buckley's argument did not settle anything. Methodists would debate the gender of laymen for another decade, before finally deciding in the women's favor in 1900. It would be another four years before they were seated as delegates. And that did not even begin to address the ordination question, which would roil General Conferences for another half century.[9]

Red-Blooded Christianity

In the meantime, worries about feminization grew more public. "No fact in the life of Christian churches excites more attention or is the subject of more anxious thought," a Baptist periodical editorialized in 1901, "than the disparity in the membership between men and women."[10] In fact by the early twentieth century male irreligion had become a crisis, this on the basis of hard evidence: the 1905 census was the first to count the relative numbers of men and women, and confirmed what most already suspected, that the Protestant churches were nearly two-thirds female.[11] Searching for the direst metaphor possible, William Jennings Bryan declared the Protestant churches a mirror image of a gender-segregated Muslim mosque, where the men sat in the main prayer room and the women were sequestered behind a petition. As he scolded a meeting of Presbyterian men in 1906, "we have been letting the women attend and the men do not even come as near the screen."[12]

One response was to insist, over and over, that a feminized Christianity was impossible, that it was based on a misreading of the Bible perpetrated by well-meaning but misguided churchwomen and clergy. In fact the Christ of scripture was manly beyond a doubt, as George Barton Cutten, a Yale psychologist explained in 1908, "marvelous in self-control" and "splendid in moral courage." Unfortunately, the church had misinterpreted his message, emphasizing the virtues of forgiveness and love, and elevating feminine strengths over masculine ones.

The whole situation was deeply unfair. "Women are not more religious than men," Cutten declared, "but they have had their wants supplied, while men who have hungered and thirsted after righteousness, have been handed something indigestible."[13] Who could blame men for avoiding Christianity? "The real cause of manless churches," said University of California president Benjamin Ide Wheeler, is "the fact that the church has been for ages cultivating the female side of religion." Religion is not, then, equally for all," Carl Delos Case, a Brooklyn Baptist pastor, agreed. The woman "finds it especially easy to be religious," but a man must struggle. "Religion is natural to woman and often unnatural to man, the more so the more masculine he is."[14]

This was not just rhetoric. By the turn of the century, social scientists were amassing scientific evidence that proved the injustice done to masculine religiosity. "Women are commonly said to be more religious than men," said George Coe, a leading authority on psychology and religion, in 1914, "but I think it can be shown that the real differences is less in the degree of religiousness than in the general make-up of the mind." Women were simply more suggestible and malleable, more attuned to feeling. Men, in turn, required a more challenging message, he said, one that would answer their intellectual doubts and harness "turbulent" emotions. "With women religion is more like the intuitive tact that helps them so much in all the relations of life," said Coe; "with men it requires the clumsier instruments of deliberation."[15] Edwin Starbuck dismissed women's supposed superiority in religion as an empty response to peer pressure. People-pleasing females were simply more susceptible to the wishes of family and friends. ("Perhaps they are more genuine when alone," he mused.) Alternatively, men needed to be compelled toward a decision. "*Conversion for males is a more violent incident than for females, and more sudden,*" said Starbuck. "The man prepares for it longer, . . .

weighs the possibilities, resists the forces which oppose his will, and when they become irresistible, the change is cataclysmic."[16]

The churches, therefore, had to provide the kind of Christianity that Christ would have approved, one that spoke to men's true nature. Reverend Case, who based his views on hundreds of questionnaires sent to men in the churches he served, was fairly certain the best kind of religion involved "skill and courage." A "virile church" was one where "strong, manly sermons are preached and songs sung which are full of vigor and vim," a prayer meeting free of "platitudes and outworn phrases," and "a campaign for men managed systematically by men with as much care as a business canvas."[17]

Fundamentalists understood this. As they sought doctrinal control of denominational schools and missionary societies—and lost battle after battle—conservatives styled themselves as courageous individualists, men brave enough to reject the mediocre majority. "Loneliness is necessary to the Christian who is like Christ," Texas fundamentalist John R. Rice wrote in 1936—which was precisely why, said his colleague Minnesota Baptist William Bell Riley, Christ chose men to be his twelve apostles, knowing "all the hardships they must endure and the suffering they must encounter." The upshot was clear: "The only churches in America that have any considerable number of big hearted brainy men in them" are those that stand for "biblical doctrines—the great verities of the good Word of God."[18]

This was the theory behind popular revivalism up through the World War I era: while the average middle-class man would not darken the door of a church, he could be reached at a high-intensity event, especially when no women were present. "Men only" meetings became a staple of big revival campaigns, drawn in by skilled, dramatic headliners like J. Wilbur Chapman, Gypsy Smith, and Billy Sunday. These were some of the most emotionally fraught, climactic moments in a weeks-long campaign, combining vigorous hymn-singing with roaring sermons against alcohol and vice, challenging men to lives of virtue. A combination of large-scale sensationalism and personal appeal became a permanent feature of revivalistic churches, many featuring massive "men only" Bible studies and Sunday school classes.[19]

Fundamentalists were not the only ones drawn to polarizing rhetoric. For a while, muscular Christianity provided cultural cover for all kinds of male churchgoers, a space where they could practice their faith without apology. In the United States, the premier effort was the Men and Religion Forward Movement (MRFM), a quasi-revivalistic campaign uniting a coalition of religious organizations aimed at men, including the Gideons, the YMCA, and denominational "brotherhoods." The "remasculinization" campaign was hugely popular. Massive rallies held in 1911 and 1912, reached nearly 2,000 cities and towns and attracted over a million men.[20]

Yet even in Bull Moose era, muscular Christianity had its limits. Masculine blustering in the name of Christ may have shifted a perception here and there, perhaps silenced a few critics. The rhetorical excesses of lonely individualists provided eye-catching and eminently quotable fodder for newspapers and novelists—and historians. But in the end all of the talk changed relatively little, at least in terms of statistics.[21] In fact, there is little reason to assume that hard-hitting, frothing sermons attracted only a male audience. It is reasonable to conclude that in the era of chiseled matinee idols like Rudolph Valentino, women enjoyed red-blooded entertainment—and religion—as much if not more than men.[22]

Mainline Protestants took a different tack. Distrusting the emotionalism of large-scale revivals, they sought to reach the reasonable man in the midst of his daily life. The best kind of "virile religion," Congregationalist John R. Scotford wrote, is "less of an emotional indulgence and more a normal aspect of wholesome living."[23] The truly muscular Christian, in other words, was a responsible, middle-class man, ideally a businessman. No cranky individualist, he was the ultimate organization man. "Remasculinizing" the churches, for the mainline churches, meant aligning Christian virtue with the emerging corporate, consumer-driven modern marketplace. "If a man's business and church mutually exclude each other," as Baptist Carl Case observed, "it is not always the fault of the business."[24] Where nineteenth-century reformers worried about the moral effects of raw competition, their twentieth-century counterparts worried that excessive regimentation would turn red-blooded men into pencil-pushing ciphers.

Mainline Masculinity

This particular version of muscular Christianity suited broad-minded, well-adjusted men, not loners or dogmatists. Reverend Case, for example, argued that men wanted a practical, ethical faith, one that emphasized the humanity of Jesus, and stayed away from dogma and doctrine. "The average man," he said, "will not go to church unless he sees practical advantage in doing so." He advised only a "moderate amount of theory," and sermons with "liberal views." They must "be free from intellectual density, and not deal with sectarian questions."[25] For their part, conservatives were already worrying in 1912 that MRFM was too much about fun and entertainment, charging that meetings featured far more dancing and pool playing than Scripture reading.[26]

Some mainline pastors were even reconsidering their opposition to lodges and secret societies, long reviled by fundamentalists for their quasi-Catholic, quasi-pagan rituals. "The fraternities are here to stay," a turn-of-the-century Congregationalist declared, explaining how his church assigned the various groups—Knights Templar, Modern Woodmen, Odd Fellows, Knights of Pythias, and United Workmen—to special Sundays, inviting them to attend in full regalia.[27]

The mainline version was less gaudy but clearly aimed at a similar clientele. The various denominational "brotherhoods" sought the well-intentioned but easily distracted layman, "occasionally in earnest for the higher things, then swept away by the tumultuous pressure of the lower."[28] They would provide for men what women had long ago established, a separate space and meaningful reasons to be together. One aim of the Presbyterian Brotherhood, for example, was to enlist men "for intelligent service," and "the diffusion of knowledge as to the history and meaning of our own church polity and government and the points of essential unity with other branches of the church of Christ." Men needed "education on the questions of social duty." The overall goal was to "promote, assist, and federate all forms of organized Christian activity of men in the churches" and to train men for "usefulness" in their local congregations through prayer, Bible study, and Christian service.[29]

Mainline masculinity also had a strong ecumenical bent, especially when it allowed laymen to try their hand at problem-solving organizational dysfunction. The MRFM was in fact much more than an evangelistic campaign—it was also an early model of interdenominational cooperation, one that ecumenical leaders followed with respect. To Charles Macfarland, Executive Secretary of the Federal Council of Churches, the MRFM was nothing short of "providential." In 1911, MRFM leader Fred Smith had chided him for lack of vision. The FCC was just "too small an affair," said Smith; it was time to think big. Though taken aback, Macfarland had to accept Smith's expertise. The MRFM was already organizing men across denominational lines and putting them to work, setting up a grassroots structure of local groups that would provide the groundwork for FCC-sponsored church federations to form.[30]

Evidence was growing that the mainline's emphasis on male camaraderie was the right one. Take, for example, a 1919 study of "religion among men," querying a uniquely captive subject group, some 25,000 soldiers at Fort Devens, Massachusetts. Surprisingly, and in contrast to the popular stereotype, the men were overwhelmingly churched—only 2 percent claimed no religious affiliation—and they were generally well behaved. The study found relatively little outright debauchery or atheism. In fact, the problem was not so much immorality as indifference: America's fighting men respected the church "as they do their grandmother." With the exception of Roman Catholics and Lutherans, this exemplary male population was woefully "illiterate" about basic religious teachings. They had little to no understanding of "the Christian idea of God," the "meaning of Christian prayer" or "the obligations of church membership." Even "the Kingdom of God," a favorite Protestant Social Gospel catchphrase, was a "meaningless term."

This was not earth-shattering information. "The situation is of course not new," the report concluded, "but in the army we have seen it with a clarity and convincingness that cannot be escaped." Clearly, the churches needed to alter their course or risk losing more men, to conduct an entire "re-examination" of church membership with masculine needs at the center.[31]

In other words, manly religion did not need to proclaim itself "red-blooded" or "virile"; it just needed to provide well-intentioned men with something useful to keep them occupied. The average man goes to church, as the *Christian Century* explained in 1922, "to avoid a weekly fight" with his wife, to fulfill a dying wish to his mother, or "because there isn't any other member of the family who can drive the car."[32] The churches could awake the "great dormant power in the unused manhood" of the churches, a Congregationalist declared, by letting men work with men, in "men's classes led by men, men's meetings, men's books, men's campaigns."[33]

Clearly, the modern man wanted a religious experience that was jolly and edifying—not unlike the secular competition offered by the Rotary Club and Community Chest. The men in a Long Island Methodist congregation in fact discovered that a set opening and closing liturgy not only added to the fun of the evening, but was appreciated by the men with "lodge affiliations," and made them "feel more at home." It also created a more productive, "business-like atmosphere." "A ritual," as the men discovered, "banishes hit-and-miss." The Long Island Methodists opened with a recitation of welcome, of their "supreme ideal" of Christ's example, and their "declaration of principles," which amounted to good citizenship and honesty. The men sang a favorite hymn ("Rise Up, O Men of God," "God Send Us Men," or "Men of the Church of the Living God") and conducted a roll call. The closing ritual included a benediction, prayer, and then a "song and hearty handshakes."[34]

But would it work? Would men take up their share of the actual work, perhaps even the missionary burden? The Laymen's Missionary Movement was founded in 1906 to parallel the work of women's groups and the Student Volunteer Movement (SVM), then mobilizing young people by the thousands to bring the world to Christ "in this generation." John B. Sleman was on his way to a SVM Convention that year when he realized that "the Christian business men of North America" could bring the young people's ambitious goal from "dream to reality." With the help of fellow Congregationalist Samuel Capen, president of the denomination's missionary society, the American Board, a spate of national conferences soon materialized.[35]

The Missionary Movement's leaders were careful to insist that it would "not duplicate the work done by any other organization"—this was, after all, an era of downsizing organizational sprawl. They would be actually enlisting "'capitalistic statesmen,'" expert professionals who knew how to raise large sums of money and would make sure that missionary work was done properly. The difference, said Capen, was that men "were accustomed to see things in the large," and it was not inconceivable that they could raise a billion dollars by their efforts. It could all be done by the power of "social influences," "calling together small groups of men and presenting to them the largeness of the opportunity, and by hand-to-hand work, the method employed for obtaining large gifts for colleges and hospitals in this country." The Laymen's Missionary Movement also promised to send out a commission of fifty business and professional men to visit all of the mission stations in the world, and report back to the home churches. "Our times are full of 'big things,'" Capen said. "The day of formal praying and petty giving is about over. The day of great consecration and self-sacrifice is at hand."[36]

Yet within a few years, the Laymen's cause had fizzled. All of the dreams of money and enthusiasm failed to materialize, and by 1919, it was absorbed into the Interchurch World Movement, tagged as one of many high-pressure "crusades" that promised much and failed to deliver. Perhaps laymen were just not as astute as some claimed: as a frustrated Congregationalist admitted in 1925, "We laymen needed the constant urge of the women to keep us in line."[37]

Hopes did not die. The Laymen's Movement for a Christian World, formed in 1941, was one more effort to put men to work. Intended as an updated version of the Laymen's Missionary Movement, it was designed to "serve contemporary needs" and "'appeal to men the ages of our sons.'" The founders had every reason to believe they would succeed. The convener of the first organizing meeting was Nobel prize–winning physicist Arthur Compton, and the attendees included department-store magnates, corporate lawyers, and civic leaders.

The Laymen's Movement is a telling contrast to United Church Women, organized that same year. In contrast to the women's program-driven planning and ambitious efforts to bring racial reconciliation and world peace, the men's slogan was "Let's try Christianity." Their initial project was Laymen's Sunday, first observed in 1942. The low-key formula appeared to work: the Laymen's Movement grew steadily in the 1940s and 1950s, attracting leading businessmen, scientists, and statesmen. It was also becoming less explicitly tied to Protestant beliefs and behaviors, and more an advocate for an emerging welfare capitalism. Members attended seminars on "Receptive Listening" and "Spiritual Growth," presented as strategies for avoiding confrontation with "belligerent union leaders" and problematic employees. Labor and capital had no inherent conflict: the Laymen's Movement advised its members to "dedicate your work to God, do the best job you know how, and pray."[38]

The Downside

By the 1920s, the word "layman" was becoming unambiguously masculine. The change was often subtle, but unmistakable, as in a handbook published in 1923, on *Preaching by Laymen*. If the title alone did not suggest a male-only readership, the examples within the text removed any question, citing parallels in the work of the Gideons and the YMCA.[39] An article in *Church Management* from 1938, described the church as a "four-horse team," composed of young people's groups, the Sunday schools, the women's organizations, and laymen, who it was argued, needed to take up their share of the load.[40] *Laymen Speaking*, a book published in 1947, featured twenty-five prominent men, everyone from J. C. Penney to John D. Rockefeller—and no women.[41]

The solidifying terminology coincided with efforts to give laymen more direct power. In 1946 the Protestant Episcopal Church elected its first noncleric, Supreme Court Justice Owen Roberts, to preside over the House of Deputies, one of two legislative bodies in its General Convention. (The other is the House of Bishops.) That same year the Federal Council of Churches amended its constitution to encourage appointment of larger proportion of laymen in delegates of constituent communions. The new emphasis on men, the FCC editorialized, "does not imply that we should take the devotion and service of women for granted. . . . The point here is to emphasize the urgency of having more men participating more actively all along the line."[42]

The National Council of Churches created its own National Laymen's Committee in 1950, a group of influential churchmen chaired by oil baron J. Howard Pew. The Committee's role was advisory, and most of the advice consisted of regular objections to the NCC's social agenda, insisting that churches had no business making economic pronouncements. After the group disbanded in 1955, the NCC created a new board, United Church Men, designed to parallel the work of United Church Women—in effect cementing once again the definition of layman as male. The men's group paled in comparison, however. Annual meetings of United Church Men were fairly tame, consisting mainly of speeches on "character building," Bible reading in public schools, and the evils of Communism. "We must face frankly the fact that the laymen in the great majority of the local churches are very badly organized," Presbyterian attorney Wilbur LaRoe told the gathering in 1954.[43]

Moreover, by the 1940s, Protestant church leaders were discovering the downside to mobilizing laymen: the boundless self-confidence of the self-appointed expert. If the churches really wanted to bring in more members and transform social mores, they needed to adopt "business values," not just efficiency and fiscal sense, but salesmanship and management techniques. One layman, advocating the importance of good advertising insisted that the possibilities were limitless. "If you have any imagination at all," he said, "you can realize that literally hundreds of advertisements can be prepared by intelligent, experienced advertising men" that will in the course of time change human behavior, to become "gradually less selfish, more honest, willing to give others a little more than their due rather than a little less." The "cumulative effect" of all that "individual unselfishness" was nearly millennial. In time, he said, "nation will no longer rise up against nation, but all will see the possibilities in co-operation, both for their own selfish good and for the good of other nations." Advertising, in other words, could be "largely instrumental in eliminating war."[44]

Church leaders had enabled a horde of critics. Local clergy bore the brunt of resentment from laymen who felt themselves being taken for granted, insufficiently recognized for their business expertise. Resentment no doubt grew among Protestant clergy, whose own professional status was coming under question. In contrast to medicine and law, the ministry's gatekeepers were fairly lax. Many denominations did not require an advanced degree or even a college education, and, alarmingly, a major study in 1934 found only a third of American clergy fully credentialed.[45] After centuries of pulpits pointing out the sins of the pews, the table was turning. If was fine to have a polished intellectually gifted minister, said a "Disappointed Layman," but I want a pastor, someone to talk with "man to man."[46] *The Layman Looks at the Minister*, published in 1947, included exceedingly personal advice on weight, personal tidiness, bad breath, punctuality, and "flashy or somber clothes."[47]

Nagging doubts about the pastor's masculine credentials persisted as well, especially in the World War II era. Young seminarians with deferments were understandably defensive about the "draft dodger" epithet. "Many of us in this school feel that ministers must be real 'he-men' if they are to win places of influence with the people of the world today," an Andover Newton student wrote in 1943. "It may be fine to be highly respected, but we want to be one of the group as well."[48]

Increasingly, the criticisms took a political edge. A Philadelphia layman, writing in 1936, complained of having leftist views "shoved" at him by his pastor—this in spite of the fact that "our money has built up a pretty good church and a pretty good country to live in." He was deathly tired of listening to the prattle of "Deacon Jones," "Pastor Brown," and "dear old mother Henderson as she drinks her third cup of coffee at the church supper." Feminized religion was soft and uninformed, and moralistic, an anathema to the layman who had earned success in the secular world. "We play cards and we smoke. Think of that! We sometimes go to the moving pictures. We dance." "The layman of today has been cursed with an education or a social nature that enables him to mingle with educated men and women," he said. "He thinks more clearly than his grandfather. He has ideas of his own."[49]

The defiance drew from growing resentments against the New Deal, blending "conservative religion, economics, and politics" into a potent stew of "Christian libertarianism."[50] Of course, the religion was not necessarily conservative: some of the most formidable Christian libertarians were not fundamentalists but mainline Protestant laymen from theologically liberal denominations. The Conference of Methodist Laymen, for example, was organized in 1935 to "fight radicalism in the Methodist Church"—hardly a monolithic threat, but certainly visible among some of the young people during the Depression era. Perhaps not coincidentally, in 1934 the National Council of Methodist Youth handed out "decision cards" to its members, in which they promised to renounce "the Capitalistic system based on economic individualism and the profit motive." "Ours is not a movement to 'muzzle the pulpit,'" the laymen announced in 1936, but to "preserve the original and vital message of Christianity." An "entrenched minority" of leftist clergy had no right to bind "an entire Church organization on political, social, and economic issues, without full understanding and agreement."[51]

Conservative laymen's resentment against clergy—and laywomen—also had an impact on denominational decision-making. One of the most dramatic confrontations took place among Congregationalists. The precipitating case was the creation of the Council for Social Action (CSA) in 1934, a department created to educate church members on Depression-era social issues—"rural-urban conflicts," problems of church and state, disputes between labor and capital, and racial justice. The purely educational mission of the CSA raised little alarm at first. In the confusing political and economic whirl of the early 1930s, "expert, objective information" from a reliable source was a welcome prospect. Within days of its forming, however, the CSA was controversial. Under somewhat murky circumstances the denomination passed a resolution condemning capitalism—both "the legal forms which sustain it, and the moral ideals which justify it"—as well as private ownership, wherever it interfered with the "social good." To outraged conservatives the connection was obvious: the CSA was behind it all, a radical left-wing stealth operation intent on using the Congregational Christian churches to bring down the American Way.[52]

The opposition crystallized among laymen, resentful over the power of liberal clergy and their feminine allies. At a luncheon discussion during the General Council meeting, the men made note of the fact that all but 48 of the 700 voting delegates to the General Council were either ministers or laywomen. In fact only a third of men roaming around the Council meeting had an actual say in the proceedings: most were "interested spectators," there mostly to provide transportation for their wives and ministers. Under a daily regimen of seminars and speeches, private irritation progressed to public protest. The so-called social relations seminar that one layman had attended was nothing more than propaganda. "The management," as he called them, had not bothered to "procure nor present anyone to discuss the other side of the 'new economics,' as it was called," and provided little opportunity for discussion.[53]

Roger Babson, an eccentric, outspoken businessman and leading layman, was not surprised to see his fellows getting frustrated. All the church meetings he had seen were poorly run, inefficient, and dull, especially alongside what the average man experienced in the business world. "Some of these men have accepted appointments to commissions and boards. They have—at genuine sacrifice—attended one or two meetings. They found the discussion trivial, the consideration of constructive measures inadequate, and they quietly dropped out—disappointed men." The "ablest men in our fellowship," said Babson, will return to work "*only when they are convinced that frank advice is desired and that they will have a genuine share in doing the job.*"[54]

In the 1940s and 1950s, opposition to the CSA broadened to a full-out campaign against the denomination's ecumenical agenda, a proposed merger with another denomination, the Evangelical and Reformed Churches. The first antimerger organizations were led by laymen from Minnesota and Southern California, businessmen and lawyers and politicians, including the Minnesota Republican Senator Walter Judd. "Big steeple" pastors also played a role, led by James Fifield, the pastor of the First Congregational Church of Los Angeles and one of the nation's most influential Christian libertarians. He was founder and leader of Spiritual Mobilization, an organization formed in 1935 to combat totalitarianism abroad and government regulation at home, the "controls and restrictions on many areas of life formerly subject only to voluntary cooperation and competition." Its founding "credo" insisted that "the state must not be permitted to usurp" the inalienable rights of citizens, and that it was "the duty of the church to help protect them."[55]

The antimerger forces were not successful—the United Church of Christ was formed in 1957—but opposition continued. Laymen in organizations like the League to Uphold Congregational Principles continued to stoke anger at overreaching, left-wing clergymen, waving lists, McCarthy style, of ministers affiliated with communist front groups.[56]

Indeed, by the 1950s, "layman" had a conservative, even right-wing connotation. The American Council of Christian Layman (ACCL) was founded 1949 by Verne Kaub, a libertarian Congregationalist. Clergymen, and presumably women, were explicitly not welcome. The ACCL was a strident anticommunist, antiecumenical voice: one of its most popular publications was "How Red Is the National Council of Churches?" Though the organization did not survive Kaub's death in 1964, it was a visible and influential part of right-wing conservatism in the 1950s, the Congress of Freedom and later the John Birch Society.[57]

Still a Man's Church

By the 1950s, laymen had come a long way, and in many different political and cultural directions. They were, by turns, self-actualizing welfare capitalists, libertarian Cold Warriors, and hale-fellows-well-met in the church social hall. The layman was antiecumenical but eager for male camaraderie, anxious for good leadership and the nemesis of many a local pastor. The fuzziness mirrored larger cultural ambiguities about manhood in American society, amplified by the stresses of war and economic hardship; it also, however, stemmed from a lack of clear direction from religious voices in an increasingly secular conversation. Mainline Protestant religion, once the vested interest in muscular Christianity, the champion of the businessman's gospel, no longer had a meaningful role in a conversation they had once led.

The long-term impact of laymen's organizations was subtle but significant. On the one hand, efforts to recruit laymen did little to rebalance a lopsided gender ratio or to convince the wider public that religion was inherently masculine. Church laymen's organizations would always be a weaker sibling of older and more robust women's groups, a pale alternative to the Rotary Club, the lodge, and the bowling league. But the attempt itself, the effort to integrate men into the work of the church, maintained, even strengthened a perception that proved difficult to eradicate. "Women have always been in the churches," a group of feminist critics wrote in 1975, "but not really *of* the churches. Women have supported the churches, carried on pastoral and relief work, but have always been auxiliary, not participants in the mainstream, in the initiating and shaping of the churches' center, its teaching and spiritual and institutional life." Writing in 1983, Methodist Theressa Hoover still saw an assumption that churchwomen's organizations were "*less than official* in status, while male-governed agencies were taken to be the *real* church organizations. This thinking," she said, "was an article of faith with the men earlier in the century, and churchwomen acquiesced to it." The idea was not only "patriarchal," it was "irrational and undemocratic for churches, where the majority of members are women." In other words, twentieth-century Protestant churches had learned to see "the church" and "women" as two separate categories, one masculine and the other forever auxiliary.[58]

6

Forming the Question

A European Critique of "Woman's Mission"

Twila Cavert was not expecting much from the trip to Geneva. She knew how these things generally went, the husband holed up in planning meetings and the wife wandering through more shops and museums than she could stand. Samuel McCrea Cavert was a star, after all. In 1948, as secretary of the FCC, he represented the American wing of Christendom, a fresh face of hope as leaders laid plans for a World Council of Churches (WCC).[1]

Momentum had been building for decades, since those first missionary gatherings in New York and Edinburgh, back at the turn of the century. Over the years the conversation had progressed beyond missionary strategy to the larger problem of Christian unity, with theologians and churchmen working through the myriad of theoretical and practical obstacles in the way. By the eve of World War II the discussions had blossomed into a series of ground-breaking international gatherings. One group, "Faith and Order," dealt with what the churches believed and how they governed themselves. The other, "Life and Work," took on practical questions about Christian faith in the modern world. The war put everything on hold, of course, but by its end the next step was clear: a WCC, a "Christian equivalent" of the United Nations, a fresh start for an old faith in postwar society. And like the UN, the WCC was heavily dependent on the American leadership—and generosity—that Samuel Cavert's presence symbolized.[2]

His wife was no sight-seeing dilettante, however. When Twila Lytton married Samuel Cavert, a widower, in 1927, she was thirty-three years old, and well into her own career as a missionary, educator, and adminis-trator. She had worked in many different settings, from the Tokyo Women's Christian College to schools in the United States, Ohio Wesleyan, Sarah Lawrence, and Lawrence University. Twila Lytton was also an experi-enced world traveler, having ventured far beyond the manicured streets of European capitals. As a young woman she had tramped across Asia, "on footpaths where no Westerners had ever been," and learned to live in

Good and Mad. Margaret Bendroth, Oxford University Press. © Oxford University Press 2023.
DOI: 10.1093/oso/9780197654064.003.0007

a foreign culture, as a teacher in Tokyo.[3] After the war she had returned to Asia and saw the horrors its people had undergone—a Korean village where the Japanese had shot all the men and burned all the buildings, the women "crazed with agony." Like her husband, Twila Cavert also had an international reputation: she sat on the board of trustees of Yenching College in China and Mount Holyoke in the United States, and was a founding member of Church Women United. She was also a board member of the world's largest women's organization, the YWCA—headquartered, as it turned out, in Geneva, Switzerland.[4]

We can imagine her frustration. Perhaps today she would have been recruited for a WCC planning committee, maybe even served as chair. But none of the men had asked her—or any other women—to do anything. "Day after day," her colleague Margaret Shannon wrote, "Mrs. Cavert waited for her husband to finish his conferences and noted that she saw only men coming in and out of the WCC offices."[5] She never put that frustration into words, however. Her surviving correspondence is uniformly buttoned-up and professional. Instead, Cavert created her own agenda, one that altered the aspirations of American churchwomen, and created an opening for feminism.

A trip to Europe made that possible. Like many American stories, this one requires a larger narrative, beyond the geographic and religious confines of the United States. As this chapter demonstrates, the awakening of American churchwomen began in post–World War II Europe, where it was profoundly shaped by the ecumenical movement's goal of Christian unity and the people working to make this possible. The formation of the World Council of Churches brought them into conversation, for the first time, with some formidable European counterparts, women who were not interested in eking out marginal equality in a separate feminine sphere. The Europeans were, in fact, openly critical of all that American churchwomen had labored to achieve, rejecting even the idea of an independent church organization as a pernicious form of enabling. In the postwar era European churchwomen had the pulpit in view, and were preparing to wage an offensive on biblical and theological grounds. Moreover, they were willing to ask questions that the Western churches had tried to ignore for much of the twentieth century, what it meant in Christian terms meant to be male and female, the theological origin and spiritual meaning of gender differences.

Restless Europeans

First on Twila Cavert's agenda was a visit to the YWCA's world headquarters in Geneva. Very quickly, what began as a courtesy call from an American board member turned into a moment of realization: the Y had taken on a job the Christian churches had largely shunned, documenting its treatment of women.[6] Cavert was both intrigued and frustrated—"bluntly clear," as one account put it, "that she considered this inappropriate."[7] All the talk going on about a grand religious reconstruction of the Christian world, a so-called World Council of Churches, had ignored one of Christendom's most critical issues. "It came to me," Cavert later told an interviewer, " . . . that there was really something ridiculous about this: why *should* the YWCA, with all the programmes it has already, deal with this? Why shouldn't the *church* get busy?"[8]

This was a timely question, and Twila Cavert was well positioned to answer it. It did not take her long to marshal important allies in Geneva, including Willem Visser 't Hooft, the visionary Dutch churchman and founding secretary of the WCC. " 'Well, go on then,' " he said "*You* do something with it."[9] This was no offhand dismissal, a genial wave of the hand to a persistent female. Visser 't Hooft's war experience had given him a deep respect for women's intellect and for their physical courage.

Madeleine Barot, whom Visser 't Hooft had met through his work with the World Student Christian Federation, was a prime example. Barot was a near legendary figure in the French Resistance, the founder and general secretary of CIMADE (Comité Inter-Mouvements Auprès Des Evacués or the Inter-Movement Committee in Aid of Evacuees). Intellectually formidable as well as physically fearless, Barot personally provided food and clothing to French Jewish refugees in German prison camps, and even helped plan some escapes. Her resistance work grew out of a deep theological conviction, shaped by an education at the Sorbonne and in Rome, and a strong commitment to human equality, Jew and non-Jew as well as male and female. "Whether her own encounter with sexism in the church affected her dedication to human rights," one scholar writes, "is impossible to prove, but it is notable that Barot, who had herself faced gender discrimination, first focused on helping the Jews during the war before turning to the rights of women." After the war she took up advocacy for young people, and would be tapped by the WCC to lead its Youth Commission.[10]

Visser't Hooft also knew Suzanne de Dietrich, another founding member of CIMADE, and like Barot a leader in one of the great student movements of the prewar era, the Universal Federation of Christian Students. She received an engineering degree from Lausanne in 1913, the first French woman to do so, but found her true vocation as an enormously popular and well-respected biblical scholar, author, and teacher. De Dietrich was also a dedicated ecumenist, and organized the first meeting of Roman Catholic, Protestant, and Eastern Orthodox theologians in 1932. She was one of three women to help write the Pomyral Theses, the charter of the French Protestant resistance to Hitler, and helped found the Ecumenical Institute in Geneva in 1946, where she taught for eight years.[11]

If these professional associations were not enough, Visser 't Hooft's wife Henriette was a passionate advocate of gender equality and a trained theologian. She published what would become a famous an essay in 1934, "Eva, wo bist Du? ("Eve, Where Art Thou?"), and used it as an occasion to initiate a correspondence with Karl Barth—a conversation in which the Swiss

Madeleine Barot, Courtesy World Council of Churches Archives, Geneva, Switzerland, B 10308-01.

theologian was at best condescending. "It was her fate," theologian Jürgen Moltmann concluded, describing this conversation, "to live in the shadow of famous men."[12]

An extroverted, well-connected American completed the circle. After her unsettling visit to the YWCA headquarters, Twila Cavert knew better than to issue a declaration or mount a protest. Instead she organized a pleasant social gathering, a tea which brought her world and her husband's together. The guests included officers of the World's YWCA and Nils Ehrenstrom, who was heading up the WCC's Study Department. The talk was specific and purposeful. Ehrenstrom confided his worries about his native Sweden, convinced that the churches' conservatism on women's issues was a dangerous misreading of the historical moment. The mere possibility of two women being ordained in Denmark's state Lutheran Church had created a full-out furor, including threats of schism.[13] Ehrenstrom agreed that the status of women should be part of the "Ecclesia Militans" series, a statement of the global churches' concerns being prepared for the opening assembly.[14]

The possibility of women's ordination was certainly pressing in postwar Europe. When the men had left to fight, many women had stepped into pulpits. The numbers, though not overwhelming, were considerable: in the Netherlands, for example, female pastors filled four of the 61 Evangelical Lutheran preaching stations, sixteen of 118 Mennonite churches, and nine of 35 Reformed congregations. Once the men returned, however, the situation ended abruptly, and often painfully, as in the Austrian state church, where a 1942 ruling allowing women to preach "in special case of critical distress" was rescinded within months of the armistice, in 1946.[15]

Many women saw the reversals as a direct affront to their wartime sacrifices and their own sense of professionalism. In contrast to the more ad hoc status of female clergy in the United States, their European counterparts were often theologically trained, regular employees of state churches, who had worked as pastors' assistants before the war. These *Theologinnen*, as they were called, did not accept demotion easily. When the Reformed Church of France rebuffed a proposal for women's ordination in 1948, emotions ran high on both sides. Elisabeth Schmidt, who introduced the proposal, sat behind a pillar in the assembly room while the men debated. She left in tears when the verdict was announced, astonished at the betrayal after her years of willing service. "My sadness," she said, was "like that of a child deceived by her mother."[16]

British women were equally on edge. The Church of England had been debating—and rebuffing—women's ordination for decades, and fueling an increasingly forceful, organized response. The undisputed leader was Maude Royden, the brilliant and charismatic founder of The Guildhouse in London, where in the 1920s she gained a reputation as "England's most famous preacher." As a leader of the League of the Church Militant, she led an intense campaign against conservatism in the Church of England, writing and speaking and traveling to all corners of the Anglican Communion.[17] Tensions peaked in 1930, when the Lambeth Conference not only rejected women's ordination but scaled back a previous ruling that allowed women to serve as deaconesses—a setback so disappointing that Royden suffered a nervous breakdown. Many of the arguments against ordination were barely theological: a Commission appointed by Canterbury and York in 1931 declared that "it would be impossible for the male members of the average Anglican congregation to be present at a service at which a woman ministered without being unduly conscious of her sex." In the summer of 1948, Lambeth retrenched again, rejecting a "Chinese Canon," a proposal from the General Synod of the Church in China, which would have allowed deaconesses a path to full ordination to the priesthood.[18]

Twila Cavert's Challenge

Twila Cavert's task, then, was to harness the vague good intentions of WCC executives and the rising impatience of European churchwomen into forward movement—all without raising alarms of a feminist uprising. The logical beginning point, as she saw it, was gathering as much information as possible in the form of a survey, with the hope that it would make the agenda of the upcoming WCC meeting in Amsterdam. It was a formidable challenge that she consistently downplayed. "I'm very pleased to note the interest in the question of 'Women in the Church' in the WCC," Cavert wrote to a friend in a pleasantly self-deprecating letter. "It appears that I'm to be mixed up in this study which is to be made—and a little later I ought to have some news to report."[19]

In reality, her undertaking was far more significant, certainly more than WCC officials expected. Instead of focusing narrowly on "problems relating to women clergy," as they had suggested, Cavert took the opportunity to document the historic relationship between "women" and "the church," a complex mix of attitudes and practices that involved missionaries and layworkers, Sunday schools and single-sex organizations. None of this had ever been documented fully: the existing picture of "women's work" was scattered and anecdotal, easily marshaled by both sides in controversies about clerical office. "Not since the Reformation," writes historian Susannah Herzel, "had systematic attention been directed to gaining a picture of the life and work of women in the church as a *whole*, both professional and voluntary, evaluating it as it is and seeing the hopes for its future."[20] In other words, Twila Cavert's aim was unprecedented: verifying the churches' dependence on their most faithful, subordinated, and silenced members.

But first she had to invent a process for doing so. In fact, we should pause a moment to consider the administrative challenge Cavert faced. Who would have the best, most reliable information about women and the church? Who should be asked?. Lacking both administrative support and direct institutional power, Cavert used her organizational skills and global connections to create a network of "outstanding" churchwomen. "Give almost anybody five moves," she later explained to an interviewer, "and they can get to anyone in the world, including the Queen of England."[21]

The questionnaire itself was a remarkable effort, an eight-page document requesting information about church offices—women clergy (including their names and addresses), deaconesses, religious orders and communities, home and foreign missionaries—as well as the myriad of other roles women filled. It queried about all types of professional work, including social workers, writers and editors, executive secretaries, musicians, architects, and educational administrators. The questionnaire asked for information about women in church governing bodies—not just the rules in place, but whether female participants were making a "distinctive contribution." It wanted to know the "theological and Biblical" bases behind those church rules, as well as "psychological considerations" that made it "difficult for men and women to work together on a plane of equality in the Church." Finally, the questionnaire was translated into German, French, English, and many other languages and dialects, and sent to 20,000 recipients.[22]

The response was astonishing: what Cavert later described as her "little home-spun effort" had touched a nerve.[23] For the next two and a half years church bodies from all around the world used the questionnaires as an opportunity to meet and talk about an old and important problem. The Scottish churches held a three-day conference, composed of men and women from seven denominations. The National Christian Council in India planned four regional gatherings. The Orthodox Church in Greece returned a 125-page set of "deeply moving documents and letters." Although the majority of responses came from Western nations, the list also included Saudi Arabia, the Belgian Congo, Brazil, Guatemala, Iraq, Japan, Manchuria, Santo Domingo, Peru, Uruguay, and Venezuela. All told, Cavert's questionnaire brought in responses from fifty-eight countries, "often from fifty to a hundred pages or more in length, with supporting documents—indicative of great ability, concern, initiative and devotion," incorporating public statements as well as "personal histories, letters, diaries, and anecdotes."[24]

In the United States, the FCC published the survey's findings as a special project, under the direction of Twila Cavert's sister-in-law, Inez Cavert. Published in 1948, *Women in American Church Life* was as comprehensive and searching as Twila Cavert's survey, documenting their official roles in 105 denominations, from liberal to conservative, as well as the content of biblical and theological debates about female clergy.[25] Though hardly the first survey of "women's status" in American Protestant denominations—executives had been piling up documentation for decades—this one was special, measuring "the attitudes of women" toward the church, not as was the custom, the reverse. Most significant of all, the FCC study was conducted and written by women themselves.

The excitement was palpable, a sense of something genuinely new. "It seems to me, as I read the report," YWCA official Rhoda McCulloch wrote to Sue Wedell, an American colleague, in June 1948, "that this project may have deep significance for the future which our imaginations are not now able to forecast." Not only would it bring "light and encouragement" to women, but "there are many men," she said, ". . . who will see between the lines of the report a new blue print of the church of the future." It will be a church in which "the contribution of women will not be labelled as 'women's work' but stuff and substance of the whole life and work of the church as a commonwealth of Christian men and women."[26]

McCulloch was definitely right in one respect: Cavert's ad hoc campaign was precipitating conversations that churches had long chosen to avoid, and documenting the ways in which Christian churches not only depended on women but routinely undercut their aspirations. The breadth of responses to the questionnaire and the quality of emerging leadership demanded a much broader, thoughtful response than yet another debate over women's ordination. It was time to break new theological ground.

The Ecumenical Problem

It is worth backing up for a moment to consider the challenge Twila Cavert was taking on: the ecumenical movement itself was a deeply embedded obstacle. In the United States church cooperation was one of the few areas of Protestant church life with a safe masculine monopoly. In his history of the FCC, its first secretary Charles Macfarland acknowledged, albeit briefly, "the negligibility of women" (pausing to wonder if the Council's "consequent neglect" might have spurred resentment).[27] Methodist Thelma Stevens was more explicit: "The 'second class' role assigned to women in the denominations was perpetuated in the new ecumenical movement," as it perpetuated and magnified the role of "denominational power groups" and "discrimination" against women.[28]

The problem was worse on the world stage: women were notably absent from all of the meetings leading up to the formation of the World Council of Churches. Some of the reasons were simply logistical: conference delegates were selected by duly-constituted national church bodies, and were therefore, by definition, clergy. Thus, the most consistent critique of the ecumenical movement was that it was "for professionals only," and not open to laypeople.

But the absence of women was also intentional. Early on, leading ecumenists decided that any talk of women's "place," which in their minds meant ordination, would hinder Christian unity. In 1916, William Temple, who as Archbishop of Canterbury would become a main architect of the ecumenical movement, wrote that though he "personally" wanted to see women ordained to the priesthood, "still more do I want to see both real advance towards the re-union of Christendom." The "general emancipation of women," he was sure, would be a byproduct, as long as everyone remained patient. "If there were no other ground for belief in a personal Devil," he wrote, it is "when a great movement gets under way" only to have its strength "sapped by another *good* movement."[29]

As a result, women were barely visible in all of the organizing meetings held before 1948. At the Lausanne Faith and Order Convention in 1927, they were a mere six out of 400 delegates, even though the meeting was to be a genuinely global gathering of the Christian churches—hopes were high that even Roman Catholics and the Orthodox Churches would attend.[30] Only two pages of the published proceedings, which amounted to some 550 pages of single-spaced text, addressed women's concerns, this as an exceedingly polite "memorial" to the men. "We do not wish to raise any discussion on the subject," the six delegates said, "but we believe that the right place of women in the Church and in the councils of the Church is one of grave moment, and should be in the hearts and minds of all." Their hope was that the churches' "quest for deeper spiritual unity" would bring both sexes to a "fresh revelation of God's will."[31]

The call for representation went unanswered. The number of female delegates to the Jerusalem meeting in 1928, sponsored by the International Missionary Council, was slightly larger, 41 out of 251, but women were only eleven of the 272 accredited delegates to the Faith and Order meeting in Oxford in 1937.[32]

The low proportion was not for want of trying. In 1936 American laywomen directly petitioned organizers for representation, even offering specific suggestions. The Woman's Commission of the FCC, for example, recommended Labor Secretary Frances Perkins, feminist Mary Van Kleeck, Wellesley College president Mildred McAfee, or British feminist and theologian Maude Royden. But they were also well aware that "the preliminary work for the Oxford and Edinburgh meetings is largely in the hands of theologians and older men." Commission members worried whether "the thinking of active young women will be in any way reflected."[33] Henry Van Dusen, a Union Seminary theologian and one of the lead American organizers, was not particularly receptive, however. The men had indeed "considered the place and contribution of women," he explained, but the subject "had not been integrated into the plans and program for the meeting." Still, not to worry. Despite the fact that the American delegation included eighty men and one woman, Van Dusen was certain that every effort "would be made to secure the thinking of women on the program."[34]

The actual reviews were mixed. From the Oxford meeting, British YMCA secretary May Curwen reported that her "feminist soul" delighted in "the high quality of the speeches given by women at the plenary sessions."[35] She was undoubtedly referring to Georgia Harkness, then a religion professor at Mount Holyoke, who gave a stirring four-minute address, though hardly a feminist manifesto. Harkness's remarks were a plea for lay people in general, for a recognition that ecumenical cooperation required more than just conversations among the clergy. And women were laypeople too. If the church was to be "*a supra-national, supra-racial, supra-class fellowship*," said Harkness, "then it should also be a supra-sex fellowship." Until the churches recognized that "in Christ there is neither Jew nor Greek, bond nor free, male nor female," it will "fall short of being a truly ecumenical body."[36] Other than that, however, the Oxford meeting was a disappointment. Women's point of view, according to one of the American female delegates, "was very inadequately represented." Still, she said, "we have something to be thankful for, that we were there at all."[37]

The 1938 meeting in Madras was more successful: fifteen of the 45 American delegates were female. Moreover, the "report on women's work" recognized their service as "ordained ministers, elders, deaconesses, members of Religious Communities and lay leaders," and called for more representation on administrative and executive boards and councils. It even acknowledged that equal access to ordination was "a conviction of many."[38] Yet the American delegates were aware of an uncomfortable truth, that it was extraordinarily difficult to find churchwomen who were even interested in attending. Was it possible that "some of the topics, such as 'The Nature and Meaning of the Church' just did not appeal" to them? Perhaps "they are more interested in the practical outreach of the Christian Message than in abstract thinking about it." Or was it because so few women were "professionally qualified," that is, members of the clergy? Did they just not want to work with men? Certainly women participated in "mixed groups" in secular settings, outside the churches. "What inhibits them?"[39]

One large part of the problem was early-twentieth century ecumenism itself. Especially as it developed in the United States in the pre–World War II years, the ecumenical ideal was deeply averse to naming social differences like race or gender. The great diversity of American religion was, according to H. Richard Niebuhr's *Social Sources of Denominationalism*, at bottom, a scandalous "accommodation of Christianity to the caste-system of human society."[40] The fundamentalist insurgence of the 1920s only deepened distaste for religious infighting, so much so that idealistic Protestants found it difficult if not impossible to countenance any kind of human division. There were simply no good reasons for tolerating disunity, no incentive to analyze the cultural, economic, or racial sources of difference, much less inequality. Far better and more constructive to concentrate on large ideals that Christians everywhere could embrace, obliterating incidental facts of outward appearance or social condition. In many ways, the ecumenical idea mirrored the "Christian internationalism" in American foreign policy, the belief that American values—democracy and capitalism—were the true aspiration of all human beings everywhere, the ultimate solution to conflict. When racial tensions emerged in the international gatherings in Jerusalem in 1928 and

Madras in 1938 the answer was a "supranational" church, "a community in which nation and race were to be transcended."[41]

After the human debacle of World War II this lofty ideal required serious recalibrating. The ecumenical movement would have to address racial inequality and nationalism in order to keep pace with African and Asian Christians in newly independent nations, and to comprehend the moral force of the civil rights movement in the United States. Gender inequality was, as yet, a secondary concern, and feminism a nearly unspeakable option. But in the months leading up to the first meeting of the WCC, in the fall of 1948, the women had started the conversation—even without a guarantee that the ecumenical movement was ready to listen.

The Baarn Meeting, August 13–17, 1948

Twenty-thousand questionnaires were just the beginning. In the summer of 1947, Twila Cavert found herself, yet again, taking on an important and poorly defined task, with limited resources. The WCC Study Department had approved a "meeting for women" as part of the pre-Assembly series, but provided no money for their travel or lodging. "We (you and I) were supposed to work on that," Cavert told Olive Wyon, who had been appointed to assist her. Moreover, though the assumption was that the group would report to the Amsterdam Assembly, WCC officials were not making any promises about an outcome. "The pressure in Geneva is so great," Henry Van Dusen warned Cavert, "that the ladies may not receive much attention."[42]

The two women were a formidable team, however. On the one hand, Cavert's personal warmth—and perhaps long experience with hosting gatherings of her husband's important guests—persuaded many women to brave the challenge and expense of international travel through postwar Europe. Her invitation letters were well crafted and personal, routinely including names of friends or acquaintances slated to attend.[43] Wyon brought a brilliant attention to detail and the strength of an international reputation. Her biographer's description is well justified, that "few were better networked across the world church." She had worked with leading British ecumenists, including Stephen Oldham and Archbishop William Temple, and helped plan the Oxford Conference in 1937. By the time she met Cavert, Wyon was also one of Europe's leading translators of theological works, including Ernst Troeltsch's *Social Teaching of the Christian Church*, which Visser 't

Hooft deemed one of the most difficult translation projects he had ever seen. During her time with Cavert, Wyon was also working on what would be the definitive English version of Emil Brunner's corpus. If that were not enough, Wyon was also part of the circle led by mystical writer Evelyn Underhill, and the author of numerous books on spirituality, including *The School of Prayer* (1943).[44]

Cavert understood the scope of their task, in both practical and human terms. As she wrote to Wyon, "one does not easily enlist the cooperation of often harassed and over-burdened women in such an enterprise as this unless their emotions as well as their minds are engaged. Sending out questionnaires," she said, "has been the least part of the activity." Nor was it enough to give the "women of the churches" a chance to "share their accomplishments, their problems and hopes," and to learn "about those of others." What they needed most was a sense of participation, a feeling of "'at home-ness' in the World Council of Churches as an ecumenical institution belonging in part to them."[45] Writing to one attendee, YWCA official Helen Roberts, Twila Cavert underlined the "sense of urgency" behind the gathering. Here was an opportunity to bring women together "for the first time really," to consider "what as women we may be led to do" in the postwar world. She was also realistic, however. "Inevitably as we consider these things," she wrote, "we shall have to face both the doors which are wide open to us and the doors which are either closed or opened somewhat grudgingly." The women would have to come "without fear or resentment, but with courage and conviction, to know 'who we are and to what we are called.'"[46]

The conference itself, though not everything Cavert and Wyon might have dreamed, was a solid achievement. Some sixty women met in Baarn, a small town about an hour by train outside of Amsterdam, at the Zendingscentrum (Mission Center) of the Dutch Reformed Churches. Due to the difficulties of travel and limited funding, nearly all of the attendees were from Europe and the United States, almost none from Latin America, Africa, or Asia. "Do you know of any women of China, Africa, the Philippines etc., who might be in Europe," Cavert wrote to Sue Wedell in mid-June, "or might be encouraged to come this way for the Women's Conference and Assembly? It is getting very late for any such planning, but it seems to me to be of the greatest importance for us all to put forth almost superhuman effort to try to make this correction in the state of affairs as it now stands." In the end, however, the women's meeting, as well as the Assembly, would end up, in Cavert's words, "primarily an Anglo-Saxon" affair.[47]

Yet those who did attend brought a diverse range of experience in Christian churches, despite uniformly elite levels of education and influence. Sarah Chakko, a member of the Syrian Orthodox Church and, president of the Isabella Thoburn College in Lucknow, had come all the way from India. A handful were ordained clergy, including British Congregationalist Elsie Chamberlain and Anna Canada Swain, who had just completed a tumultuous term as president of the Northern Baptist Convention. Margaret Wedgewood Benn (Lady Stansgate) was a leading advocate of women's ordination in the Church of England. Most of the European delegates were theologically trained, some the intellectual companions of well-known husbands—Else Bremer (Mrs. Martin) Niemoller and Henrietta Visser 't Hooft. Nearly all of the American delegates represented women's organizations: Georgiana Sibley, Mildred Horton, and Mossie Wyker had all held positions with Church Women United.[48]

Even without strong personalities and diverse backgrounds, the conversation was going to be difficult, especially for the American delegation. Lady Stansgate was "very much in evidence," Reinhold Niebuhr wrote to his wife, Ursula, about their personal friend, "though I understand is being criticized somewhat for placing too much emphasis on the ordination of women, rather than the wider problems of women in the church."[49] But the level of debate relegated many American churchwomen to watching from the

The Baarn Assembly, Courtesy World Council of Churches Archives, Geneva, Switzerland, D3334.

sidelines. "Imagine my surprise," Mildred Horton later told a churchwomen's gathering, that "the question of the ordination of women was 'hot' on the continent and it was being discussed with vigor on strictly theological and biblical grounds." Anna Swain was even more emphatic. "I told Mrs. Cavert before the whole thing started," as she wrote to her husband, "that 'women in the ministry' would produce unnecessary heat and get us nowhere."[50]

Surprisingly, however, the Baarn meeting produced a report which Visser't Hooft described as "very cautious." Declaring that gender equality was "the concern of the Church as a whole," the women called for a greater voice in ecclesiastical decision-making, as well as more biblical and theological training for "professional church workers"—directors of religious education, parish workers, and missionaries, and youth leaders. Women's ordination did not appear until the end of the document, as a recommendation rather than a demand. Acknowledging the vast range of teaching and practice in Christian churches, the report recommended "further careful and objective study."[51]

If anything, the Baarn report's biggest challenge was to American churchwomen, suddenly forced to defend the very foundation of "woman's place" in American Protestant churches, the separate space they had tended with dogged persistence for over a century. "I was told," said Horton, "that French women dread the influence of American women lest we introduce the pattern of segregation of women which they consider very 'backward.'" Even the mention of women's "place" was unacceptable, setting women back a thousand years.[52] In fact, the last thing the Baarn delegates wanted was a women's caucus. The "problems relating to women in the Church are problems of the Church as a whole" they declared in their report, and "should not be delegated exclusively to women." In an unapologetic affront to the Americans present, the report came down heavily against gender-segregated church organizations: while beneficial as a "training-ground in Christian leadership," they threatened to become "substitutes for a wider participation in the life of the Church." Their hope for the WCC was across-the-board representation on all of the newly forming Commissions and Committees, and a full study of the responses to their questionnaire. They dared hope for a Commission composed of men and women, internationally representative, "with adequate budget and executive leadership," to give further consider to the work of women in the church.[53]

The Amsterdam meeting would prove historic, and not only to the hundreds of male ecumenists who attended the august assembly. As the next chapter shows, it was also an important moment in the history of women in Christian churches, and we can also say, in the history of modern feminism. Though frustrating, even angering to the tiny group of women who presented the Baarn report to a skeptical Assembly and squared off with the irascible Karl Barth, Amsterdam would provide much needed institutional traction. Though the story has been largely forgotten and the participants mostly invisible to history, modern Christendom's first serious conversations about faith and feminism took place in the World Council of Churches during the late 1940s and 1950s. Even less well known is a small irony, the role of an American churchwoman, Twila Lytton Cavert, in facilitating a set of conversations that would, over time, challenge some of the most time-honored—and unexamined—beliefs about "woman's role" in American Protestant churches.

7

Pursuing Answers

Ecumenism and Feminism in the World Council of Churches, 1948–1953

The first gathering of the World Council of Churches (WCC) was nothing if not a masculine spectacle. On August 22, 1948, hundreds of excited "Amsterdamers" gathered outside the Nieuwe Kerke to witness a "stately procession of archbishops, patriarchs, moderators, and other church dignitaries." Men of God paraded past in clerical collars and business suits, black robes and bishops' mitres, some sporting jeweled medallions and embroidered stoles, others with beards flowing down across their chests. They marched in solemn formation, a visual display of Christianity's reach across space and time, from Eastern Orthodox to the Society of Friends, from Egypt's ancient Coptic churches to the United Church of South India, founded a year before. The gathering included the leading lights of western Christendom, John R. Mott and the Archbishop of Canterbury Geoffrey Fisher, world-famous theologians Emil Brunner and Karl Barth, Cold War statesmen John Foster Dulles and Joseph Hromadka of Czechoslovakia. The Assembly was a truly global array: 352 delegates from 147 church bodies from 44 nations, including six behind the "iron curtain."[1]

Six of those 352 delegates were women. "Of all the things which I anticipated about the meeting of the First Assembly of the World Council of Churches in Amsterdam," Mildred Horton recalled, "the last on the list would have been any particular concern about the responsibility of women for the life and work of the church." Women were at best a "welcome but curious novelty," and, not surprisingly, many were "terrified for fear they would seem to be demanding feminists."[2]

Given all this, Sarah Chakko was an inspired choice to present the Baarn report to the Assembly. A physically striking woman—there was "something a little royal about her," said Visser 't Hooft—Chakko was a college president with a prestigious academic track record that included studies in education at the University of Chicago and in international law and colonialism at the

Good and Mad. Margaret Bendroth, Oxford University Press. © Oxford University Press 2023.
DOI: 10.1093/oso/9780197654064.003.0008

University of Michigan. She was also used to the podium and to international gatherings, having served as chair of the Student Christian Movement in India for six years. Chakko's personal background was striking as well: she grew up in southern India in a family of converts to the Syrian Orthodox Church, and accustomed perhaps to standing out in a crowd. Dressed in an Indian sari, she was an uncommon figure in an assembly hall of dark-clad male clerics, and an intellectually formidable one.[3]

Nevertheless, the response to Chakko's presentation was an object lesson in genteel, public sexism. She began with a disclaimer: "there seemed to have been some misunderstanding" that a "women's committee" was bringing the report, she said. In fact, the "basic assumption" was that this subject was "the concern of the church of the whole and not the problems of a group of women." Chakko also acknowledged that her report would be brief and provisional. "It did not contain all that one would wish," she said, and no doubt contained errors and omissions. But the Baarn meeting had made clear that women were "greatly interested in the ecumenical programme," and "it was

Sarah Chakko, Courtesy World Council of Churches Archives, Geneva, Switzerland, D122.

important to capture their imagination" quickly. "The time element was an important consideration."[4]

The men, however, heard Chakko's nuanced report as a demand for ordination. George Bell, the Bishop of Chichester complained that though "the facts in the report were generally agreed to be of great value," there was insufficient "unanimity" on a subject "which always caused controversy." Did anyone even know "how many and what theologians" had guided the women's discussion? Another colleague agreed: why raise the ordination question "when it was fully known that there was no hope whatever of anything like agreement"? Without "substantial corrections" it would "give a wrong impression to people and lead them to think that there would be more general consent to the ordination of women than was actually possible."[5]

Chakko was courteous and firm, insisting first of all that the ordination of women "was only a minor part of the whole problem." The central issue was "the service of women," and "surely it could not be so very dangerous to discuss." In fact, the recommendation for more reliable information about women's work would "help to develop the ecumenical interest" of both sexes, and "would not appeal merely to a rather peculiar species of woman."[6]

Though the Assembly did finally adopt the interim report, the public wrangling continued. Because the Life and Work of Women in the Church had been identified as a core concern, it was scheduled for an afternoon follow-up discussion. Expectations—and anxieties—were high: the great Karl Barth had volunteered to attend. The famous theologian had already been a cantankerous presence at the Assembly, pouring skepticism on liberal hopes for Christian unity and human betterment in a keynote address. Without a firm dose of humility, he warned, the World Council of Churches would amount to little more than a "Christian Marshall plan."[7] But the women saw Barth's presence as a hopeful sign: at that time he was the only serious Christian thinker who had given systematic attention to a theology of gender. The Baarn group had considered at length his analysis of the creation story in the third volume of his major work, *Church Dogmatics*, and many, though not all, saw him as a potential ally. Mildred Horton recalled that Barth "interested us very much" because he had "recently discovered women" and appeared to find "a great future" for them "within the framework of biblical authority." Others, however, were dubious, "not sure what Karl Barth means and in any case are not sure they agree[d] with him."[8]

The others were probably right. At the Commission meeting Barth went out of his way to muddy the waters, insisting on both the "equal dignity" of the sexes and women's subordination to men. Georgia Harkness found it all deeply unsettling. It did not help that "without warning" Sarah Chakko had asked her to open the conversation with a theological summary of the Commission's work. Harkness scrambled a bit: "I said briefly that in the O[ld] T[estament] it is stated that both male and female are created in the image of God; in the N[ew] T[estament] Jesus assumed always that men and women were equal before God, and in our Christian faith is the chief foundation of sex equality." Barely had she finished when Barth "claimed the floor," and declared it all "completely wrong." And the discussion went downhill from there. "There was great disappointment and opposition," Visser 't Hooft recalled, when Barth "asserted that while the Bible did indeed maintain the equal dignity of men and women, it also spoke of women's subordination to man." They were, simply put, made from Adam's rib and subject to male authority as the church is to Christ. "Then followed a lively interchange," said Harkness, "in which I did little but to quote Gal. 3:28," while "the room buzzed."[9]

Barth lived to regret being so outspoken. He had provoked some formidable opponents, including not just Harkness, but Chakko, Horton, and Wu yi-Fang, all three college presidents. Though hardly "feminist extremists," as Visser 't Hooft wrote, these women were "heartily sick of being told that subordination meant, *de facto*, the sole sovereignty of the male." Barth did not help his cause when he joked about the interchange in a press interview.[10]

This was gallows humor. In fact, the confrontation apparently left a "deep impression" on Barth, one that continued long after Amsterdam. "To hear him speak of it," said Visser 't Hooft, "the women had really brow beaten him," and "never in his life had he been so terrified as at that meeting with a group of women who he felt were ready to 'extort the last ounce of flesh from me.'" Barth was reportedly "*especially* scared" of Sarah Chakko, according to Visser 't Hooft. Georgia Harkness received her own satisfaction a year later when "a friend of mine asked him if he recalled meeting a woman theologian from America." His "cryptic reply was, 'Remember me not of that woman!'"[11]

What is a Woman?

Despite this rancorous beginning, the conversation continued. In fact, in the 1940s and 1950s the WCC was the most important, if not the sole, site of theological discussion about gender roles, first through the Commission (later the Committee) on the Life and Work of Women in the Church, and then after 1953, in the Department of Cooperation between Men and Women in Church and Society. Both groups were well stocked with highly educated, sophisticated churchmen and women eager to open new theological ground and build a Christian dialogue with the contemporary secular thinkers.

All of it was new ground for American churchwomen. Pragmatic to the core, they had rarely paused to theologize, let alone tackle the biblical texts that had roiled the Christian world since the days of St. Paul. Though hardly uneducated or anti-intellectual, women like Margaret Horton and Anna Swain saw little practical value in reopening long, and likely fruitless discussions about their proper role. Thanks in part to their hard-earned institutional experience and skill, the mainline churches had come to see gender as an administrative issue, a matter of calculating women's "status" and ensuring their proper representation on denominational boards and committees. Now the foundational question, a query posed and then dropped in the post-suffrage era, arose again: What is a woman?

The WCC's Commission on the Life and Work of Women in the Church inaugurated and led the discussion. It was a remarkable group, a well-credentialed, intellectually diverse gathering of men and women: Cornelia van Asch van Wijk, the former president of the World's YWCA; Arne Fjellbu, the Bishop of Trondheim, Norway; as well as Sarah Chakko, Visser 't Hooft, and Kathleen Bliss, a British woman with years of ecumenical experience, missionary work, and a theological degree from Cambridge. Additional expertise came from Gustav Bally, a psychiatrist from Zurich and Elizabeth Schwartzhaupt, a jurist and legal adviser to the Evangelische Kirche in Germany. Mary Ely Lyman, professor of English Bible at Union Theological Seminary, was the sole American participant.[12]

One primary task was allaying fears of a feminist uprising. The situation was still "very delicate," Twila Cavert reminded Sarah Chakko, urging her to practice the "Christian graces of restraint and of moving forward at the same time." The Commission might well risk the progress of "those who have labored and suffered" for so many years.[13] Visser 't Hooft was equally cautious: "People may fear that we are going to make an onslought [sic] on the whole tradition of some churches or interfere with their life," he warned. The Commission's work would require an "immense amount of tact."[14]

This meant making sure that conversation included both men and women—another major challenge. The Executive Committee had appointed only a handful, and their attendance tended to be spotty. As an alarmed Kathleen Bliss wrote to Sarah Chakko, "it looks as though it will be a women's commission for all practical purposes unless steps are taken to redress the balance"—even removing women if necessary.[15] Men had to carry their share of the work, and not just for the sake of perception. The women were mostly outsiders to the world of ecumenical theologizing. Whether for lack of interest or lack of an invitation, few had attended a meeting of the Faith and Order Commission, which would have been the logical setting for any discussion of gender equality. Without conscious effort, men and women both might revert to old habits, "a man's Church related to doctrine, Church order and organisation and a woman's Church which takes care of missions, works of mercy and the social life of the Christian community."[16]

The final challenge was the limited intellectual resources available to the Commission members. As Visser 't Hooft reminded them in 1951, they were "entering a field in which little thinking has been done by the churches and in which no ecumenical thinking has been done at all."[17] The Baarn meeting had raised the question, whether "responsibilities in the Church [should] be determined by the sex of individuals." But the participants had balked at any discussion of innate differences, rejecting "oversimplifications" about the gentleness and tact of women or the strength and courage of men. It was, after all, a "well-attested psychological fact" that "every human being, male or female, has within him an admixture of both masculine and feminine qualities." Moreover, the Baarn discussion had only touched on biblical material, noting the gulf between Paul's declaration of freedom in Galatians 3:28, and the restrictions imposed on the Corinthians. "We were too naïve in thinking that we could put something out quickly," Visser 't Hooft concluded; "we must first do some real ecumenical thinking ourselves."[34]

Nuanced, fresh ideas were definitely rare. Beyond Barth, the conversation was dominated by conservative Lutherans who insisted that God's "order of creation" destined women to a permanently subordinate role.[18] Their manifesto was Fritz Zerbt's published dissertation, *The Office of Woman in the Church: A Study in Practical Theology*, written as a riposte to the perceived liberalism of the WCC on gender issues. Zerbst argued that the subjection of women was coded into creation itself: Adam was the ruler, and Eve the follower. The divine order was not only "unchangeable and irrevocable," it was biological. "Woman always remains woman," weak, dependent, and nurturing, argued Zerbst. Though he allowed that some women might be intelligent, capable, and perhaps even good preachers and pastors, it made no difference. Hierarchy was the divine decree, and the church was duty-bound to "always set forth clearly the Creator's will concerning women."[19] Soft-hearted egalitarians were not just wrong, they were dangerous. Without order, said Zerbst, men and women would "battle for leadership and supremacy"; life would descend into sexual chaos and competition, "a breeding ground for sin." Everyone therefore was better off with male leadership, a "protective wall" against the "demonism of sin, lusts, and passions."[20]

The alternative was Karl Barth, who had already proved himself an uncertain ally. Like Zerbst, he based his theology of gender on the creation story in Genesis, but drew a different conclusion, emphasizing complementarity rather than difference, unity more than competition. "How is it possible," Barth wrote in Volume 3 of *Church Dogmatics*, "to characterise man except in his distinctive relation to woman, or woman except in her distinctive relation to man?" Gender differences were part of the "breath-taking dialectic" at the heart of creation, a "dialectic of difference and affinity, of real dualism and equally real unity, of utter self-recollection and utter transport beyond the bounds of self into union with another, of creation and redemption, of this world and the next."[21]

Commission members understood that though Barth was not ideal, he offered an important starting place. Unlike many other theologians on the subject," Sarah Chakko explained, "Karl Barth indicates that woman was not created as an extra or an afterthought, but that man and woman together form the image of God." She understood Barth to argue that man is not the "archetype of the human being," but that men and women are "of equal worth." The "di-unity" of the human pair, said Chakko, reflects the divine image.[22] Barth was no feminist, of course: Chakko was aware that he interpreted sexual difference in a negative light, as "a sign of limitation proper to the creature"— only the three persons of the Trinity were both distinct and equal, a "perfect union with one will and freedom." Yet though Barth allowed that the union of the sexes required some form of "superordination" and "subordination," he did not believe that gender differences were obstacles to human thriving, or that their fundamental bent was toward competition and chaos. Human beings are "ordered, ranked, and determined," like everything else in creation, but "men and women also create themselves, including their social roles. They belong together."[23]

Barth, however, was not going to be the final word. The Commission members were also, if not more, interested in what non-Christians were thinking about gender roles. They delved into the works of secular thinkers, circulating reading lists and reviews of Margaret Mead's *Male and Female* and Simone de Beauvoir's *The Second Sex*, even Ferdinand Lundberg and Marynia Farnham's antifeminist polemic, *Modern Women: The Lost Sex*. Henriette Visser 't Hooft also translated and summarized Philip Lersch, *On the Nature of the Sexes*, which argued that "male and female are meant to be and act as two opposite poles, whose tension guarantees growth and balance."[24] The Commission members received their reading assignments with enthusiasm. Kathleen Bliss wrote to Chakko of her desire to "come to grips with Simone," because she was "the very best type of modern pagan who presents and absolutely fundamental challenge to Christian belief." Bliss was truly inspired by the prospect of having de Beauvoir "heard, read and understood in its full depths, and then challenged from a Christian point of view."[25]

Yet feminism, as Commission members understood it, was not an option. They were well aware, first of all, that the barest mention of the term conjured fears of ruinous debates over women's ordination. They also recognized that word itself was problematic in the postwar era, suggesting a welter of contradictory political, economic, and social threats to the social order. Popular psychology tagged feminists as either sexual libertines or sexually maladjusted malcontents, women who hated men or wanted to become just like them. In the United States, the feminist movement itself was struggling for coherence, insisting on the one hand for equal treatment of the sexes, and on the other advocating protective legislation for working women. This was the "feminist paradox," described by historian Nancy Cott, "of women mobilizing as a class to defeat discrimination against them as a class."[26] In Europe, the reference point for "feminism" was even more problematic: Stalin's Russia, where women worked in fields and factories alongside men. Commission members specifically decried the "superficial egalitarianism found in Communism," riding roughshod over "the different charismata of men and women." After fighting a war against fascism for the right of individual expression, many Europeans were wary of any rules about gender relationships. Even a regime of absolute equality was a risk not worth taking.[27]

A new vocabulary was necessary. In 1953 the Committee on the Life and Work of Women in the Church became the Department of Cooperation between Men and Women in Church and Society—two lengthy titles that indicate a shift in philosophy. In many ways "cooperation" was implicit in the discussions that began at Baarn, and strengthened as the Commission worked to enlist men and fight the perception that gender issues were for "women only." By the mid-1950s, it was much more. The Davos Statement, issued by the Department in 1956, declared the concept of cooperation between the sexes as "revolutionary," part of the general emancipation of women taking place in the postwar world. Madeleine Barot, who headed the Department until 1964, emphasized the uniqueness of this approach, one that "intrigues everybody with whom we work." "The WCC is the only organisation, as far as I know," she said in 1959, "which stresses the idea of cooperation," which is neither "part of the classic feminist position" nor a "hidden retreat for the idea of the subordination of women."[28]

Cooperation was neither feminist nor antifeminist. "Some men feel uneasy in their minds about what seems to them a new feminist attack," the Davos Statement explained, "while on the other hand, some women believe that this is one of the last efforts of certain men to keep women in a subordinate and junior position." In fact, the idea was one of mutuality, that men and women are "incomplete" without each other," and only become "truly themselves as they continually respond in partnership," one of "equal grace and equal responsibility."[29] In other words, the Department was advocating a model of gender relationships that dovetailed with the WCC's ecumenical agenda. "The churches are called to undertake in the particular field of relations between men and women," said the Davos Statement, "a work parallel to the one they are now engaged in for unity between the churches." Harmony between the sexes was in fact a precondition for the unity of Christendom.[30]

But what were those gender differences? In the late 1950s, the Department hosted a series of lengthy discussions between leading theological and social science experts, who proved themselves much better at framing lofty questions than formulating practical answers. At times the conversation skirted perilously close to the oversimplifications the Baarn meeting had rejected in 1948. "What is the fundamental nature of woman?" the members of a 1956 consultation wondered, before concluding that there was no "real answer," "except to say that the physiological can be defined," and that "tenderness, upward-looking, compassion seem to be feminine characteristics, which vary greatly from person to person." Though these differences were "God-given," they were neither absolute nor consistent from one individual to the next: "no man nor woman is either 100% male or female."[31]

The European Critique

American churchwomen entered this conversation on the defensive. Already in 1928 Maude Royden had observed that they were too pragmatic, too focused on being useful. "Filled with the desire to serve," she said, "the American woman sets about the building of the City of God, and often fails, because, born organizer and administrator that she is, she does not perceive that organization is not enough." But who could blame them? Religion in the United States was, of course, generally lacking, a largely shallow affair, "lack[ing] the spiritual depth and the sense of eternal things which comes only from intensive spiritual discipline. In other words," said Royden, "it has in building the City of God, neglected the making of saints."[32]

American churchwomen heard that criticism again at the Baarn meeting in 1948, and two decades after Royden, little had changed. "There was some doubt expressed in many quarters," Sarah Chakko wrote in 1951, "as to whether the average woman in the U.S.A. will be interested in the study of "Man-Woman relationship." In her visit to the United States, she was gratified to find more interest than she expected, but realized that the only way to catch "their full interest in support" is to "put these problems into simple understandable language," without "high sounding theological terms."[33]

Mary Ely Lyman attempted to defend the American position. "We are a practically minded people," she explained to Commission members in 1952. Given all the latitude American women enjoyed in "the great denominational women's organizations," most would find any "theoretical discussion" unnecessary, and uninteresting. Writing to an American audience, Lyman was gently encouraging: "this approach through theology to what appear to us to be pressing practical issues may seem the long way around which may not prove to be the shortest way home." She reminded American churchwomen that "it is the very nature of the ecumenical movement that we are *not* left to ourselves, to pursue only the tasks most congenial to our own temper of mind. No national group can any longer live unto itself alone."[34]

The strongest rebuke came with the publication of Kathleen Bliss's report, *The Service and Status of Women in the Churches*, in 1952. Drawing from the survey information compiled by Twila Cavert, the book was an unambiguous achievement, providing an in-depth, panoramic view of gender roles in mid-twentieth century Christianity, as well as lengthy consideration of secular modernity and its impact on women. It chronicled the diversity of Christian ideals and practices across the world, all the while underlining the fact that Europe and the United States lagged behind the rest. While the Church of England, most American Protestants, and Roman Catholics refused to ordain women, the United Church of Christ in Japan had 103 female clergy, one of whom was minister of one of the largest churches in Tokyo. Bliss devoted relatively little space to ordination—her concern was the larger question of status and opportunity—but she did make clear her own position, that the overwhelming conservatism of the churches was getting absurd. "Why should the Christian ministry be the only or almost the only position barred to women on the grounds of their sex?"[35]

Most of all, Bliss demanded new thinking about gender roles, beyond old tropes about dominant males and oppressed females. "It is nonsense," she

Kathleen Bliss, Courtesy World Council of Churches Archives, Geneva, Switzerland, D4401.

said, "to say that women have never had any power in the Churches; they have immense power, but power in the form of influence, which is irresponsible power. Nobody can call to account the wife or mother who gets her way with her husband or son and is known to be the real director of his opinion and vote." In fact, said Bliss, "women have wielded influence with very great skill over the centuries and many still prefer it to any form of responsibility which brings them out in the open. But the choice between influence and responsibility is one that women have to make."[36]

Anyone who had attended the Baarn meeting would have understood the practical implications of Bliss's critique, and the main transgressors. How would American churchwomen respond? The new conversation about gender no longer focused solely on institutional markers of "women's status"—how many served on national boards, the extent of control over budgets, rules about ordination. It was going to be about ideas—theology and feminism, perhaps even sex, topics long forbidden or ignored in mainline churches. Would it be enough, however, to move the dial, to introduce actual change? Chapter 8 explores that important question.

Georgia Harkness, Courtesy United Methodist Commission on Archives and
History, Madison, NJ.

PORTRAIT

Georgia Harkness and the Spirit of Heaviness

Georgia Harkness was sick and tired. In fact, she was so close to the end of her rope that in the spring of 1943 she asked H. G. Smith, the president of Garrett Seminary, for mercy—some time off, a course reduction, anything. It didn't even matter if she had to take a cut in pay. The pain had been so unrelenting and for so long, for three years now, tormenting her literally from head to toe. Most of the afflictions came without a cure or even a clear diagnosis, an unending round of strep infections, "glandular imbalances," aching feet, and insomnia, and then the fog off too many sedatives, too much medicine.

Harkness believed it was nobody's fault but her own. My own "inability to get well," she confessed to President Smith, was pulling her under, turning her into a terrible colleague, an abysmal teacher, a second-rate scholar. Her letter included a list of humiliating failures: canceled speaking engagements, mediocre classes, and intellectual torpor, her mind too tired to keep up with any of the latest ideas. Even worse was the shame, worrying about her own pain while a world at war was in so much deeper anguish. It was a particularly loathsome affliction for a dedicated pacifist. "I feel as if my personality were disintegrating," said Harkness, "and instead of being able to live and work with enthusiasm and zest as I once did, I endure existence. And this is no way for a Christian to be!"[1]

Georgia Harkness had already treaded ground few women had dared, not only graduating from Cornell University, but earning a master's in religious education and a PhD in theology from Boston University. She got an academic post, and then began to publish books; her reputation grew, alongside the awards and plaudits. She became a professor of theology at Garrett Theological Seminary, one of only two women in the United States who could make that claim (Mary Ely Lyman at Union Seminary was the other). Eventually she was invited to important meetings, sat with the big names in the theological establishment, and got to know them by their solidly Germanic first names—Reinhold, Paul, Karl.[2]

It was never enough, though. Her first position was at Elmira College, a small school in upstate New York, far from the Ivy League. Her next post at Mount Holyoke was a step up, but still a good distance, and then she went to Garrett, where her students were mostly undergraduates or would-be ministers, not brilliant scholars in the making. None of them would ever become famous, never even close to the stratosphere inhabited by those of Reinhold, Paul, and Karl.

And so Georgia had always worked hard, harder than she needed to. She was the one who took on the extra course when the dean asked her to, gave a talk to the women's group when her colleagues were giving academic lectures, and wrote articles for Methodist papers and books for laypeople when she should have been putting together something dense and scholarly. And for her pains, she was dismissed as a popularizer, "sound, but not overawingly profound."[3]

One night, in college, Georgia fell off a cliff, into one of the deep river gorges that frame the Cornell University campus. No one saw. For a terrifying moment it appeared she would drown alone in the dark. And then, miraculously, a rescuer heard her call for help, shimmied down the cliff into the water, and pulled her to shore.

An unselfish act of bravery, certainly—but in truth, the river was not all that wide or deep. Georgia hadn't been injured by the fall, and perhaps if she had held on for another minute she would made it to the shallows on her own. It seemed her fate to end up the damsel in distress, depending on the gallantry of a man, whether a Cornell undergraduate or a seminary president, to play the hero.

Many women, especially the high-achieving ones, punish themselves with sickness. In the nineteenth century the advice-givers chalked it up to neurasthenia, a type of nervous strain only curable through enforced bedrest and a total avoidance of anything remotely intellectual. When Georgia was in college, some educators were still insisting that the life of the mind damaged women both inside and out: the real cost of a woman's college education, they warned, was insomnia, depression, and even loss of fertility. Is it surprising that after graduating from Cornell University in 1912, Georgia Harkness used her Ivy League degree to teach high school, for six years in small-town upstate New York?[4]

Religious faith has helped women manage pain, though at considerable cost. It is no accident that the great healers in American Christianity were female sufferers: Mary Baker Eddy, bedridden with a spinal injury before she founded Christian Science; Ellen Harmon White, the inspiration for Seventh Day Adventism, disfigured by an accident; Pentecostal evangelist Carrie

Judd Montgomery, all but paralyzed by chronic pain until she experienced miraculous relief. Yet for every one freed from sickness many more accepted the equation between faith and physical misery. It had to be God's will, going back to the curse in the Garden of Eden promising suffering in childbirth for Eve and all of her female descendants. The assumption burrowed deep into American Protestantism, that women were "naturally" more attuned to religion—and more likely to be bedridden.[5]

Georgia Harkness described the price she paid in a talk titled "The Spirit of Heaviness." She was speaking to clergy, giving advice about helping people in emotional and spiritual pain during the weary depths of world war, speaking personally yet obliquely. "Many of us, I suspect, do not need to have it described for us because we know it all too well." In the Middle Ages they called it *acedia*, the sin of sloth; in the twentieth century the name for the affliction was "depression, or the blues, or the loss of nerve." She described the experience as one who had lived it: "To know that one ought to eat, and yet remain inactive; to know that one ought to enjoy one's work and one's family and friends and the beauties of nature, yet be weighed down with a heavy heart; to know that one ought to put one's trust in God and put away worry, yet still be enshrouded with dark clouds that seem to hide God from our sight—this is not only one of the most common but one of the most baffling of human experiences."[6]

The solution, at least for that gathering of clergy, was a contradictory mixture of firm resolve and accepting one's psychological fate. *Acedia* "is neither a sin nor a disease," said Harkness. "It is both. The complexity of the problem arises from the fact that depression lies at the border-line of our freedom." Healing from depression thus began with a "willingness to emerge," what Harness called "cooperating" with God. It meant battling spiritual indifference as well as all that couldn't be helped, the economic, physical, and psychological circumstances that "limit personality." As a hard-working Methodist, Harkness also believed that sufferers did have to fight back: "in all most every instance," she said, "*something* can be done," even if it is just remembering to stand straight and tall. "For example, faulty posture in connection with the corpulence of middle life can induce strains that throw one's spiritual stature out of balance and make the grace of God seem inaccessible." Ultimately, though, the suffering Christian had to "accept without inner rebellion that in the external situation which cannot be altered," staying active and engaged and finding meaning in service."[7]

All that moral striving was profoundly worth the effort. "Work is such an important component of Harkness' theology," one scholar writes, "that it even colors her understanding of life after death." The "moral task" was simply endless, as was the human capacity to grow and develop. Like a good mid-twentieth-century liberal, Harkness saw no value in emphasizing original sin, a built-in limitation on one's ability to improve.[8]

Georgia Harkness knew about realities that could not be changed. She was the one who had described the mainline churches as "the most impregnable stronghold of male dominance" in 1938. Though the Christian gospel had "done more than any other agency for the emancipation of women," the twentieth-century Protestant establishment was conspicuously lagging behind the secular world, where female professionals "receive[d] recognition at least roughly commensurate with the kind of work they do." What could women do? There was "no value in railing against the situation," so deeply rooted in the social and theological tradition of the churches; nor could women simply acquiesce. The only path forward, Harkness wrote, was to "keep on doing the best work we can because it is worth doing—without expecting much recognition or reward. The women of the future," she prophesied, "may reap the results."[9]

In mid-life Harkness found a measure of psychological equilibrium in mysticism and poetry. She wrote a book on *The Dark Night of the Soul*, using the ancient title that sixteenth-century mystic St. John of the Cross had given to his own search for God through spiritual pain and powerlessness. For Harkness, the book was, quite plainly, a way to avoid a complete nervous breakdown. She spent more time at her lakeside cottage, and in the company of her beloved partner, Verna Miller.

Perhaps this is why Harkness was silent in 1956, when Methodists finally gave women full clergy rights. It was definitely a dramatic moment, as Bill Rose, an old friend, recalled, bringing a "lump to my throat and tears to my eyes." The room was still buzzing as the delegates drifted off to dinner destinations, a "jubilant and milling throng." And there in the middle of the commotion was a "talented and silver-haired lady—alone," just "standing there looking to the front of the huge auditorium overwhelmed by it all." When the crowd thinned, Rose finally made his way to Harkness for a personal word of congratulations.

Her response was as laconic as her presence during the debate, but no doubt filled with private meaning. "'Bill, it was more than I expected. More was done,'" said Georgia Harkness, "'by keeping still than speaking.'"[10]

8

Assuming Equality

American Churchwomen in the 1950s

Perhaps Madeleine Barot liked to shock people, perhaps she had simply earned the right to say what she thought. At any rate, the stocky, no-nonsense Frenchwoman had little patience for the bland social courtesies of middle-class American culture. Was it surprising, then, that many of her colleagues in the United States found her bewildering, even irritating? Certainly the churchwomen and clergymen who encountered Barot in Mossie Wyker's living room, one very long evening in the summer of 1954, found her hard to forget.

The discussion was elevated, thick with theological abstractions and exegetical arguments about Genesis and Galatians—the type of conversation that busy, American Protestant church leaders generally avoided. Suddenly, as Presbyterian churchwoman, later head of Church Woman United, Margaret Shannon later described the moment, "Dr. Barot introduced a startling concept using the words, 'the sexuality of God.'" We can imagine the awkward hush that followed, the gallant efforts to restart the conversation on safer ground. "The one layman present," said Shannon, "remained in a state of shock for the rest of the meeting."[1]

Divine sexuality was only one of Barot's concerns, however. She was on her way to Evanston, to the second Assembly of the World Council of Churches, where she would present a status report as director of the Department on the Cooperation of Men and Women in the Church. After Sarah Chakko's untimely death—a heart attack on a basketball court in India—Barot had stepped in to head this Department, which in 1953 had superseded the Committee on the Life and Work of Women in the Church. She was, in short, one of the most educated, influential, and opinionated women in postwar Christendom, and about to deliver a blistering critique of the American mainline churches.

How would her words resonate? This chapter is an extended answer to that question, a deep look into the culture of mainline Protestantism in the 1950s.

Good and Mad. Margaret Bendroth, Oxford University Press. © Oxford University Press 2023.
DOI: 10.1093/oso/9780197654064.003.0009

This religious era is normally dismissed as conservative and dull, especially in the shadow of the sudden changes in the offing. Certainly, by all kinds of measures, there was complacency, buttressed by skyrocketing membership in the years after World War II. "Never before," as one historian describes it, "had as many Americans belonged to, attended, or associated themselves with religious institutions." By the end of the 1950s, nearly 70 per cent of the population claimed to be church members.[2]

But Barot was no outlier: the mainline churches were starting to think long and hard about the role of women. In 1956 two major denominations, northern Methodists and Presbyterians, approved equal rights to ordination. Churchwomen's organizations were flourishing, and laywomen were inching into denominational power structures, gaining seats on top boards and committees.

Beneath all these signs of progress, however, were powerful constraints. The idea of "cooperation" between the sexes, which Barot and her European colleagues heard as a radical call to action, resonated more softly, more conventionally in American mainline churches. To a considerable degree the reason was cultural: we generally hear what makes the most sense within our surroundings, and the rest tends to get muffled. Much of this chapter, then, deals with elusive but important matters of context, the social and intellectual framework that filtered what church people and denominational officials heard—and didn't hear—in the WCC language of mutuality and wholeness. This means going beyond the usual markers of the decade, the easy shorthand references to Billy Graham and anti-Communism, fox-hole patriotism and all those church pews bulging with happy nuclear families. The 1950s made clear, as never before, the particular strengths of mainline churches, the fact that they were essentially moderating institutions, never built for adventure at society's cutting edge. Indeed, like any religious culture, from medieval Catholicism to Tibetan Buddhism, mainline Protestantism came with its own folkways, from rules for raising children to the conduct of personal piety. Most important, the churches of the moderate middle had their own language of religious belonging, a grassroots theology of church life that accounted for a good deal of their popularity in the post–World War II era. It was this religious culture, with all of it social conventions, spoken and unspoken, that both defined and limited "women's role" on the eve of second-wave feminism.

Evanston, 1954

Late summer in Chicago was hot and humid, a challenge for international delegates unused to the extremes of American climate and packed into a crowded assembly hall for far too long. A few of the presentations had gone over time, and by the middle of the evening on August 23, the agenda was well behind schedule. Madeline Barot was slotted to speak at 8 pm, and she graciously, and perhaps wisely, agreed to wait until the next day. As the official report noted, "The large audience breathed a sigh of gratitude." Not so grateful were the busloads of American churchwomen who had come up to Evanston that day to hear Barot speak, only to return home disappointed.[3]

Barot's presentation would not have made them any happier. A mature, self-confident woman, she was not intimidated by "this impressive assembly, largely dominated by men," as her biographer writes.[4] She challenged the Assembly to take gender inequality seriously, to grapple with the economic, social, and political forces that were transforming relationships between men and women. Instead of lagging behind secular society, said Barot, the churches should be leading the way, changing the world rather than simply coping with it. This meant fresh thinking, systematic consideration of "what equality means when it is applied to men and women." Barot was calling Christians to a new intellectual project, to reject both sentimental notions about womanhood and an "aggressive feminism" which denied gender differences. True ecumenical unity, she said, required "a more complete integration of both sexes into the life of the Church, ensuring that all people may freely put their gifts at its disposal." The great possibility of "hope and renewal" was "a truly feminine influence," extending to "all spheres of life, in the Church as well as in society."[5]

Then came a more discordant note. "The great danger of the women's organizations," said Barot, is that they are "too independent." They had become a "shadow church," little more than a weak parallel, caring only for its own narrow concerns, lacking any commitment to the "ecumenical movement as a whole."[6]

American churchwomen were immediately stung by Barot's remarks. Margaret Shannon, who had received an advance draft of the Evanston address, was so exasperated that she vented at length to Mildred Horton before sending a reply. "Those of us who are working among women," she said, "have always found considerable irritation in the interpretations that frequently come out of the 'studies' of such things by the World Council." Barot and her colleagues approached the role of women as "a psychological study with a sociological solution," not as a "spiritual force which the church could use." The idea that American women flocked to serve the church "in lieu of status" was particularly offensive. Not everyone was cut out for the kinds of changes Barot was proposing. "Long after all the women that can preach are ordained for the ministry," she said, " . . . there will be the women who stutter," and plenty of others "whose husbands are less cooperative" than Barot's ideal would have them.[7]

In her letter to Barot, Shannon was still angry, and pushed back forcefully against the suggestion that churchwomen's organizations existed only to compensate for powerlessness elsewhere. She scoffed at Barot's belief that "when the full 'cooperation' of men and women is achieved or women are given status in the ecclesiastical structure, there will be no more need for women's organizations." Far from an independent "shadow church," church-women were the ultimate team players, providing invaluable "second-mile service," beyond the scope of conventional church programs. Rather than imply, Shannon said to Barot, that women should seek integration into male-dominated church structures, the WCC should recognize that separate organizations were a means to "wholeness," indispensable to a well-rounded social agenda.[8]

The situation was delicate. The Europeans were well aware that the American churchwomen who felt dismissed by their criticisms were also funding their efforts. Financial support from the WCC was a perpetual problem for the Department, and by 1957, the parent organization was providing less than half of the barebones budget allotted. United Church Women (UCW) made up the difference.[9]

What Barot was really countering, however, was a widespread insistence among American churchwomen that sex discrimination was not a problem. Cynthia Wedel remembered her first trip to a WCC meeting in 1952, "flying over in the plane thinking to myself, 'Who's worried about the role of women in the church?'" Her own experience, as a Presbyterian and in UCW, had been nearly conflict-free: "I could do anything I wanted, had had leadership offered to me," she said. It only remained to explain to the "poor benighted women from other parts of the world" how to organize "women's work." "So we were all set." Then she arrived in Geneva. As Wedel told her interviewer, meeting Sarah Chakko, Madeleine Barot, and other women from Europe, Asia, and Africa was a "mind-blowing experience."[10] It was time, Wedel told

American churchwomen, to "realize that we, too, have problems." "[D]on't talk," as Barot told her, "listen."[11]

Not all American churchwomen had the benefit of Wedel's transatlantic travel, however. The assumption of equality was deeply entrenched within the mainline churches, reinforced by the belief that gender differences did not—should not—matter. That is clear from yet another denominational survey, conducted by UCW and the National Council of Churches in the early 1950s.[12] The findings, which were presented at the UCW meeting in 1953, were frustratingly evasive. On the one hand was direct evidence of a male monopoly on denominational boards and committees, and on the other, a confident insistence (from both sexes) that there were "few limitations on including women in policy making bodies." Not to worry, though: what looked like an injustice was really a commitment to fairness, to a gender blind process that elevated women, "on the basis of their qualifications rather than their womanhood." Not surprisingly, the report found "few basic objections" to women's ordination, most unrelated to biblical prohibitions or theological principles. The remaining barriers were "non-theological," little more than amorphous objections by lazy traditionalists.[13] When asked to speculate why so few American Baptist women were on policy-making boards, the New Hampshire Baptist Convention insisted vaguely that there was "no prejudice against women serving on these boards. It just happened."[14]

Mildred McAfee Horton wrote most of the report and added her own gloss in a concluding paragraph. This was the work of a woman at the peak of a stellar career, having served as president of Wellesley College (she resigned in 1948 when she married Congregational ecumenist Douglas Horton) and during World War II, as director of the Woman's Reserve of the United States Navy (WAVES). When she was elected a vice president of the National Council of Churches in 1949, the first woman to serve in that position, Horton was already a veteran of corporate boards and committees. She was the first female trustee of New York Life Insurance, the National Broadcasting Company, and the Radio Corporation of America, and served as chair of the National Social Welfare Assembly.[15] Mildred Horton, therefore, was not interested in excuses from American churchwomen. In her view, their fundamental problem was not male opposition but capitulation to "womanhood as defined by secular society," and its ensuing rewards. "We like its perquisites— we react heartily to chivalry, gallantry, flattery. Maybe the time has come," the former military commander declared, "to do our duty," to "face the fact that the acceptance of responsibilities is the duty of a child of God."[16] All that the situation required was an attitude adjustment, a commitment to forge ahead as if there were no obstacles in the way, to believe that hard work and persistence would eventually lead to equality.

Mossie Wyker, then president of UCW, wrote an entire book to press this point. *Church Women in the Scheme of Things*, published in 1953, was an extended argument for positive thinking about sexism. It was time to end the "charm school approach," Wyker advised, and get to work. Too many women were "baffled and insecure," realizing that they could no longer blame men for their situation. "Absolute honesty requires us to say that whatever a woman wants to become she can," if she follows God's "directives."[17] In fact, the biggest obstacle was staring back from the mirror, "women who have restricted other women as they struggled to serve the church in its full ministry."[18] Of course, hard evidence insisted otherwise, and Mossie Wyker knew it. Her book contained page after page of stories about sex discrimination, of misogynistic statements and practices, even a lengthy critique of her home denomination, the Disciples of Christ. Yet Wyker reassured her readers that she was not a "'frustrated female,' demanding rights in the church"; she was merely lifting "an area of concern."[19]

How do we understand this? Mossie Wyker and her colleagues were seasoned church professionals who must have had some inkling of what Betty Friedan would call "the problem with no name." Yet they rarely pushed back, even when, at least in theory, they had the right and the ability to do so. And so it is worth taking a moment to consider their position.

Mainline Protestants Thinking about Gender

First of all, there were some substantial conversations about gender issues in mainline Protestant circles. The late 1950s saw an array of conferences and presentations, in the United States as well as Europe, bringing together major scholars and top church officials to consider knotty questions about the "man–woman relationship." The conversations drew from anthropology, from studies of the family, and from recent history, all demonstrating the fact of structural inequality. Speaking alongside Madeleine Barot in 1954, Boston University professor Walter Muelder reminded the Evanston Assembly that the church shared the "dominant cultural patterns of a nation, or of a civilization." Given the scope of the problem, the insights of secular scholars working on gender and race—Simone de Beauvoir, Melville Herskovits, and

Talcott Parsons, to name a few—were necessary for a thorough Christian housecleaning, a faith-informed challenge to both church and society.[20]

Ursula Niebuhr thought it was high time that Protestants talked about sex. The churches had had enough of the "sub-Christian" view of women's sexuality, she said, in a groundbreaking article, the assumption that they were a "lower order of creation," destined only for motherhood. Though history remembers her famous husband Reinhold, Ursula Niebuhr was every bit an able partner. Sharply intelligent and highly educated, she had graduated from Oxford College with honors and was the first woman to receive a fellowship to Union Theological Seminary, where Reinhold was on the faculty. Ursula Niebuhr went on to teach religious education at Barnard College, and is credited with founding the school's religion department. In 1951 she assembled a gathering of graduate students, professors, and clergy for an intense three-hour discussion of "Women and Church" that, unlike many other mainline Protestant colloquies, dared to bring up the subject of sex— and the fact that no one was talking about it. The lack of conversation was in fact the problem, leaving the discussion to secularists and a host of amoral advertisers and media figures. The churches needed to construct a Christian ethic on solid ground, with "detailed sociological, psychological, theological research." The fundamental obstacle to equality, it was clear, was not the "indefensible use of the Bible to quote proof-texts, divorced of their historical setting," but "an adequate sex ethic in Christian doctrine."[21]

Ursula Niebuhr was right, of course. Mainline Protestants had spent the past several decades doing their best to pretend that sex did not exist. While evangelicals and fundamentalists railed about the sins of the flesh, specifically and frequently, their liberal cousins maintained an air of polite detachment. Samuel McCrea Cavert articulated the general discomfort in 1931, when he denounced an interdenominational study guide that appeared to encourage open conversations about physical urges. "The idea that young people should be encouraged to make problems of sex the subject of public discussion and debate," he declared, "is one which I emphatically repudiate." Not surprisingly, mainline Protestants produced almost no literature on birth control before the 1960s, much less advice about sexual ethics. The primary focus was on the family, and the proper comportment of Christian family life. A conference on the Church and Family Life, conducted by the National Council of Churches in 1958, found the intellectual larder completely empty, except for the insistence "ad nauseam that family that prays together stays together without a glimmer of criticism to that claim." The conference itself was a first step forward, concluding with a call to the churches to think deeply about marriage and sex "in light of biblical theology and scientific findings," and to create a "positive Christian ethic on sexual behavior."[22]

Serious conversations were taking place on other fronts as well. In 1957, what we would now call structural sexism was the agenda for leading scholars at Yale Divinity School conference. Cosponsored with the WCC, the consultation's ambitious goal was to consider "Theological and Scientific Perspectives on the Role of Men and Women and Its Implications for the Cooperation of Men and Women in Church and Society." The participants included a range of specialists, both secular and church-related—theologians, biblical scholars, and psychologists—and a working committee of internationally known scholars—the Dutch theologian Hendrikus Berkhof, French pastor André Dumas, and Boston University's Walter Muelder. Churchwomen were also at the table: Americans Mossie Wyker and Cynthia Wedel, as well as well as Marion Royce, director of the Women's Bureau of the Canadian Ministry of Labor, and Mary Whitelaw, representing the World Presbyterian Alliance. At Barot's request, the agenda focused on big questions requiring theological clarity, including first off the Bible and its teachings on women. The participants sailed through that long-standing problem, however, only to founder on a second. Were the differences between men and women were "ontological or only functional." What would equality really entail?

The answer was elusive. The Yale consult called for "renewed honesty, a renewed freedom to attack the stereotypes of what people think it means to be 'masculine' (for example, 'a man doesn't cry') or 'feminine' (for example 'a woman isn't and shouldn't be efficient')."[23] Modern psychology, after all, found that all men have some feminine characteristics and women masculine ones. But what did gender differences really entail, in practical terms? "We recognized that there are differences between men and women," said Cynthia Wedel after a meeting in Odense, Denmark, in 1958, "but we are not sure what they are. They are hard to define, but impossible to ignore." The goal was to help both sexes express their uniqueness, "men masculine, and women more completely themselves—women feminine."[24]

It appears the discussion had circled back to the imponderable that Zephine Humphrey had posed back in 1920: "is there such a thing as a woman?" This time, however, some serious theological resources were being brought to bear, examining fundamental questions about gender differences in light of the Bible and Christian tradition. Certainly the conversation was a step beyond what secular American culture had to offer. One of the bestsellers of the postwar era was an antifeminist diatribe by psychologists Ferdinand Lundberg and Marynia Farnham. Like so much of the advice literature of the late 1940s and 1950s, *Modern Woman: The Lost Sex* leaned heavily on Freudian categories, drawing a dismal picture of neurotic career women and overprotective mothers. A conservative functionalism picked up whatever pieces were left, with psychiatrist Helen Deutsch urging that "normal femininity" required the sublimation of "masculine strivings" and identifying with one's husband "as a means of relating to the outside world."[25]

All of which underlines the bigger question, why these budding theological conversations did not gain more traction. Why was change so slow? And why do we no longer remember that they even took place? Many of the reasons are historical, drawn from a mainline Protestant world that would be eclipsed, forgotten, and misunderstood in the shadow of the turbulent 1960s.

A Culture of Cooperation

When Madeline Barot talked about "cooperation" she meant something radical. In her world, a postwar Europe that had been devastated by powerful men, mutuality between the sexes was a heady, even optimistic, idea. Far more than just a model for intrapersonal relationships, it challenged every social structure, secular as well as religious, blighting the lives of women. Even more, it made men an essential part of the solution, not just an obstacle to be overcome. Under the right circumstances, especially where discrimination against women was an unapologetic social fact, as it was in most European state churches, an ethic of cooperation between the sexes was genuinely progressive, opening the way for bigger, searching conversations about religion, gender, and structural injustice.

Cooperation meant something different on the other side of the Atlantic. The mainline churches have been criticized, and rightly so in many cases, for being bland and rule-abiding, content with their suburban captivity. Yet there was more to the homogeneity than mere social conformity. Cooperation— that is, the will to compromise for the sake of the whole—was bred deep in the bone.

The postwar years marked the peak of what sociologist Robert Putnam has dubbed the "we" era in American history. This was a time when social institutions—government, schools, labor unions, and churches—enjoyed extraordinarily high levels of public trust. Before the culture wars and the rise of identity politics, those institutions appeared to work for nearly everyone, bringing people together instead of splitting them apart.[26]

Not all of the harmony was real. As Putnam admits, African Americans and, to a degree, women paid a high cost for the social consensus of the postwar era. An "effective" institution could also be adept at quashing protest and perpetuating equality. Moreover, togetherness took a nefarious turn in the service of anticommunism, as a rationale for ostracizing critics and punishing dissenters. One of the ugliest episodes in American history, the Red Scare was not, however, a coordinated government effort that destroyed all civil liberties in its path. Some of it was simply self-imposed. As historian Stephen Whitfield writes, Americans "imposed a starchy repression upon themselves" to ward off fears of internal subversion.[27]

Yet much of that public trust had been earned. World War II was, after all, one long object lesson in the virtues of systematic coordination, a broad strategic effort of American, European, and Asian military forces that thoroughly vanquished two authoritarian powers. The lesson was not lost on the business world either, where a Progressive-era zeal for efficiency had given way to tolerance for institutional diversification and spread. A certain amount of bureaucratic sprawl was now considered healthy, a strategy for growth by balancing losses in one sector against the strength of another.[28] By the 1960s, as Godfrey Hodgson writes, there was a sense that "the businessman and the unskilled laborer, the writer and the housewife, Harvard University and the Strategic Air Command, International Business Machines and the labor movement, all had their parts to play in one harmonious political, intellectual, and economic system."[29]

Mainline Protestantism was a particularly powerful force for belonging. During World War II, for example, patriotic Protestant homes sported window stickers that declared "this family is cooperating," a religious take on the New Deal's iconic "blue eagle." The sticker came with a pledge, defining "cooperation" as regular church attendance and prayer, and, even more important, an agreement to resolve interpersonal disputes with "family councils." In explicit contrast to fascist authoritarianism, American Christian families embodied democratic principles of mutual respect and shared decision-making.[30]

After the war, mainline congregations became sites of literal togetherness, as flush church budgets allowed for ambitious building projects. State-of-the-art educational wings and gleaming kitchens and fellowship halls signaled that these churches were open every day of the week, not just Sunday. The "activity church," as sociologist Robert Wuthnow describes it, "encouraged people to spend more time on sanctified turf by sponsoring socials and pot-luck dinners, young people's groups, Sunday school classes, men's prayer breakfasts, and ladies' aid societies."[31]

Cooperation was a social strategy undergirded by an explicit theological rationale. An entire infrastructure of Sunday schools and family advice literature, going back to the mid-nineteenth century, rested on the assumption that authentic religious belief could not be coerced. Indeed, if the mainline churches could have claimed a patron saint, it would have been Congregational theologian Horace Bushnell, whose idea of "Christian nurture" profoundly altered the theory and practice of white Protestant child-rearing. Bushnell's immediate target was evangelical religion, in his view a particularly insidious form of emotional terrorism, forcing sinners into the arms of Christ through threats and intimidation. Even worse, it was all unnecessary. Genuine faith emerged gradually, fostered by parents who taught "the way of submitting to wise limitations" through their own godly conduct. Everything mattered, down to the last detail of healthy food, clean clothes, and adequate ventilation. "Bring every thing, in the training, even of his body," said Bushnell, "and it will be strange, if the Christian body you give him does not contain a Christian soul."[32]

A century later, Bushnell's advice had become more therapeutic than theological. A Baptist author, writing in 1950, defined the true "marks of a Christian home" as respect for individuality, warmth and affection, and a "general atmosphere of cleanliness and neatness." Knowledge of the Bible and Christian doctrine was secondary, especially if done in a heavy-handed manner. After all, "brainwashing" was a Communist tool, not a child-rearing technique. "A child should not be made to have a sense of guilt," a Protestant expert counseled, but of "temporary failure that he can overcome." In that sense, Christian parenting in fact echoed the assurances of Dr. Spock, that if wise parents followed the proper guidelines, confrontation and punishment—and uncomfortably negative emotions—were simply unnecessary.[33]

Cooperation was more than just a principle of child-rearing, however; it was also the watchword of an ecumenical movement reaching the peak of success in the postwar era. Among mainline Protestants, institutional togetherness signaled a deep faith in religious institutions and the power of careful, incremental change. Years of coordination and planning brought about a major reunion in 1958, with a newly created United Presbyterian Church in the United States of America (UPCUSA) bringing together northern and southern wings separated before the Civil War. The most exciting achievement came in 1957 when an entirely new ecumenical denomination was born. The United Church of Christ melded four separate Protestant traditions into an "organic union," a triumph that in the end heralded bureaucratic skill and patience as much as visionary leadership.[34]

Yet this faith in institutional processes also meant that mainline churches were slow to recognize, if not respond to, genuine social division. Dissenting voices did not resonate very far, and far too often protecting institutions overruled the missions they were supposed to enable. Amid the rising drama of the civil rights movement, for example, the National Council of Churches followed a "cautious, evolutionary, go-slow approach." As historian James Findlay writes, decisions about the pace of change remained "in the hands of whites, which usually meant little or no change," and little commitment to the long-term strategies that racial inequality required. A statement condemning the murder of Emmett Till in 1956 languished for months in subcommittee; even in the wake of the 1954 school desegregation decision, the National Council did little more than encourage further study. The mainline churches, says Findlay, were simply "unprepared" to affect "in any lasting way the course of the racial struggle in the late 1950s and 1960s." Change was in the offing, of course, but it would arrive painfully and suddenly—and from the outside.[35]

Feminization and Tokenism

Then there is the matter of churchwomen themselves, and the ways in which Protestant institutions both accommodated and limited their aspirations. By the 1950s most denominations agreed, in theory at least, that women should be allowed to serve on national policy-making boards. According to the study conducted by Inez Cavert in 1948, the proportion was over two-thirds—75 of the 110 denominations responding to the survey had no formal barriers against gender equality. Yet the actual numbers of women serving were small, however, especially in proportion to their membership. American Baptists, for example, had three women on its Governing Council, alongside 33 men; the 36 women on national committees (alongside 178 men) filled slots in traditionally female areas like religious education.[36]

The story behind these numbers is complicated. To a large degree, the presence of women on national boards was a legacy of quota systems instituted in the 1920s and meant to appease the loss of independent missionary societies. Token representation was hardly unique to churches, as many women making their way up ladders in business, law, and medicine could attest. Yet in many mainline denominations tokenism put women at the top rather than the bottom of the ladder.

Many leading churchwomen no doubt assumed their access to power, however limited, was justified. After all, they possessed not only advanced degrees and career experience, but influential, often wealthy husbands. The examples are not hard to come by: Mildred Horton's husband Douglas was the Dean of Harvard Divinity School and a nationally known theologian and ecumenical leader; Cynthia Wedel's husband Theodore was the canon chancellor of the National Cathedral and in 1952, the president of the National Convention of the Episcopal Church. Georgiana Farr Sibley was born into wealth and married Harper Sibley, a department store magnate who also served as director of Western Union, and President of the United States Chamber of Commerce. Leaders with financial resources were critical, of course, especially after the 1920s, when women's church organizations could no longer count on the direct generosity of their members or access to denominational budgets. As Thelma Stevens noted in a candid interview, even as idealistic a group as UCW was "oriented toward women with money." "The whole organization," she said, "was dependent on how many wealthy women you could get in by giving them a job."[37]

Yet well-to-do women did more than boost an organization's bottom line. They also provided a model of feminine church leadership, a careful balance of competence and conformity. In practice this meant following the rules of gender performance, not just wearing a pillbox hat and white gloves, but eschewing any identification with feminism. Mildred Horton, Cynthia Wedel, Twila Cavert, and "Mrs. Harper Sibley" openly preferred to go by their husbands' names, happily defending their decision in public interviews. "My husband is a wonderful man," as Mrs. James D. Wyker (aka Mossie Alman Wyker) explained in a typical response. "I'd rather do my work in his name."[38]

Good behavior mattered, in the churches and in the corporate culture they mirrored. As historian Nancy Cott writes, in the years before feminists began to challenge the rules, professional women in male-dominated settings had to adopt a strategy of "proving loyalty and shoring up the guild in order to shore up their own position as participants." A show of allegiance was essential; open criticism of the established order was a risk not worth taking. Above all, professional women had to avoid appearing too feminine. The "tenet of sex neutrality," says Cott, made questions of power "unspeakable."[39] The anthropologist Margaret Mead, writing in 1949, put it more baldly: "The mannish woman, the ugly woman, may be treated as a man in disguise, and so forgiven her successes. But for the success of a feminine woman there are no alibis; the more feminine she is, the less she can be forgiven."[40]

Elite churchwomen in a feminized church treaded with extra care, avoiding at all costs the appearance of a special interest group seeking power. As Mildred Horton told a male colleague in 1962, "Nothing can jeopardize the participation of women more effectively than having them prevent the participation of responsible men!"[41] "Women want to be treated in the church simply as *persons*," said Mossie Wyker. "They want to be appointed to positions not just because the rules say they may or must be, but because they are fitted to fill those positions."[42] Horton was routinely adamant about even the appearance of special pleading. In her view, women should even be subject to the military draft. "Drafting women would not be pleasant for girls from 18 to 23," she said in a radio interview; "but it is not pleasant for boys 18 to 23 either!"[43]

The message filtered through the organizational ranks: above all, churchwomen were ladies. Thus, Baptist women received not only instruction on parliamentary procedure but also emotional etiquette ("Do not interrupt a member while speaking. Do not become excited. Do not be rude or unjust to a troublesome member."). They also learned appropriately feminine "platform posture and mannerisms" ("Sit correctly with head and shoulders up, and both feet on the floor. *Legs should never be crossed on a public platform.*").[44] Ruth Graham, president of the UCW chapter in Detroit and on staff at the local John Robert Powers School, also insisted on "the importance of poise and good grooming in church activities" and, above all, good posture. Graham advised checking oneself by standing against a wall with heels together. "If the hand can pass through the space between the middle of the back and the wall, correction is needed." Platform stance required even more precision, with the back foot at a 45-degree angle to the front and the hands falling gracefully, "with one just enough behind her hip to be invisible from the front" and the other "falls with the narrow part, thumb forward, showing." When seated, one hand rested on the palm of the other, "both palms upward and in the lap," thus countering the urge to fidget with hair or hat or glasses.[45]

The rank and file might have asked, however, whether their leaders actually represented them. Trivialized in the denominational press as "Mrs. Housewife," the "mistress of pots and pans," as one Methodist periodical described her, the typical laywoman lived a considerable social distance apart from part from the churchwomen sitting on national boards and committees.[46] The typical American Baptist, according to a survey published in 1961, was solidly middle class, white-collar with a high school education. Less than 5 percent identified themselves as wealthy.[47] Moreover, their world was changing. American women began moving into the workplace in the 1950s, not the 1960s, albeit to stereotypically, low-paid female occupations. By 1955, their numbers exceeded those from the World War II "Rosie the Riveter" era. By 1960, 30 percent of American women were employed outside the home, a third with children below the age of eighteen.[48] Though Protestant denominations did not keep statistics on female employment, there was no doubt that an old order was passing. "So many women with family responsibilities are now working" Thelma Stevens wrote to a colleague in 1959, "that some of the jobs they formerly did as volunteers must now be neglected or left for someone else to do." Methodist women in Southwest Texas saw an even more challenging trend: "As women, in large numbers, have entered employment," a circular letter explained, "they have dropped out of the Woman's Society. . . . These women are being lost to the women's organizations of the church."[49]

Churchwomen's organizations recognized the trend, and puzzled over it. In 1958 UCW helped sponsor a Consultation on Employed Women and the Church, bringing together a distinguished array of economists, psychologists, sociologists, and church leaders to consider "what the changing picture of the employment of women will mean to all of us, and what the Church and church women's groups should do about it." According to one expert, the vast majority of women in the work force, some 75 percent, were there out of "social need" or psychological satisfaction, not for economic reasons. The implications for volunteer organizations were plain: "Case studies and the personal experience of many of us here," she said, "bear eloquent testimony to the fact that the way of the volunteer in our world is apt to be narrow, rocky, and all too often a dead end."[50] Working women were more than "potential cookie bakers," as one churchwoman described them, but only in passing did one Methodist pilot study note that in two-thirds of local churches, the facilities and programs were "inadequate" for families of working mothers.[51]

Ordination and Feminization

All of these disparate tensions gave leading churchwomen good reason to avoid pressing the rank and file, especially on matters of equality. As Congregationalist Lillian Gregory remarked in 1955, "It is the women who do not want a woman pastor," adding, "We needn't blush."[52] Elsie Thomas Culver, another shrewd observer, concluded that a women in church leadership was "never quite sure whether the rank and file of the women in the church will stand by her" to demand equality. "Far from being appreciative and responsive, they may only find ways to demonstrate that they consider her forward."[53]

Not surprisingly, then, the prospect of women's ordination was surrounded by ambivalence—a muddy situation that in many ways allowed two major rulings, by Methodists and Presbyterians, to succeed. In the 1950s, access to pastoral credentials was more of a career opportunity than a spiritual right, certainly not the beginning of a social revolution.

In 1956 the General Assembly of the Presbyterian Church U.S.A (PCUSA) voted to add a single sentence to the Form of Government, Chapter IV, Section 1, "Of Bishops or Pastors, and Associate Pastors": "Both men and women may be called to this office."[54] Margaret Towner, the first woman to be ordained in the PCUSA, typified the air of determined calm. When members of her Allentown, Pennsylvania, congregation approached her with "worried looks" after the ceremony, she reassured them that life would continue on as before. Formal ordination was, in her case, she insisted, only a lateral career move, a way to further her work as director of Christian education. Her relieved parishioners were happy to confirm Towner's prediction. "No one has seemed disturbed about the change in Miss Towner's status," *Presbyterian Life* reported. "She has received hearty congratulations from everyone, including the session, all of whom are men."[55]

The debate leading up to the decision had been similarly undramatic. What discussion took place served mostly to confirm that nothing particularly momentous was in the offing. Writing on behalf of women's ordination in *Presbyterian Life*, John Burkhart, a campus pastor at the University of Southern California, glided past centuries of biblical debate in a few brief paragraphs. Reminding his readers that the Bible "says many things," Burkhart dispensed with St. Paul by pointing out the inconsistencies of early church practice and the dangers of "legalistic" interpretations. Just as Presbyterians did not use wine in Communion services or baptize by immersion—both specifically practiced in the Bible—they could also relativize Pauline prohibitions on women as specific to first-century circumstances.[56] John Craig, a Houston, Texas, pastor, spoke against ordination, albeit tepidly. "Scripture opposes it," he said, and then devoted five columns of text to a summary of biblical evidence before landing on a general defense of gender differences. "It is complimentary to speak of a feminine woman and a masculine man," he said. "Reverse the adjectives and you have terms of opprobrium and insult. I am opposed to Presbyteries making men out of women."[57]

If the letters to the editor of *Presbyterian Life* are any indication, Craig lost the debate, mostly, however, for a lack of conviction. A St. Louis pastor complained that his argument was "scripturally unsound, intellectually careless, and just poor stuff." All told, an Ohio laywoman agreed, "Brother Craig effectively illustrates the poverty of Scriptural authority against the overture."[58]

The Bible simply was not the issue. The real sticking point was institutional stability, making sure that the rulings would not topple the already precarious gender imbalance in Protestant churches. Would laymen leave if women became ministers? "Some men might," admitted Burkhart, "but for the wrong reasons. Some left our Church when it opposed racial segregation." In fact, the best argument for women's ordination was that it did not really matter. "The years have punctured the ballooning fears of feminism," Burkhart argued. Presbyterians would know to reject any woman seeking ordination "belligerently," just as they would a man.[59] Even Craig admitted there was little to worry about, pointing out that the numbers of female ministers were a "tiny fraction" of the whole, and mostly from "fringe sects hovering on the edge of Protestantism" like the Christ United Spiritual Science Church and the "Holy Rollers" of Aimee Semple McPherson's Four Square Gospel Church. If trends in other denominations were any indication, said Craig, "we Presbyterians are putting ourselves through all this costly fuss and fury for a potential fifteen or twenty women ministers by the year 1970."[60] The *Christian Century* agreed. Presbyterians were "not likely to be subjected to any sudden onslaught of lady applicants."[61]

Methodists hid their anxieties with bemused exasperation. In fact, a lighthearted mood prevailed at the 1956 General Conference, even after grueling hours of debate. No one worried that biblical authority was under threat: most everyone viewed the issue as an adsministrative adjustment, a final tweak to a process that had begun decades earlier. Up until then a female ministry was theoretically possible—as of 1924 they could be ordained as deacons and elders—but it was also rare. The 1956 ruling was certainly consequential, however, granting women membership in regional conferences, which meant access to voting rights in denominational decisions as well as pensions, and, most controversially, guaranteed appointments in local congregations. Yet time and time again, the delegates had to be reminded not to laugh. "This is a very serious question that is before us," a New Jersey woman implored, "and although we have had some funny things happening, I think we should consider it in a very serious light." Please, she said, "no more joking around."

She was only partially successful. The delegates certainly understood that barring women from ordination was a form of "discrimination." That word had appeared again and again in their deliberations, especially in regard to race. Just two days before they approved ordination rights, Methodists had finally dismantled the racially segregated conference created during the 1939 merger with their southern wing. One of the male delegates, Lynn Radcliffe, made an explicit comparison: after moving forward against "discrimination in one realm," the denomination needed to move ahead on another, "with equal seriousness and similar Christian spirit."[62]

The biggest Methodist worry was, like the Presbyterian, about gender balance. Writing in the fall of 1955, Emory Stevens Bucke, a prominent editor and writer, admitted that "it is fear which prompts our opposition." The top concern was Barot's "shadow church," whether ordination would strengthen separatist energy instead of promote equality. "Through their national organization," said Bucke, "the women of Methodism have organized, in effect, a separate church within a church, with its own national and world missionary programs. We are not at all sure whether this is a debate on the rights of women as women, or on the powers of the national organization of Methodist women. We fear that it is the latter."[63]

Rejoinders to Bucke did not deny the "latent threat of organized women," as a Kansas pastor put it, but insisted that the ordination was at most a minor change in procedure, a theoretical effort toward equal opportunity in the workplace. "I doubt if there will be a great rush of women for conference membership," a Massachusetts pastor wrote.[64] Georgia Harkness responded wearily, reminding Bucke that the General Conference had considered ordination in 1948 and 1952, "chiefly as a joke." The Woman's Division had every right to press for "elemental Christian justice." "Is there any reason," she said, "why those who comprise half the membership of the church should not examine their own status within it and express their convictions in memorials if they so desire?"[65]

Most Methodists did not, however, see their decision within some long arc of gender justice, much less a protest against middle-class convention. Whether by accident or design, the published account of the General Conference proceedings, on the very pages covering the ordination debate, featured a photograph of two female delegates at the "lost and found" desk. One was thanking the other for returning a lost earring.[66]

Response to the ruling was emotionally complex, typified by Georgia Harkness, who remained silent during the hours of debate. After the vote, when one of the delegates moved to salute her, expressing appreciation for the "valiant fight she has waged for this cause for many years," she gave only a brief word of thanks. This was not a moment for triumph, perhaps. "Some of you wondered why I didn't speak this afternoon. It says in the Bible there is a time to speak and a time to be silent. I thought we would do better if we let the rest of you speak."[67]

Or perhaps it was just hard to know what to say. The Presbyterian and Methodist rulings, for all their backhandedness, did open an important door. The achievement owed much to the perseverance and professionalism of leading churchwomen and the organizations they led. Yet, behind it all was reluctance born of anxiety, an unspoken fear that empowering women in the short term meant long-term damage to the future of American Protestantism.

9

Finding Feminism

A Prehistory of Women's Liberation in Mainline Protestant Churches

Nelle Morton was incredulous. Here it was, the largest feminist demonstration ever, ten thousand marchers filling the streets of Manhattan, and not a single church organization in the mix. The March for Equality was a joyous, defiant public spectacle, marking the fiftieth anniversary of the suffrage amendment, a raucous coming together of white, middle-class members of the National Organization for Women (NOW) and a rising radical wing. According to the *New York Times*, the event brought out "limping octogenarians, braless teenagers, Black Panther women, telephone operators, waitresses, Westchester matrons, fashion models, Puerto Rican factory workers, nurses in uniform, young mothers carrying babies on their backs"—and even a few men.[1]

But no Protestant groups. Addressing a gathering at the Interchurch Center in New York, Morton could not contain her disappointment. "Why is no church officially on the long sponsoring list for this celebration?" she demanded.

It was a good question. Why were the mainline churches so passive? In 1970 Morton represented their best claim for a veteran feminist, a professor of Religious Education at the Drew University School of Theology, and a strident and articulate critic. She was still a loyal Methodist, but with one foot inching toward the door. "We have learned," she told the gathering, "through heartbreaking disappointments and dehumanizing work inequities, that competence, creativity, and efficiency are not enough to deal with a male supremacy that has become a pervasive structured force in our church."[2]

Would Morton, who died in 1987, be surprised at the distance mainline Protestants have traveled since then? Perhaps. Though the liberal flagship *Christian Century* "overlooked" the emergence of NOW, and virtually ignored women's rights until the Senate was considering the ERA in 1970, the mainline churches have certainly changed.[3] Feminist theology is now a

Good and Mad. Margaret Bendroth, Oxford University Press. © Oxford University Press 2023.
DOI: 10.1093/oso/9780197654064.003.0010

standard in seminary curricula, taught by female professors to classrooms full of female students. In mainline worship liturgies God is no longer war-like nor male. "Onward Christian Soldiers" rarely makes the cut in most pro-gressive hymnals, and the old standard "Faith of Our Fathers" has become "Faith of Our Parents." Moreover, most of the mainline denominations sup-port working mothers, abortion rights, and equal pay for equal work. Though critics point out that the commitment to gender equality tends to be soft and episodic—the majority of female clergy still sit under a "stained glass ceiling," underpaid and overqualified—it is safe to say that change has come. Like so many other American institutions, from advertising to higher education, sports to medicine, mainline churches heard the call for gender equality, and drifted earnestly in that direction.[4]

Certainly mainline Protestants are a world apart from their conservative evangelical cousins, for whom antifeminism has become an organizing prin-ciple, if not an article of faith. The Presbyterian Church in America (PCA), now one of the largest conservative denominations, was born in opposition to feminism, formed in 1973 in reaction to moves toward women's ordina-tion in the main body of the Presbyterian church. Some forty years later even a proposal to study women's roles met created a sustained uproar, fueled by suspicions of a feminist stealth campaign. "We would, of course, all agree," a PCA commentator declared, that no matter the pressure, "we would never abandon the principle of Christ as the Way, the Truth, and the Life. The same is true for women in ministry: This issue has been studied by the PCA and we are clear on what Scripture teaches."[5]

Yet Nelle Morton's frustration with her peers was genuine. Mainline Protestant feminism did not arrive on schedule, certainly not at the fore-front of the rising liberation movement being led Jews and secularists and a few pioneering Roman Catholics. Equality emerged incrementally. Where their nineteenth-century predecessors had been on the ground floor of the women's rights movement—the 1848 Seneca Falls meeting was in a Wesleyan Chapel, after all—most twentieth-century mainline Protestants watched the emerging social revolution from a safe social distance.

Where did change come from? The story of the 1970s and 1980s, the trans-formation of biblical studies and theology, the rise of Christian feminism, and the march toward ordination rights, has already been well documented, more than once.[6] We know much less about what preceded feminism, the fuzzy time of transition in the late 1950s and 1960s, when an old order was giving way to a new one. Clearly the conversation had to shift, to take on a new vocabulary, one that was less focused on gender balance in church institutions—issues of administrative parity—and ringingly clear about gender justice.

As we see in this chapter, the words had to come from a particular set of outsiders, not the secular critics of the churches but trustworthy religious partners. One of the most important was the World Council of Churches (WCC), specifically Christian feminists losing patience with the old ethic of male-female cooperation. The others were Roman Catholics, here an articulate, theologically driven opposition party battling with an unapologetically conservative establishment. In a sense, these allies provided permission to venture further, to dare to be uncooperative, and to set aside old institutional loyalties for the sake of something new.

Too Many Women?

Before any woman could ascent to the pulpit, however, feminism required a reckoning with feminization. "Ancient fears and prejudices" still prevailed, even in the 1960s, said Doris Hunter, Counselor for Women at Boston University School of Theology. Young women came to theological seminaries with a "masculine voice" ringing in their ears, "saying, 'There are enough women in the church already.'" The "masculine leaders of the church," said Hunter, "often feel that their virile qualities are in danger when [women] assume leadership in this field."[7]

Real progress, as it was symbolized in a push for women's ordination, required a different sense of historical trajectory. "[T]ime and time again," Norma Ramsey Jones wrote in 1970, "women are told that it is their moral duty to restrain themselves from making a full contribution to the life of the church because they will thereby avoid scaring off potentially committed men." Writing in one of the first feminist statements directed at mainline churches, Jones declared it was time to "break away from the old stereotype of a 'good churchwoman.'"[8]

The first inklings emerged in the mid-1960s. A 1964 survey of Illinois churches, for example, made the explicit point that church "participation" was not a reliable indicator of gender imbalances. Certainly by the obvious measurements—joining a congregation, attending services—women outnumbered men, about "6 ladies for every 4 men," as the survey report put it. And true, the average congregation consisted of "a small men's group struggling to survive" and a "thriving women's group containing several 'circles.'" Moreover, everybody knew that most Sunday school teachers were female, and that church choirs were always running short of tenors and basses. But, what if the measurement were different? What if participation reflected "active membership," that is, the actual number of men on church boards and committees? In that respect, the survey declared (without really explaining the calculus involved) that the problem was not all that bad. From a slightly altered angle of perception, with perhaps a bit of a squint, feminization was a myth.[9]

By the early 1960s, that conclusion was increasingly plausible. The religious revival of the 1950s had, at the very least, made male churchgoers more visible. Norman Vincent Peale and Billy Graham were Protestant celebrities with a secular fame and following. The marriage and domestic life of the Chaplain of the Senate, Peter Marshall, was a best-selling memoir, written by his wife, Catherine. This was an era in which rugged-looking theologians graced the cover of *Time Magazine*; figures like Reinhold Niebuhr and Paul Tillich were nearly household names, certainly well known among the cultural stock of public intellectuals. Even more important, the Cold War elevated the profile of Protestant laymen, stalwarts like the Presbyterian Secretary of State John Foster Dulles, and the Disciples of Christ war hero and president Dwight D. Eisenhower.

It is also conceivable—though membership statistics cannot provide sufficiently fine-grained evidence—that on any given Sunday churchgoers simply saw more husbands and fathers in the pews. Their presence was, to a large degree, a function of the family-centered ethos of mainline churches during the postwar era. Convinced that the old Sunday-school approach, age-graded lessons aimed only at children, was outmoded and ineffective, religious educators pushed for total family involvement. Protestant families of the 1950s received weekly torrents of advice literature, magazines, and instruction manuals from experts who insisted that "home religion" was beyond essential, more perhaps than actual churchgoing. "The absence of prayer at home," wrote popular authors Elton and Pauline Trueblood, "is more damaging than is the absence of prayer at Sunday school."[10]

Aunt Jane on the Defensive

Mainline familism coincided with growing skepticism toward women's church groups, new permission to say the unsayable. The scrutiny came from many quarters, from *New Yorker* cartoonist Helen Hokinson's popular send-ups of large-bosomed clubwomen to searching self-criticism among mainline women themselves. Writing on the "feminine crisis in Christian faith" in 1965, biblical scholar Elizabeth Achtemeier was sharply critical of women's organizations, especially their "naïve tendency to 'think big.'" "Our efforts on behalf of our faith," she said, "seem to have been marked by a certain unaware simplicity at times. And this simplicity has made us more the objects of amusement than of interest in our cause." The solution, in her view, required a great deal of intellectual shoring up, a deeper understanding of Christian thought, and a hard-headed assessment of what was truly possible in a time of world crisis. "Whatever we may think of this attitude toward women in society—and heaven deliver us from the professional feminists!—the fact is that it has left many of us women with an inner frustration and sadness beyond expression."[11]

Achtemeier was a conservative critic, but she was not a lone voice. In 1964, Peggy Way, at the time a social welfare consultant with the Chicago City Missionary Society, criticized churchwomen from the left, decrying their "self-satisfaction, contentment with what exists, and great defensiveness at the slightest hint of criticism." Women's church groups were, in her view, one of the greatest impediments to church renewal, "not only because of their structured power, but also because of their naiveté regarding the real task of the Church in the contemporary world." From the local church to top interdenominational boards, women's groups "tend to chart their own course, set their own pace, establish their own patterns, and write their own theologies. The leadership is deeply entrenched and brooks no interference—particularly from pastors." Clearly, said Way, "a great deal of power is involved—financially and socially," and not used to further prophetic aims.[12]

In many ways, churchwomen's organizations were already a soft target. The "Aunt Janes," as they were called, were facing some stiff institutional headwinds in the late 1950s and 1960s. Money and resources were shifting toward empowering the "laity." The use of that term represented a quiet but intentional shift, replacing the masculine "layman" with a gender-neutral category that included both men and women. Emphasis on the laity came out of the ecumenical movement, in a response to criticisms that it was a self-perpetuating clique of clergy and religious professionals. Training and equipping the laity was a worthy goal, but, as Eileen Linder points out, it created an "awkward and uneasy" situation for women's organizations. The ecumenical movement's desire to close the gap between pulpit and pews "obscured the question of gender inclusiveness," and, Lindner argues, delayed serious conversation about women's ordination.[13]

Take for example, the steps taken by the newly formed United Church of Christ (UCC). Its Department of the Laity drew directly on the model of cooperation advocated by the WCC. (In fact, an earlier proposed name was "Council for Cooperation of Men and Women.")[14] The creation of this lay group was an explicit loss for the two women's groups from the merging denominations, the Evangelical and Reformed Women's Guild and Congregational Christian Women's Fellowship. Leadership supported the merger, but with a clear "tug of regret."[15] Congregationalist Lillian Gregory used the metaphor of highway construction to explain the organizational change to her rank and file, reminding them about the "vast demolition" required for the building of Chicago's Northeast Expressway. "The destruction was monumental," she wrote, "eliminating residential units, industrial buildings, and, one imagines, playgrounds, shops and neighborhood landmarks which had welded the communities into havens of security." And admittedly, the process was far more costly and complicated than anyone expected. But the results were worth the trouble. Now, said Gregory, "traffic flows at an amazing pace" and drivers routinely reached their destinations "with speed and comfort." "If anyone longs for the old roads," she said, "he never mentions it."[16]

The expectation was that, as part of the laity, women would be equal partners in the leadership of the UCC. The appointment of Helen Huntington Smith to lead the Council for Lay Life and Work was certainly auspicious, the "first woman to head a United Church Instrumentality and the first lay person to head one of them."[17] Yet, as Mildred Horton observed, though the idea was "appealing" it "didn't work very well for very long."[18] The push for lay involvement certainly did not appear to benefit lay women, at least judging from the near complete absence of women in UCC executive offices and policy-making boards and committees. "One actually wonders sometimes," a critic wrote, "why the male element of the church so tenaciously holds on to its formal and yet rather specious control. Why not pleasantly accept the facts of contemporary life and accord competent laywomen responsible posts in the furtherance of the Christian cause and in the strengthening of the church?"[19]

Episcopalian women encountered some of the same frustrations. In 1967, after decades of debate, women were finally allowed to serve as deputies to the national body, the General Convention. Put simply, they had finally become fully enfranchised in denominational decision-making, from local vestries to diocesan and general conventions. (The constitutional change ratifying the decision took place in 1970.) Yet that decision coincided with another that effectively undermined women as a group, when the denomination dissolved the General Division of Women's Work and transferred its responsibilities to the Standing Committee on Lay Ministries. Episcopal Churchwomen, the national organization, was no longer a voice for women. As historian Mary Donovan writes, "the 'integration' of women into the national administrative structure resulted not only in the demotion of women officers to subordinate staff positions but also the complete dissolution of women's separate power base." Hopes of equal representation on the new laymen's organization were denied. Not surprisingly, the Lay Ministries Committee that was drawn from the Executive Council, which was still a clerical body, ended up with "one clergyman, one layman—no women."[20]

The dissolution of the General Division of Women's Work came with an ironic consequence, however. Behind the attention-grabbing public battles over ordination in the Episcopal Church, was a quieter change with significant long-term consequences. The loss of financial support from women's groups meant the closing of separate training schools for female church workers—and as a result, more Episcopalian women in theological seminaries. Moreover, the one remaining area of women's financial control, the four million dollars raised as their United Thank Offering—also facilitated ordinations. Special grant funds for an "enabler" to work with female seminary students supported Reverend Suzanne Hiatt, a deacon and key founder of the Episcopal Women's Caucus. Ultimately, as Donovan writes, the integration of women into church structures brought them "face to face with the crucial reality of the distribution of power within the Episcopal Church." No longer "isolated in their parallel structure," where they had "been able to avoid the reality of patriarchal power," Episcopal churchwomen "found themselves confronted with a series of issues they had scarcely imagined."[21] In the end, efforts to eliminate gender differences ended up magnifying them, clearing the way for a new network of denominational women's caucuses and commissions and departments, all overtly feminist in their goals and rhetoric.

The late 1960s were also a moment of truth for Church Women United (CWU, renamed from United Church Women in 1966). "As church women with a commitment for involvement in legislative action, theological investigation, urban affairs, adult basic education, and all kinds of social programs,"

Ruth Weber, editor of the *Church Woman*, declared in 1969, "we are going to have to make up our minds about this male-female thing." It may be, she said, "that we will start with questions: Is real equality possible? Have we examined all the ramifications?" In other words, the members of this large and successful women organization had to face the reality that, despite all of the progressive social causes they had supported, they were female.[22]

Meanwhile, CWU's deteriorating relationship with the National Council of Churches (NCC) required an aggressive response. Bureaucratic tensions had been growing since CWU joined the NCC in 1950, fueled by theological differences as well as administrative infighting. But the fit was bound to be awkward from the start: unlike other ecclesiastical members of the NCC, CWU was not a denomination sending duly appointed delegates. Margaret Shannon called it a "movement" of individual women working toward common goals. The tensions of the 1960s only exacerbated that fundamental difference. In 1969 a Commission on Women in Today's World, bringing together leading figures like Nelle Morton, Pauli Murray, Sarah Bentley Dooley, and Charlotte Bunch Weeks, began to plumb the question of "women's identity." The Commission also pushed CWU to take stands on the ERA and abortion rights, as a "retrieval center for stirrings among women." In 1971 CWU's alliance with the NCC, which had always been rocky, was over.[23]

Still, CWU struggled to adjust to new social realities. "The phases of women's liberation came so rapidly and spontaneously," said Shannon, "that no one had any way to count the cost." Many of the rank and file objected instinctively to the argument that they had to possess a "male attitude" in order to "exert power in society." The problem, as it was discussed in the pages of the *Church Woman* in 1968, was not so much gender identity as the possibility of direct, uncomfortable confrontation. "Nothing would be more disastrous to the cause of feminine power," a Texas woman wrote, "than if women went about behaving like men. The early suffragettes did, and their crude methods have made woman-power a comic phrase for years. The sly old ways we've always known are far more effective." There was nothing wrong with a little feminine misdirection, a New York woman added, since "passivity is often an element in the use of power."[24]

Searching for a New Paradigm

Histories of second-wave feminism point to several catalysts for rebellion, moments when the realities of sexism emerged with dramatic clarity. The federal government played a role documenting and publicizing economic inequality, with the 1963 Presidential Report on American Women and the Equal Pay Act (Title VII). On the other end of the spectrum the unrepentant sexism of left-wing men spurred radicalized women to separate protest, to "speak bitterness" and develop a "critical consciousness of the language of masculinity." And for untold numbers of isolated, quietly angry wives and mothers, the publication of Betty Friedan's *Feminine Mystique* (1962) was a call to revolution. It all pointed to the need for systematic, widespread change. The manifesto of NOW, formed in 1966, put it succinctly: "We believe the time has come to move beyond the abstract argument, discussion and symposia over the status and special nature of women." It was time to "confront, with concrete action, the conditions that now prevent women from enjoying the equality of opportunity and freedom of choice which is their right, as individual Americans, and as human beings."[25]

That call to action outlined a powerful trajectory, from theoretical analyses of social problems to the deeply personal realization that everyday slights and frustrations were manifestations of a system skewed toward male dominance—that "the personal is political." The evidence was often subtle. African Americans, Jews, and other people of color could point to evidence of their oppression in segregated housing, racial violence, and outright bigotry. But American women, especially those of the white, privileged middle class who would turn toward feminism in the 1970s, had some hard thinking to do.

For most feminist activists, consciousness-raising came as a series of reframings, each one opening the way to the next. The first, what became known as the "click," was the sudden awareness that one's self-doubt and self-hatred were "not just me," but the cost of systemic injustice. A passing remark or irritating encounter, once accepted as normal daily wear and tear, opened a new door of perception, an understanding that the entire framework of reality was tilted against women. Yet to make a difference, the "click" had to create a yearning for justice, an "oppositional consciousness" that led to action. What was previously seen as "unfortunate but perhaps tolerable" had to be redefined as unjust and immoral. And finally, the emerging feminist needed to see herself as female, in moral solidarity with all women everywhere. Collective identity required a new set of symbolic boundaries separating "us" from "them."[26]

At times it all sounded like a religious conversion. Some consciousness raising accounts even used classic Protestant tropes of being "lost and found" or entering a "promised land." As Virginia Brereton has shown, an evangelical language of spiritual transformation has been used to define all kinds of personal growth stories, from deliverance from addiction to lesbian "coming out" crises.[27]

Yet the comparison only goes so far. Women with religious commitments may have been every bit as angry as secularists, but they did not arrive with a blank slate. Historian Mary Henold writes of the "multiple, conflicting loyalties" of Roman Catholic women who were both loyal to the Church and convinced of its errors. Feminism was never a "self-evident" reality they could choose to adopt or reject. Conversion was fraught, episodic, and costly, and often involved losses of deeply held beliefs, spiritual communities, and in some cases economic livelihoods.[28]

Some consequences were more dramatic than others. Evangelical feminists who made even the barest suggestions of contextualizing St. Paul's prohibitions against women speaking faced withering accusations about their fidelity to the word of Scripture. As *Christianity Today* editor Harold Lindsell wrote in 1976, feminism meant "directly and deliberately denying that the Bible is the infallible rule of faith and practice." And there was no arguing with the result: evangelical feminists "have ceased to be evangelical."[29]

Mainline churchwomen faced more nuanced choices. To be sure, debates about biblical texts had lost their purchase decades ago, relegated to the backward world of "funny Fundamentalists," as one of Anna Swain's colleagues described her critics.[30] Whatever back-and-forth continued was more about logistics than ideology, more about the dangers to administrative procedures than biblical authority. What should higher-ups do if a local congregation refused to hire a female candidate? What would women wear in the pulpit?

It is easy to mistake these conversations as bureaucratic sandbagging, efforts to protect the status quo by relentless nit-picking—or worse, a Protestant "establishment" buttressing itself against change. But as we have seen, the regard for institutions was instinctive, and authentic. But there was genuine work to do. While evangelical feminists wrestled with the infallible word of Scripture, mainline churchwomen had to redefine old loyalties to congregations and denominations, and along with them the norms of service and cooperation that had so long defined their role.

Change required a new set of ideas about belonging. And in that respect mainline Protestants were no different from anyone else searching for self during those rule-bending years. The thirst for personal experience was a major fault line of the 1960s, driving not just feminism but the evangelical revival and seeker-style mysticism. Yet, the mainline churches did not—perhaps could not—generate a language of individual dissent on their own. Nor could they simply turn to secular sources. They needed allies with sharp shoulders and a theological vocabulary, women and men they could trust, with an understanding of how faith both helped and hindered liberation.

It is telling that when NOW's Task Force on Religion put together a reading list for its members, the books came primarily from two sources, the WCC and Roman Catholics.[31] The first was familiar: since the 1950s, most of the hard thinking about gender roles had come from people like Madeleine Barot, Kathleen Bliss, and Sarah Chakko. The other is surprising, a departure from the long historical mistrust between Protestants and Roman Catholics, brief perhaps, but consequential.

The World Council of Churches

Within the WCC, faith in cooperation between the sexes was already growing thin in the late 1950s. The criticisms were out in the open by 1960: a conference on "Responsible Cooperation between Men and Women" found the model far too soft, far too eager for middle ground. "Co-operation *per se*," the participants declared, is not a solution, especially when it was framed as "complementarity," the idea that the sexes together formed a human whole. Instead of vague hopes for mutuality, the churches needed reality, facing the intractable "polarity of interests" between men and women, the historical fact of male domination.[32] Moreover, the WCC conversation was growing leery of any generalizations about gender, no matter how balanced and careful. The dividing lines had always been fuzzy, of course; now they were becoming detrimental. A 1964 conclave declared that it was "obviously time to abandon the general traditional distinction between men and women in favour of a more nuanced differentiation between human *individuals*." It would be a "sin," they noted to "hamper anyone" from developing his or her particular gifts.[33]

Much of the change in perspective reflected Madeleine Barot's travel itinerary. She made her first trip to Africa in 1958, to women's gatherings in Madagascar and Cameroon. The visit not only tempered her views on gender-segregated church organizations, it made her see "what women at every level had to accomplish to share responsibilities with men."[34] In cases of rank oppression, where women were denied basic rights to education and economic independence, Barot had to wonder whether female solidarity was a more effective weapon than cooperation. Subsequent trips to Mexico, Argentina, Uruguay, and Brazil revealed, as she wrote in 1964, that "the Christian life cannot be lived, nor a social problem answered, in the same way in Finland as in the U.S.A., in Moslem Algeria as in Buddhist Thailand, in over-populated and highly-industrialized Japan as in the Congo, in Russia, Brazil or Indonesia." Christians outside the Western world, said Barot, "must find their own Christian way," reexamining "their own cultures and traditions, in order to discover what can be preserved and what is incompatible with Christian life." When a women's consultation at Kampala in April 1963 asked the African churches to consider ordaining women, Barot and her Department tried to help, but recognized that they could not impose a single answer. The question for each church to decide, she said, is whether "the admission of women to the ordained ministry is a good and profitable thing for the present situation."[35]

At the same time, women's ordination was moving back into the realm of possibility, albeit indirectly. When the Third Assembly in New Delhi commissioned a study of the "theological, biblical, and ecclesiological issues" in 1961, the question was taken up by both the Department of Cooperation and the Faith and Order Commission—in other words by the ecumenical world's leading theologians and churchmen. After decades of deference to more conservative partners, ecumenists were finally ready to tackle the issue, as both a theological and practical concern. Women's ordination was not just the preoccupation of feminist agitators, but related directly to "the total understanding of the ministry of the church and therefore has deep theological significance."[36]

The changes solidified in 1967, when Brigalia Bam succeeded Barot. A Black South African with extensive experience in human rights, Bam "brought a new emphasis on solidarity," insisting that women needed separate space to "discover their own identity and work out their own contribution." "Earlier statements and declarations on man-woman relationship[s] were dealt with mostly in terms of theology," Bam reported in 1968. "Now, we are emphasizing the urgency of the main concern of the Department on Cooperation in light of the social revolution of our times." It was time to free men and women "to complement each other without the exploitation of either one by the other," so that they might enjoy "self-expression in all phases of life."[37]

The Fourth Assembly in Uppsala in 1968 marked a clear transition, when talk of cooperation gave way to a new emphasis on "equalizing the participation of men and women." Though still, at least outwardly "establishment-focused, male-dominated [and] European led"—the meeting had very few women present, only 0 percent of the delegates—the event was clearly groundbreaking. James Baldwin denounced the churches' "betrayal" of Black Christians and urged the "spiritual daring to repent" of racism. The delegates listened to folk singer Pete Seeger, watched Czechoslovakian films, and drafted a statement against the war in Vietnam. And the Assembly asked the Department of Cooperation to study "problems preventing the partnership of women and men" and to take up the ordination question.[38]

The final argument against cooperation was practical: all the talk on male–female mutuality had not changed anything. Here the significant benchmark was Marga Buhrig's essay, published in 1970, "Discrimination against Women." Buhrig was a WCC veteran and would become president of the WCC in 1983. Her involvement went back to Madeline Barot's Evanston address in 1954. As director of a lay academy in Zurich, the only woman in German-speaking Switzerland at that level of achievement, she had thought long and hard about male and female power. Her article was an unsparing critique of cooperation. "[N]ow, twenty years later," she wrote, "it would seem that the real balance of power within the churches has changed scarcely at all," especially if judged by the number of women participating in meetings of the WCC. "Making allowances for a measure of exaggeration," said Buhrig, "one might almost say that these meticulous theological and psychological inquiries into the 'true nature of woman', her intrinsic gifts, the mission entrusted her by God, and the correct appraisal of the unalterable contrast between man and woman which is part of creation," and have made it impossible for the churches to admit that " 'discrimination' against women exists." All the talk seemed to have led nowhere. "It may well be," Buhrig noted wryly, "that lucid theological insights make people blind to the practical conditions which require change."[39]

Change was coming quickly, however. In 1974, the WCC "grasped the nettle of sexism," with a major international conference in Berlin. Significantly, no men were invited—the gender inclusive conversation that the Baarn meeting attempted to begin was over. As General Secretary Philip Potter told the gathering (before departing), "We are incapable of understanding from within what sexism means because we are mainly responsible for it." Under Potter's direction, the 1975 Assembly included for the first time, women in a variety of leadership roles. By 1983, according to one report, they were "visible and actively present—as worship leaders, as plenary speakers, as Bible Study leaders, as moderators and rapporteurs of committees and subsections." Their impact on "the agenda of the ecumenical movement was sealed!"[40]

One of the 200 women present at the Berlin conference was Constance Parvey, a graduate of Harvard Divinity School and ordained to the Lutheran ministry in 1972. "Many of us had been at world gatherings before, but had never been at a meeting of women who were all our peers from many continents, churches, and professions," she wrote. "For many, the Berlin experience was a turning point." Parvey offered to chair a working group on theology, an idea initially resisted by the conference organizers. "There was a strong sentiment," Parvey later recalled, "that theology had nothing to say to women," another clear departure from the Baarn agenda. But the initiative proved surprisingly successful. "As we shared our own stories," she said, "we discovered that though we were all very serious and committed Christians, we were marginal to the church's institutional life. Few doors were open to us." The outcome was a Community Study, focused on "the implications of theology and church structures" for women in "theology, ministry, and church life."[41]

Parvey was part of a task force in Boston, a formidable gathering of theologians, biblical scholars, and churchwomen who finally put to rest the possibility of cooperation between the sexes. "Relationships between women and men are not complementary, but reciprocal," the group agreed. "*Reciprocal implies equal.*" Or in Parvey's words, "there can be little hope for women and for men in solidarity until women, without dependence on men, find their own identity." The new imperative was to "cultivate and nurture their own needs, their own creativity, their own contribution."[42]

In one sense, these Christian feminists were circling back to an earlier era. They were staking down an end of an arc, in fact, taking up questions about "women's nature" that had been all but sidelined in the United States since the 1920s, considering the possibility that women, as well as men, could be individuals. A conversation about gender that had revolved mostly around institutions—women's status in churches, their role in families— was finally becoming personal. Now the words of Elizabeth Cady Stanton, Virginia Woolf, and the feminists of bohemian New York began to resonate. "Those who are seeking to discover their own power as Christian women," Letty Russell wrote, "must first learn that sisterhood is beautiful and powerful.[43] Most of all, however, women had to see church institutions for what they were, to insist on "nothing less than a total revolution." They needed to realize, said Parvey, "that theirs is an alien experience, alien in the way that the imposition of Western Roman Catholic church life and dogma on Latin American peasants to their experience, identity, and life situation."[44]

Roman Catholics

And indeed, the Roman Catholic Church was a powerful counterexample for mainline Protestants. Anti-Catholicism had deep roots in American culture and American religiosity: a despotic papacy was the standard against which nineteenth-century native-born Protestants defined their commitments to democracy. Even as tensions faded in the increasingly pluralistic twentieth century, old suspicions remained. They were voiced more quietly, of course, often in lawyerly arguments about public schooling and taxation, but were nevertheless widely acceptable within middle-class Protestant circles.[45]

It is surprising—and not surprising—that the early voices of feminist liberation were Roman Catholics rather than Protestants. Their finely honed, passionate critique of religious sexism was already well under way by the early 1960s. One of the only women at Vatican II—as an observer, not an official delegate—was Mary Daly, acutely aware of the ironies in that historical moment. The meetings themselves, taking place in Rome from 1963 to 1965, certainly looked like a harbinger of change. The message of openness to other ideas and the possibility that the Church did not speak with one voice was not just a "shocking concept for Catholics," as historian Mary Henold writes. It was an "invitation . . . to grow up." An old ecclesiastical order, dominated by a hierarchy of priests, bishops, cardinals, and popes, was giving way to vigorous leadership by laypeople. Yet, as Henold writes, it became clear very quickly that "the general use of the term 'laymen' meant just that."[46]

Mary Daly had both the language and the scholarly credentials for a stinging critique. She went back to the United States, to her position in the theology department at Boston College, and put it all down in a book. When *The Church and the Second Sex* was published in 1968, Roman Catholics had both a "comprehensive overview of Catholic sexism" and a "new vision of Catholic feminism." Daly's belief that the Church contained its own seeds of liberation would sour in years ahead, but by that time the Catholic library of protest was strong and growing, a formidable mix of mainstream and academic voices, from Sidney Callahan's *Illusion of Eve* and Sally Cunneen's

Sex: Female, Religion: Catholic to Arlene Swidler and Rosemary Radford Ruether.[47]

Roman Catholic women also had institutional resources that Protestants lacked. Nuns and sisters were, after all, trained religious professionals. They were certainly a world apart from most mainline churchwomen, largely volunteers with limited access to theological education—seminaries that did not outright exclude female students routinely shuffled them into vocational tracks like religious education and counseling. Women religious were also busy professionalizing and modernizing, well before Vatican II. The Sister Formation Conference, established in 1954 to promote teacher training and credentialing, fostered conversations about updating "anachronistic" dress and opportunities for service in the secular world. Already in the early 1960s, "new nuns," as they were called, were shortening veils, working in inner cities, marching in Selma, and receiving graduate degrees in theology.[48]

Catholic laywomen also had access to theological training at Grailville, a center for religious education in Loveland, Ohio, founded in 1940. The Grail movement promoted the "lay apostolate," a way for laywomen to devote themselves to the Church, short of joining a religious order. Seekers came to Loveland for weeks, sometimes years, to be part of a female community that promoted liturgical celebration and a monastic lifestyle. Grail conferences and workshops brought together clergy and laypeople, academics and schoolteachers, young and old—even male and female—on an equal footing. Years later, a laywoman still remembered a 1963 meeting: "[There were] women in positions of academic leadership . . . no evidence of chauvinism." The atmosphere, she said, "was one of collegiality and mutual regard."[49]

Protestant women were impressed. Sarah Cunningham, editor of the Presbyterian magazine *Concern*, wrote wonderingly of a Grail gathering she attended as a guest at Cornwall-on-Hudson in 1965. "After dinner, the co-ordinator of the group did what I thought was a strange thing for such a sophisticated assembly," Cunningham wrote. "She asked each of us to tell a bit about ourselves. What had brought us to this place?" A ritual that was partly feminist consciousness-raising and partly evangelical personal witnessing left this liberal Protestant utterly baffled. "I did not even understand the question," said Cunningham. But by the end of the evening, when life stories had been shared around the room, she understood the power of shared experience. "[W]e were made aware of how our accumulated past had brought us to this particular present," and the "pain of separation." "By the time we had left the house on Hudson on late Saturday afternoon," said Cunningham, "many of us acknowledged that we had participated in an event beyond our immediate comprehension."[50]

Grailville introduced Protestant churchwomen not just to theology as a discipline but also to theology as cultural critique. The *Churchwoman* reported with some amazement a meeting in 1968, led by both a Protestant and Roman Catholic scholar, on the biblical and theological framework for "Christian Faith in a Secular Society." In addition, Presbyterian educator Nelle Morton led three afternoon sessions on "the role of women." Though, reportedly, some of the attendees were not sure this was a "valid subject for discussion," they began to see that "this, too, is an area that reveals much about accepting the full humanity of all persons."[51]

Roman Catholic women also made the first formal alliances with secular feminists. The NOW Task Force on Religion can trace its origins to a meeting of "the two Bettys" in 1966, when Elizabeth Farians, a veteran of the Catholic Worker Movement and theology professor at Sacred Heart University, decided it was time to get to know Betty Friedan. The two met in a bar in a railroad station near the University of Bridgeport, where Friedan had just spoken, and as Farians remembered, talked "theology over drinks." Farians was no mere supplicant: she had a doctorate in theology from St. Mary's College in Indiana, the only Roman Catholic school that awarded that degree to women. She was the first female member of the Catholic Theological Society, and a close friend of Mary Daly's. Farians was also well aware of the risk she was taking with Friedan. "For feminists in general," she said, "religion was irrelevant and for the women in religion feminism was irrelevant. It became the job of the NOW Task Force to point out that one of the root causes of the oppression of women was religion."[52]

Roman Catholic women took the lead. The Task Force, which Farians helped form in 1966, met in Mary Daly's apartment, "rather raucous events" aimed at "unmasking and undoing patriarchal religion." Their principle target was the Catholic hierarchy. The first protest, the so-called Easter Bonnet Rebellion of 1969, called on women to go to Mass without head coverings, the traditional symbol of feminine submission. Other protests featured "liturgies of anguish" and in 1970, the burning of the Roman Missal, specifically the section that only allowed women to participate in worship services from outside the sanctuary gates. Feminists sent the ashes, in a box tied up with a pink ribbon and a protest poem ("Pink and Ash") to the National Conference of Catholic Bishops.[53]

And then, in the early 1970s, when feminism was first beginning to flower in Protestant seminaries and churches, the Catholic pioneers were finished. Daly and Farians left the Task Force on Religion in 1972—and soon after the Catholic Church itself. There were reasons for despair, coming from both sides, from secular feminists as well as conservative churchmen. In 1971 Ti-Grace Atkinson had stood on a stage at Catholic University and denounced the Bishops as "Motherfuckers," a statement that typified NOW's growing impatience with religious institutions in general. That same year, NOW's fifth national conference passed a resolution declaring that "religious teachings and practice are a major cause of the oppression of women" and encouraged the diversion of financial contributions from churches to the NOW Ecumenical Task Force on Women and Religion. On the other side of things, in 1976, the Church closed the door completely and firmly to the possibility of ordination with a papal encyclical, "Declaration on the Question of the Admission of Women to the Ministerial Priesthood."[54]

The transition to Protestant leadership was unmistakable. After Daly and Farians departed, the first action was a protest on Reformation Sunday that included the posting of "115 Feminist Theses." The list, a "call to the churches to complete the Reformation," was written by Protestant women—two Lutherans, an Episcopalian, and two Presbyterians. The change in leadership was not revolutionary, however. Despite the hat tip to Martin Luther, Protestant protest adopted Roman Catholic themes, excoriating "the church" for its history of oppressing women, and "all those who are deprived of power and status within patriarchal-ecclesial systems," including the laity as well as children, and racial, ethnic, sexual, and economic minorities. The charge that "males dominate the Christian churches" was certainly true historically and in regard to the Roman Catholic hierarchy—but it did not necessarily reflect American Protestant reality. "Domination" was borrowed rhetoric at best, a far from accurate description of the Protestant landscape, a diverse network of sprawling denominations thinly governed by a male minority.[55]

Cooperation versus Authenticity

Liberal Protestant feminism, in other words, had some work to do, developing a vocabulary and an agenda that reflected the mainline's particular realities. Without a doubt the United States, and the world, was undergoing a social transformation that, even in retrospect, was sudden and cataclysmic.

We are still parsing through the many difference sources of unrest: the baby boom, the opening of colleges and universities to the many rather than the few, racial unrest, drug culture, even television. Religious institutions were particularly hard hit, sustaining mortal losses in membership and social power, zigzagging between earnest desires to be relevant and a conservative evangelical backlash. But they were more than mere battlefield casualties: each religious tradition came to the 1960s with its own set of historical burdens.

Of all the profound challenges mainline churches encountered—intellectual, demographic, theological—the demise of the ecumenical movement is one of the most significant, and the least understood. Although the rhetoric of ecumenism remains, the mechanisms of unity have eroded. Religious tolerance and interfaith cooperation are still articles of faith among liberal Protestants, but so is a lack of trust in the very church institutions charged with making that possible. Vietnam War protesters and Black Power advocates had no patience for the stately pace of change in Protestant churches. The NCC was, in their eyes, a particularly egregious example, little more than a "bloated bureaucracy of divisions, departments, committees, and task forces." It all began to look like nothing more than conservative foot-dragging, a particularly insidious form of opposition.[56]

Certainly by the late 1970s, feminists were losing patience with the ecumenical movement, this despite long strides toward support for women's ordination. The general timidity and organized resistance, especially in conservative bodies like the Eastern Orthodox, suggested that gender justice was still secondary—and that religious institutions would never be true instruments of change. "As important as union is," UCC minister Elsie Gibson wrote in 1978, "it can never come at the expense of truth."[57] To a growing number of feminist critics, the ecumenical movement was "simply a confirmation of a patriarchal status quo, with new agreements reinforcing an old-boy network of episcopal and other ordained authorities."[58]

The new ethic was authenticity. At the heart of 1960s protests—and the therapeutic culture that followed in their wake—was a desire for social traction, the experience of being "real." Personal honesty emerged from doing, by choosing to forsake comforting myths and mindless loyalties and doing the hard work of social justice. Despite the secular image associated with the New Left, the impulse was as much spiritual as political, a "search for meaning" that drew a rising generation of mainline Protestant churchgoers into radical social causes.[59]

An important leading edge was the Student Christian Movement (SCM), an outgrowth of the YWCA, the YMCA, and the ecumenical movement. Especially for young women, raised in churches, the SCM was a "subversive thread within mainstream Protestantism," nurturing a generation of activists and "feminists before their time." Women associated with the SCM would become influential figures in mainline churches—Peggy Billings, Nancy Richardson, Dorothy Height, and Valerie Russell. In the 1950s and early 1960s, the SCM was a "vehicle for the postwar generation's search for meaning and authenticity," hosting theological discussions, sometimes massive conferences, on leading figures like Dietrich Bonhoeffer and Paul Tillich as well as Jean-Paul Sartre and Albert Camus.[60]

Not everyone found connection between Christianity and feminism. Charlotte Bunch, who came up through the YWCA and Methodist Student Movement as a Duke University undergraduate, was the first president of the University Christian Movement, an activist arm of SCM. With her close friend Sara Evans, who became a well-known feminist historian, Bunch was a prominent campus voice for civil rights and opposition to the Vietnam War. After graduating she was a youth delegate to a Church and Society conference in Geneva and traveled to Beirut and Jordan, where she met with leaders of the Palestine Liberation movement. Feminism came next, as Bunch experienced open sexism in leftist circles, finding herself ignored by the "mostly secular and highly intellectual" men at the Institute for Policy Studies. At the same time, she was drawn into radical lesbian protest. A founding member of the Furies, she was part of a "movement within a movement," challenging the sexual boundaries of feminism—and also "less sure I was a Christian," in her words. By the 1980s she was in a committed lesbian relationship, a campaigner for human rights, and though she attributed her "activist temperament" to her Methodist upbringing, alienated from religious institutions.[61]

Some breaks with organized Protestantism were more dramatic, and more painful. Most of the women who met at Grailville in 1972, at a conference on "Women Exploring Theology" sponsored by CWU, were excited and hopeful, many deeply involved in church organizations or pursuing a seminary education. The group included Elizabeth Farians, who described herself as a "professional trouble-maker" and "bishop badgerer," as well as influential academics, including Elisabeth Schüssler Fiorenza and Rosemary Radford Ruether. Behind the positivity, however, was a thread of disillusionment, or, as one participant wrote, an "increasingly great and murderous rage against the institutional church." "I'm mad as *hell* at the church institutional, another woman testified; "questioning and rebelling—angry! Against the bondage of institutions," yet another described herself.[62]

Yet for women born and raised in the institutional church, the path to feminism was not easy. For many it required an experience of isolation, of being the lone woman in a man's world—in other words, enrolling in a Protestant seminary. "For the first time," UCC clergywoman Davida Crabtree wrote in her ordination paper in 1972, "I was in a situation where there were few other women. And despite most people's persistence in believing I must love it that way, I didn't."[63]

Many of these female seminarians had never questioned their loyalty to institutional religion. A good proportion were there to pursue degrees in religious education, a female track to the ministry, fast becoming an established profession requiring educational credentials.[64] "Even when I first began to study theology," said Parvey, "the idea that the Christian faith could be anti-woman never occurred to me." Only "vaguely aware of women's status in the church," she, like most of the female seminarians she knew at Harvard, "took our position for granted. We were doing what was possible. What we wanted to do, and we thought that other women would exercise their freedom of choice as well. It was only when we graduated," she said, "that we saw how differently we were treated from our male colleagues."[65]

The decision to pursue ordination did not come lightly. In fact, many twentieth-century seminarians resonated deeply with their nineteenth-century predecessors, that rag-tag array of female preachers and evangelists who insisted that they were simply answering a divine call. Anguish and turmoil were standard steps toward acceptance of God's will, the cleansing and clarifying necessary on the way to obedience. Their modern descendants also described wrenching doubt and painful decisions, both rendered endurable by a persistent belief in a divine calling—though with an emphasis on personal self-realization that would have been unintelligible to their preaching predecessors. "My religious quest," one young woman declared, "is to live authentically and holistically."[66]

Certainly the pulpit held indisputable symbolic importance. As Nelle Morton wrote, "I believe that women preaching, more than any other aspect of the church's ministry, threatens to expose the church and its seminaries as primarily masculine institutions." Indeed, "once the pulpit is de-sexed," she said, "it can no longer be labeled as the phallic symbol in the sanctuary with the Book on top to give it authority."[67]

But preaching was not everything. For many female seminarians, the call to ministry dovetailed with an enthusiasm for liturgy, an urge springing up across mainline churches in the midcentury decades. Tired of bland, preaching-centered worship, many Protestants sought spiritual inspiration through ritual, which meant returning to ancient practices in denominations with closer ties to Roman Catholics, particularly the central role of Holy Communion, or the Eucharist. This is one reason why some of the earliest and strongest demands for ordination came from women in denominations with priests instead of pastors. Lutherans and Episcopalians had long argued against women in the priesthood because female clergy could not, by definition, meet the essential requirement of the role. They would never be able to represent Christ, who was, as everyone knew, biologically male. Yet the "'tug' of the Eucharist," as one Lutheran woman described it, was hard to deny. "Each time it was celebrated," she said, "there was the haunting feeling of being drawn to the mystery but somehow also to responsibility."[68]

Yet perhaps the highest hurdle was an invisible one, the transformation of servants into leaders. Along with the visible changes—women in the pulpit, serving communion, teaching in seminaries—had to come a new set of attitudes about the church itself, a new theology of women's role. Valerie Saiving Goldstein articulated it the most eloquently, in an article initially overlooked when it was first published in 1960. She was a struggling graduate student at the University of Chicago when she wrote "The Human Situation: A Feminine View," critiquing Reinhold Niebuhr's theology of sin. Preoccupied with a young child and a deteriorating marriage, Goldstein had, in her words, absolutely no desire to "make waves" or attract attention. Her theology professor, Daniel Day Williams, was the one who recommended publication.[69]

Goldstein's argument was comprehensive and compelling, drawing on Margaret Mead's anthropology and an emerging scientific consensus that sex differences were far more cultural than biological. Perhaps, as Niebuhr would have it, selfishness and the need to dominate were problems for men, but hardly for the average woman. If anything, most women, especially those in churches, had the opposite problem. Instead of a masculine "will-to-power," they committed feminine sins of passivity: "triviality, distractibility, and diffuseness; lack of an organizing center or focus; dependence on others for one's own self-definition; tolerance at the expense of standards of excellence." Instead of a domineering self, most women tended toward an undeveloped one, one satisfied with "sentimentality, gossipy sociability and mistrust of reason." Salvation, therefore, required a certain selfishness in women, a refusal to compromise or to be content with serving instead of being served.[70]

Perhaps one of the reasons why Saiving's argument went unnoticed for so long (even though it was quickly featured in *Time Magazine*) was that it came just slightly too early. For the next decade it circulated in mimeographed form through theology departments and scholarly seminars, until it was "rediscovered" in the 1970s and 1980s. By then, it all made more sense. Saiving's argument spoke eloquently to the uniqueness of women's experience, and the male-centered agenda of so much Protestant theology. In 1960, however, churchwomen were not insisting on their "uniqueness" or openly criticizing men. Cooperation still seemed a viable strategy and service a worthy goal. Change would come gradually, and it would not include everyone.[71]

Not Feminists, But . . .

Take, for example, Ruth Peale, a woman with a famous husband, and an ego to match. Norman Vincent Peale was the preeminent pastor of the 1950s, the best-selling author of *The Power of Positive Thinking* and minister at the Marble Collegiate Church in New York City. But she knew better. Looking back on their relationship in 1971, Peale was certain that "my own listing in *Who's Who in America* has nothing to do with being Norman's wife." Early in their marriage she took it upon herself to study the organizational structure of his church and learn how to conduct meetings. "I practically memorized Robert's Rules of Order," she said. The idea was to help with the burdens of a busy pastorate, but "in the process I made a surprising discovery about myself: I was rather good at that sort of thing! What began as a slightly apprehensive decision to do something useful for Norman became a whole new dimension in my own life, one that has expanded steadily ever since."[72]

Ruth was indispensable. She not only ran her household to polished perfection, she also managed Norman's business affairs, editing and transcribing his sermons. It was Ruth, in fact, who started the Foundation for Christian Living in 1945, the immensely successful direct mail operation that, some 40 years later, had supplied subscribers with 350 million inspirational pamphlets and letters. That same year she cofounded, with Norman, an equally uplifting project, *Guideposts* magazine, also serving as publisher and board chair. Within a few years circulation reached over half a million, as *Guideposts* became an enduringly popular centerpiece of American religious culture. Ruth Peale was equally successful on her own, serving as a vice president of the NCC and president of the North American Missions of her home denomination, the Reformed Church in America. She also made a career of encouraging her husband, who was prone to moments of crippling self-doubt. His biographer in fact concluded that the confident and outgoing, Ruth was "the real possessor of positive thinking in their household."[73]

But she was no feminist—at least as she understood the meaning of that word. Ruth was proud of her success, and she agreed that women should receive equal pay and equal opportunity. She joined the feminists denouncing the chic misogynism of *Playboy* magazine. But Ruth Peale also made no bones about managing her famous husband. The key was avoiding confrontation. The smart wife got her way by creating a "climate of acquiescence," to act as "emotional blotting paper." "For instance," she advised, "listen but don't listen—let it go in one ear and out the other and above all, don't react emotionally to it." Patience was the best strategy: "look at your husband and thinking how much you love him. Don't say that aloud. It isn't the right moment. Just think it." At all times, the smart wife kept a "wary eye on his masculine ego, which can easily be bruised or damaged." Feminists just didn't understand how this worked. "Unless a woman is willing to look and act and be feminine," said Peale, "she's never going to be a success as a wife and mother or even as a person." The demand for equality was counterproductive: "instead of viewing the male-female relationship as complementary and mutually supportive," they insist on a competitive struggle. Her word to militant feminists was clear: "Ladies, your real enemy in your search for happiness is not masculine prejudice, or masculine exploitation, or masculine anything. Your real enemy is the lack of femininity in you."[74]

Ruth Peale was an outlier, perhaps, but also a churchwoman of an earlier generation, women who believed in ecumenical cooperation and the necessity of gender-segregated organizations. They endorsed the new order gingerly, or opposed it outright. If anything, Georgia Harkness told a Methodist gathering in 1964, the times called for "*more cooperation between the men and women*" of the denomination. This meant full clergy rights and greater acceptance of women in Methodist pulpits, but also "the right of women to have autonomous voluntary organizations like the Woman's Division." Shortly before her death in 1974, Harkness was still leery of feminism. "I suppose I am," she admitted to a group of female clergy and seminarians. "I have worked for years for larger recognition of the place of women in the church."

But she also drew certain lines: "I think it is perfectly silly that you should hesitate to speak of God as 'He' or as 'Our Father.'" The pronoun simply indicated that God was a person, not one sex or the other. "I certainly don't want to call God 'She.'"[75]

Mildred Horton was equally frank. "Some of us who have been liberated almost by accident," she told a group of New Hampshire churchwomen, "certainly not by any personal virtue—must be a problem to hard-working feminist leaders who find us as difficult to understand and more difficult to work with."[76] It seemed nonsensical to abandon a strategy that, in the long run, was achieving equality. Citing the women in leadership in Congregational circles—Helen Kenyon as moderator in the 1950s, Ann Bennett on the Council for Social Action—Mildred Horton argued that separate women's organizations helped to "demonstrate competence," training leaders "for larger spheres of influence."[77]

For their part, the new generation felt little connection with the immediate past. The "contemporary church's view of women," a UCC seminarian wrote, "is that she is an aesthetically-minded, child-centered individual who has no talent for or interest in ordained ministry, administration or policy-making positions."[78] Others criticized existing women's church organizations as "irrelevant, irreverent, and banal," and "lethargic, condescending or openly critical of women seeking after new ways in the service of the living Lord." Genuine spiritual renewal required "serious consideration" of their role in "the contemporary world" and "in professional and lay ministries within the Church."[79] Female seminarians in the 1960s found that "the old feminism had so waned that role models were nonexistent."[80] "Nobody really knows what will come of our presence," an Episcopalian student wrote in 1974, "because there's no touchstone from the past. . . . We're on the ground floor of creating role models for ourselves."[81]

In many ways they were right: a revolution was in the works. The exploding numbers of female seminarians in the 1970s are only one part of the story, a 340 percent increase for the decade, thirteen times greater than male enrollments. Yet, as Mark Chaves and James Cavendish have demonstrated, the ordination question is hardly new for Protestant churches; moreover, the conflicts that took place before the 1970s, from the 1920s onward, were more likely to result in equality than those afterward.[82]

Forgetting had consequences, and not just for Protestant churches. "One tragedy of feminism in the twentieth century," writes historian Jill Lepore, "was the way its history seemed to be forever disappearing," and along with it an understanding of the women who had paved the way. That much was clear in 1969, when Shulamith Firestone and other younger feminists visited the aging Alice Paul, who as founder of the National Woman's Party had drafted the Equal Rights Amendment in 1923. Paul had been an uncompromising radical voice in the years leading to the passage of the Nineteenth Amendment, part of a rising generation fed up with gradualism and compromise. In explicit rejection of their predecessors' tactics, they went on hunger strikes and chained themselves to fences in front of the White House. The walls of her parlor were covered with portraits of suffragists—and when she asked her guests to identify them, "they couldn't name a single one."[83]

Forgetting happened in mainline churches too. Feminists there had living predecessors, churchwomen who had won ordination battles in the 1950s, studied theology, and made transatlantic alliances that changed the course of the ecumenical movement. That earlier generation had done so believing, sometimes simply hoping, that they were institutional insiders. In a sense, they might be tagged as religious elites, women married to influential men or exceptionally independent and talented on their own. But they represented a genuinely grassroots movement of socially progressive women in local churches, many adventurous enough to forge interracial friendships, and train themselves for leadership.

Perhaps the difference simply came down to attitude, one group committed to an ethic of cooperation and another prepared for conflict. "[W]hen I speak to women," said Peggy Way in 1968, then a social welfare consultant with the Chicago City Mission Society, "I am addressing them NOT as church women or as women organized into women's work in the Church. I am speaking to you as persons, who happen to be female." The churchwomen who had so long devoted themselves to tasks of institutional upkeep were, to Way, little more than custodians of a "museum filled with relics of a passing age."[84] To feminists coming of age in the 1970s, the older generation looked like enablers, women who had maintained a status quo by appeasing men in power, the female counterpart of the "organization man." And in many cases they were right.

The error was assuming that they were not angry.

Cynthia Wedel, Courtesy Presbyterian Historical Society, Philadelphia, PA.

PORTRAIT

Cynthia Wedel and the Limits of Cooperation

It's possible that Cynthia Wedel was incandescently angry in 1969 as she sat locked in a Detroit hotel room, on the verge of a career-topping success. She was about to become the first woman president of the National Council of Churches (NCC), the "highest symbolic post in American Protestantism," according to the *New York Times*.[1] But she had been kidnapped—her word— by rival forces. The National Committee of Black Churchmen opposed her candidacy and nominated Albert Cleage, pastor of Detroit's Shrine of the Black Madonna, for the post. This was the first time a slate of nominees had ever been challenged. At a luncheon reception Cleage had "forcefully urged" Wedel to withdraw, "declaring that the women's liberation movement must not stand in the way of the black liberation movement."[2] When Wedel refused, as she later confided in a private interview, a group of Black churchmen "kidnapped" her and "locked me in a room at the hotel and said they would not release me until I agreed to withdraw my name." Wedel stood firm, she said, because she had agreed to run "and would not go back on my promise." After an "uncomfortable and tough time," she was finally released, on the condition that she engage in a public debate with Cleage, which she did. And she won in the end, 387 votes to Cleage's 93.[3]

The whole meeting had been emotionally painful, not just for Wedel but likely everyone who attended. Alan Geyer, reporting for the *Christian Century*, was frustrated beyond measure, denouncing the proceedings as "an almost insufferable orgy of confusion." "The ecumenical and denominational establishments have suffered five days of severe shock from which they can recover only through deliberately courting more pain and trouble."[4] To others it was nothing short of an uprising, as a host of angry constituents— African Americans, but also "other ethnic minorities, women, youth, [and] laymen (especially wage earners)"—vented their rage on the "white over 40s" who had, until that moment, run the NCC and, for all intents and purposes, the ecumenical movement itself.[5]

To an older generation on the defensive, the assembly was simply bizarre. Suddenly they were no longer earnest do-gooders, but variously charged with "racism, militarism, materialism, legalism, hypocrisy, heresy, cowardice, deceit and other gross failings." Their introduction to 1960s-style Guerrilla Theater was Jonathan's Wake, a merry band of pranksters who marched a coffin through the proceedings, declaring the death of establishment religion. When a resolution against the police failed to carry, one protester ran through the hall crying, "Crucify me! Crucify me!" Another doused the speakers' table with a can of red paint after the NCC voted against shielding a draft resister, "covering papers and folders and splattering the presiding officers." The "joy box" sponsored by Aquarius-Age Episcopalians only added to the dislocation, a dark, curtained cubicle containing a mélange of colored flashing lights, bells, gongs, and other "sensation-producing devices."[6]

In any other year, Cynthia Wedel's election would have been assured. She was the first woman to become an associate general secretary of the NCC, where she took charge of ecumenical relationships. The *New York Times* marveled at her ability "to hold her own in dealings with the all-male hierarchy of the Roman Catholic Church." She had also served as president of UCW from 1955 to 1958, and held major positions in the Red Cross, the Episcopal Church, her home denomination, and the World Council of Churches. President John F. Kennedy appointed her to his Commission on the Status of Women. If that were not enough, Wedel also held a PhD in psychology, and in 1969 was associate director of the Center for Voluntarism of the Institute for Applied Behavior Sciences, the organization that pioneered sensitivity training. Not least, her husband Theodore Wedel was dean of the College of Preachers at the National Cathedral in Washington, DC.[7]

She was also proud of her track record on race. Wedel's first involvement with UCW was as chair of the committee on Christian Social Relations, where she led pioneering work for integration in the 1940s. "I have all kinds of delightful memories," she told an interviewer in 1972, "of going to totally illegal interracial meetings in Mississippi and South Carolina," which "church women just quietly held without telling anybody." As UCW president in the late 1950s, Wedel led an organization at the forefront of an emerging national awareness of racial injustice. UCW sponsored workshops around the country in the wake of the 1954 *Brown v. Board of Education* Supreme Court ruling, with the assistance of a major grant from the Fund for the Republic in

1957. In 1960 additional funding led to the creation of Assignment: RACE, the first large-scale religious effort toward racial integration, involving some twelve million church women in thirty-four states. CWU had criticized the Black Manifesto for its "lack of concern for women disadvantaged by poverty" and the sexism in Black denominations, but clearly supported the document's intent. After her election in 1969, she even had kind words for Cleage, declaring him "brilliant" and praising the Manifesto's "honesty."[8]

We might even call Wedel a feminist. After her election, she announced that though she deplored "discrimination against black people," she believed that women were also "victims" of prejudice. Her election, she said, was "a belated recognition of their importance in the church."[9] As CWU president she had taken on the issue of women's employment, and directly advocated for equality in the churches, including the right to ordination.[10]

Yet she was still a woman of an earlier era, admired for her poise and personal grooming more than her moral and intellectual fortitude. According to one admirer, this "slim, attractive, auburn-haired dynamo" effortlessly managed eighteen-hour days filled with speaking engagements and thousands of miles of travel. She even did her own housework—or most of it. When Wedel retired from her UCW presidency, friends and colleagues praised her "dynamic casualness and naturalness," her "simplicity, humility, and warm sincerity," and "warmth that comes from one who is at home with people," her ability to lead "with tact, understanding, and discernment worthy of an expert in group dynamics."[11]

They were actually praising Wedel's abiding faith in the power of cooperation. She had represented the Episcopal Church in the WCC Department on the Cooperation of Men and Women and consistently advocated for consensus and conciliation. In 1958 she received a Togetherness Award from *McCall's* magazine. Wedel had also led UCW during the difficult years as part of the NCC, later admitting that the strength of that conviction had made it difficult to understand the conflict, "because there was perfectly good will on both sides." The "eagerness to be cooperative and to go in as a part of the NCC," she said, meant overlooking "the fact that we were different."[12]

Once she was NCC president, Wedel continued her low-key style, encouraging the press to call her "Cynthia." She stood up with the other women delegates at the Assembly in support for "woman power," but was "not terribly militant about that cause." "Possibly because she is a woman," one reporter concluded, "Mrs. Wedel can get away with much stronger statements on issues than most male ecclesiastics dare make." But she courted her opponents with "so much enthusiasm, charm and humor" that "people wind up being grateful to her without quite knowing why."[13]

Cynthia Wedel's moment of triumph was actually the passing of an era. The center of gravity was moving on, beyond her direct influence. The same year that she was elected NCC president, feminists formed a Women's Caucus. Peggy Billings read a public manifesto, as one hundred women rose in support. The statement declared solidarity with African American protest, declaring a direct parallel between the "erratic swellings of outrage" from both groups, a similarity that was "both understandable and also extraordinary." Statistic after statistic on salary figures and board memberships confirmed the NCC's commitment to sexism—and feminists' intention to change everything. "Many times," the statement read, "evidence such as the above is turned aside by the reminder that, after all, women do comprise a numerical majority in the churches." That argument no longer worked: it was finally time for women to "exercise the prerogative" of their greater numbers. "We must do this."[14]

And they did. In the years ahead feminists made a deep impact on the NCC, and in the mainline Protestant world, as women's caucuses formed in all the major denominations. In 1974 Claire Randall was elected to the NCC's highest post, as general secretary. "There is a new kind of woman emerging in the church," she declared in a 1972 report. "An increasing number of women with varying interests, many backgrounds, old and young are working to free themselves, internally and externally from centuries of limitations to a new sense of identity, a new sense of the validity of their insights and Christian experience and of their ability to contribute to the main stream of the church's life." This is Pentecost, said Randall, when the "formerly scattered, isolated, obscure, and unheard" found a "new language and strange speech." "Whatever the institutional church may or may not decide shall be the place women shall have in structures," she declared, "the Spirit is alive and well among women of the church and they are, therefore, on the move."[15]

What role in this new movement was there for a woman who "escapes all the 'isms,'" as one admirer described her?[16] Did Cynthia Wedel watch the formation of the NCC Women's Caucus with joy or regret? Did she recognize all that the Protestant churches—and she herself—we gaining and also losing? For many reasons, most of which we will never know, she did not say.

Afterword

Stubborn, Unlaid Ghosts

Everyone was afraid of Ann Hibbins. It wasn't just because her husband was one of the most powerful men in the Massachusetts Bay colony, a wealthy merchant and member of the Court of Assistants, its highest governing body. And it wasn't just because she was argumentative and stubborn, though that reputation was well deserved: even the saints at Boston's First Church had thrown up their collective hands and excommunicated her. Ann Hibbins scared people because she was deeply, constantly, excessively angry. And therefore, she was more than likely a witch.

In colonial New England, and around the world, witches came in different shapes and sizes. Some were young, some were old, a considerable number were male. Some were wealthy and some were poor. All of them, though, were angry, possessed by "malice and envy," to use the seventeenth-century term. The quintessential witch, as historian John Demos describes her, was driven by "deeply-rooted, intensely negative feeling." Jealous wrath was her "emotional wellspring."[1]

Angry women are nothing new, of course. They have been raging up and down the hallways of history for a long time now. They are the twentieth-century suffragists who chained themselves to fences in front of the White House and then went on hunger strikes in prison, too furious to eat. They were scientists denied credit for their discoveries, novelists forced to write under assumed names; poisoners and plotters and revolutionaries. No wonder that the angry woman stereotype stuck so fast to feminists, tagged as repellant "man-haters" when they rejected the advertisers' ideal, burning their bras and refusing to shave their body hair.

There's just so much mystery. "Multiple experiments reveal," one commentator writes, "that an angry woman's face is one of the most difficult for people to parse."[2] Religion only makes things more complicated: female rage becomes wrath. The secular anger of women who have been historically underpaid, politically disenfranchised, and sexually exploited, is a justified

Good and Mad. Margaret Bendroth, Oxford University Press. © Oxford University Press 2023.
DOI: 10.1093/oso/9780197654064.003.0011

response to injustice. Male chauvinists can accept or minimize the data, but they can't deny it. But witches are a different story, women angry enough to consort with the Devil, unhinged enough to transgress every known moral boundary. When Ann Hibbins's powerful husband died, her fellow Bostonians promptly hung her for witchcraft. She was not just a social irritant, she was a threat to the community—literally a mad woman.

What happened to the danger in the twentieth century? Did churchwomen ever become angry? In all the pages of this book, up to this one, we have seen them protesting and working to effect change, but mostly by preaching cooperation and avoiding confrontation. They had to have understood what was going on, even been furious beyond measure at being belittled, patronized, and ignored. Who would not seethe over years of education and talents wasted, while feckless male bureaucrats rose through the ranks, acting as if they had earned every silly promotion? Somehow these churchwomen were too canny, too repressed, too loyal, or too artful to make more than a mild fuss.

So a short epilogue is necessary. It's relatively easy to track rebellion among the spiritually unconventional, the outspoken women who demanded what they knew was theirs. And, it's a fairly short leap to conclude that an angry woman must be a feminist, even if just in the making. But well-behaved women make history too, if only to define the boundaries that others will one day transgress. And they have stories of their own that need to be told, in all their historical and emotional complexity.

Churchwomen's anger is hard to see. A Congregationalist, writing in 1953, borrowed a phrase from the puritan poet John Milton, describing gender inequality as a "stubborn, unlaid ghost" who breaks his "magic chains at curfew time," and sets out to terrorize.[3] It is an apt metaphor, and not just because it evokes the supernatural fears that brought so many women to stakes and gibbets. An unlaid ghost is both real and not real, probably not capable of doing anyone any harm, but can you be sure? Perhaps the worst outcome would be a few broken dishes, some kitchen cupboards left inexplicably ajar. Or in another case the specter might be bent on revenge, perfectly capable of bringing down the entire house. The frustration and fury of religious women "lurk[s] in the background like ghosts of a past that has been abandoned," writes Roman Catholic feminist Carol Osiek. The ghosts lie in wait in the basement, chained to the wall, for "once they get out, they wreak havoc on a tightly-controlled upper story."[4]

How do we understand that anger? It is not the fury of the oppressed, not open rage at injustice, says Osiek. The anger of churchwomen sometimes searches for its object, groping for clarity in a fog of misdirection. It is directed at rules that do not make practical sense for anyone, male or female, but somehow maintain their power. It comes to those who have arduously supported church institutions that "would be forced to face its need for reform much more quickly if they simply abandoned it."[5] It's the underside of loyalty—to God, to church, to husband or friends. Loyal churchwomen knew the open secret, that the church, at least in its everyday business, was female, and men at times window-dressing. "For believe or not," a canny Methodist wrote in 1946, "the mind of man fears the power of woman, though it covers fear with mighty thunderings. Woman does not fear man; she only resents— that is 'feels indignant displeasure at'—him!"[6]

Mainline Protestant rage—or the lack of it—is also a function of privilege, a sign of social class that is certainly not unique to religious organizations. "The real entitlement has never been anger," Leslie Jamison writes; "it has always been its absence." Refusing rage is a "luxury" most often reserved for the economically at ease, the culturally comfortable.[7] We should remember that before the 1960s, before *The Feminine Mystique* fundamentally altered middle-class perceptions, women were not a minority group. A few sociologists, writing against the background of an emerging civil rights movement, considered that surprising. Gunnar Myrdal included a brief appendix to his magisterial study of *An American Dilemma*, musing about parallels between race and gender, their common source in a "paternalistic order of society." Both groups labored under patriarchal assumptions, for African Americans that they were "unassimilable," and for women "the function of procreation," the eternal disability of fertility. Sociologist Helen Mayer Hacker, writing in 1951, wondered why women could not see what was as plain as day. Just like any other minority, they were excluded from decent-paying jobs and then subjected to "ceaseless propaganda" reminding them why they deserved unequal treatment. The "marginal woman" suffered the same "psychological ravages of instability, conflict, self-hate, anxiety, and resentment."[8] Unlike African Americans, however, women were not rising up; the conflict was there, but sublimated into low-grade emotional warfare. The "dissociative process between the sexes," said Hacker, included mostly "rebuffing, repulsing, working against, hindering, protesting, obstructing, restraining, and upsetting another's plans."

We could also say, though, that this behavior signals a certain kind of hope, belief in the power of persistence. As we have seen Protestant churchwomen were acutely attuned to the dynamics of social institutions, in a way that most of us have lost. They had a knowledge of how those institutions worked, and why they were so hard to change. They lived in a world where it was better to be smart and at least outwardly loyal—to persist in fact—than to rail. In our world, on the other side of the 1960s, their doggedness looks like repression, their cooperation like capitulation. So much of their emotional language is familiar: they were white, middle-class Protestants, kind of like me, but it's a dialect, an inflection, that is difficult to understand in retrospect.

I remember being surprised, many years ago, when I made my first presentation about women and fundamentalism to a small group of male colleagues. The experience was nerve-wracking enough for a young, female scholar, but the question that stumped me was one I should have anticipated but had not: Given all the nasty things fundamentalist men said about women, why in the world would any self-respecting female go anywhere near one of their churches?

Looking back, I am beginning to understand why I did not ask that question myself. It just never occurred to me. Like so many women, particularly those with young children, I had learned to bracket out negativity. Every day I had to maintain my emotional balance in impossible situations. There is no "win/win" when a toddler is melting down in the produce aisle—you cut your losses and head for the cashier. That peculiar mortification of the flesh had become so second-nature that I barely recognized it, an inner discipline that would go on to shape life decisions without much awareness on my part. What's interesting in retrospect is that it took a man to pose the "why" question, to recognize and call out the sheer effrontery of the fundamentalist men I was writing about. Why would anyone stand for that?

Women do, of course, and all the time. We simply fail to recognize that patience is not the same as capitulation and cooperation does not rule out anger over injustice. The problem is our one-dimensional vocabulary, the way we assume that the purpose of anger is to separate the one from the many, that it is a refusal to conform, a rejection of rules. I hope this book has shown, however, that even the behavers get us somewhere. Despite their flaws and deficiencies, their missed opportunities and limitations, they made history.

Notes

Introduction

1. "Religion" is absent or tied to patriarchy in the indexes of two major compendiums, i.e., Ruth Rosen, *The World Split Open: How the Modern Women's Movement Changed America* (New York: Penguin Books, 2001), and Estelle Friedman, *No Turning Back: The History of Feminism and the Future of Women* (New York: Ballantine Books, 2002). More focused histories are similarly thin, e.g., Rosalind Rosenberg, *Divided Lives: American Women in the Twentieth Century* (New York: Hill and Wang, 1992); S. J. Kleinberg, *Women in the United States, 1830–1945* (New Brunswick, NJ: Rutgers University Press, 1999). William Chafe, *The Paradox of Change: American Women in the Twentieth Century* (New York: Oxford University Press, 1991) does not even have an entry for "religion" in the index.
2. Rosen, *The World Split Open*, xiii.
3. Daniel Horowitz, *Betty Friedan and the Making of the Feminine Mystique: The American Left, the Cold War, and Modern Feminism* (Amherst: University of Massachusetts Press, 1998).
4. "Mrs. Fred Bennett, A Church Worker, 85," *New York Times* April 12, 1950. Her first name was Mary Katherine.
5. "Thelma Stevens, Social Worker, 88," *New York Times* December 19, 1990, D21, https://www.nytimes.com/1990/12/19/obituaries/thelma-stevens-social-worker-88.html, accessed November 12, 2020. On the secularity of twentieth-century history, see Jon Butler, "Jack-in-the-Box Faith: The Religion Problem in Modern American History," *Journal of American History* 90 (March 2004): 1357–1378.
6. Ann Braude, "Women's History *Is* American Religious History," in *Re-Telling U.S. Religious History*, ed. Thomas Tweed (Berkeley: University of California Press, 1997), 107.
7. The literature on the twentieth-century mainline is large and growing. See, for example, William Hutchison, ed. *Between the Times: The Travail of the Protestant Establishment, 1900–1960* (Cambridge: Cambridge University Press, 1989); David Hollinger, *After Cloven Tongue of Fire: Protestant Liberalism in Modern American History* (Princeton, NJ: Princeton University Press, 2012); Elesha Coffman, *The Christian Century and the Rise of the Protestant Mainline* (New York: Oxford University Press, 2013).
8. I refer to the mainline as "liberal," in the theological rather than political sense, and even though these denominations were by no means uniform in belief or behavior. Theologically they ranged from moderate to liberal on key issues like the authority of the Bible or the exclusivity of Christianity, with considerable debate and variety in

between. The term is useful still to distinguish mainline churches from evangelicals and fundamentalists. "Ecumenical" is another useful description, coming increasingly into use, and another way of distinguishing cosmopolitan and culturally sensitive mainliners from separatist, sectarian evangelicals. Regretfully, I have not used it, largely to avoid confusion as so much of this narrative deals with the actual ecumenical movement—the institutional and theological structures that created the World Council of Churches.

9. See, for example, Peter Dobkin Hall, "The Rise of the Civic Engagement Tradition," in *Taking Faith Seriously*, ed. Mary Jo Bane, Brent Coffin, and Richard Higgins (Cambridge, MA: Harvard University Press, 2005), 21–59. In that respect this narrative follows the larger arc of the twentieth century recently described by sociologist Robert Putnam, charting a steep rise of civic engagement from the World War I era through the 1950s, and then a sharp decline in the mid-1960s and 1970s. Putnam calls this the "I-we-I" of American history, a U-shaped curve that reflects the success of the early-twentieth century Progressive movement and the New Deal in decreasing economic inequality and political tribalism, and then the erosion of that success in the past several decades. Mainline Protestant churchwomen clearly shared, and benefited from that that mid-century communitarian ethos—and struggled to adapt to the individualism of the post-1960s world. See Robert Putnam, with Shaylyn Romney Garrett, *The Upswing: How American Came Together a Century Ago and How We Can Do It Again* (New York: Simon and Schuster, 2020).

10. Take, for example, recent statistics on racial attitudes, where mainliners are more similar to evangelicals than to secularists. Only 9 percent of mainline Protestants attend racially diverse congregations, compared to 16 percent of evangelicals. Both groups are majority Republican, far more similar to each in social and political attitudes than to African American Protestants. See Robert Jones, *White Too Long: The Legacy of White Supremacy in American Christianity* (New York: Simon and Schuster, 2020), 174. See also Robert Putnam and David Campbell, *American Grace: How Religion Divides and Unites Us* (New York: Simon and Schuster, 2010), 257, 274, 292. On mainline and evangelical versus African American beliefs and practices, see Pew Research Center, "America's Changing Religious Landscape," May 12, 2015, https://www.pewforum.org/2015/05/12/americas-changing-religious-landscape/

11. For a useful overview, see David Kling, *The Bible in History: How the Texts Have Shaped the Times* (New York: Oxford University Press, 204), 269–308.

12. Dana Robert, *American Women in Mission: The Modern Mission Era, 1792–1992* (Macon, GA: Mercer University Press, 1996), and *Gospel Bearers, Gender Barriers: Missionary Women in the Twentieth Century* (Maryknoll, NY: Orbis Books, 2002); Kathryn Kish Sklar and Connie Shemo, eds., *Competing Kingdoms: Women, Mission, Nation, and the American Protestant Empire, 1812–1960* (Durham, NC: Duke University Press, 2010).

13. Willard, *Woman in the Pulpit* (Boston: Woman's Christian Temperance Union, 1888), 39.

14. Braude, "Women's History *Is* American Religious History," 94.

15. See US Bureau of the Census, *Religious Bodies, 1906*, 2 vols. (Washington, DC, 1906), https://www.thearda.com/Archive/Files/Descriptions/1906CENSCT.asp; H. K. Carroll, *The Religious Forces of the United States* (New York: 1912), lvii–lvix; US Bureau of the Census, *Religious Bodies: 1916* (Washington, D.C., 1919), 40–42; US Bureau of the Census, *Religious Bodies: 1936*, Vol. 1 (Washington, DC, 1941), 23, 451f; also Luther Fry, *The United States Looks at Its Churches* (New York: Institute of Social and Religious Research, 1930), 14, 24.

16. Sarah Imhoff, "The Myth of Jewish Feminization," *Jewish Social Studies: History, Culture, Society* n.s. 21 (Spring/Summer 2016): 134.

17. Ann Douglas, *The Feminization of American Culture* (New York: Avon Books, 1977), 327, passim. Also Barbara Welter, "The Feminization of American Religion, 1800–1860," in *Dimity Convictions* (Athens: Ohio University Press, 1976), 137–152.

18. For example, the charge that late-nineteenth-century American religion lapsed into "effeminacy and infantilism" in William Clebsch, *From Sacred to Profane America: The Role of Religion in American History* (New York: Harper and Row, 1968), 102–103. On critiques of feminization, see, for example, David Schuyler, "Inventing a Feminine Past," *New England Quarterly* 51 (September 1978): 291–308; David S. Reynolds, "The Feminization Controversy: Sexual Stereotypes and the Paradoxes of Piety in Nineteenth-Century America," *New England Quarterly* 53 (March 1980): 96–106. For more recent and thorough analysis, see Jan De Maeyer et al., eds., *Gender and Christianity in Modern Europe: Beyond the Feminization Thesis* (Leuven, Belgium: Leuven University Press, 2012).

19. Callum Brown, *The Death of Christian Britain: Understanding Secularisation, 1800–2000* (London: Routledge, 2001), 192.

20. Rod Dreher, "The Feminization (and Decline) of Religion," *American Conservative* April 2, 2018, https://theamericanconservative.com/dreher/the-feminization-and-decline-of-religion/ Accessed January 3, 2021. Dreher was discussing Leon Podles often referenced book, *The Church Impotent: The Feminization of Christianity* (Dallas: Spence Publications, 1999).

21. Virginia Lieson Breton, "United and Slighted: Women as Subordinated Insiders," in Hutchison, *Between the Times*, 143–167.

Chapter 1

1. Zephine Humphrey, "The Modern Woman's Home: Recording Some Doubts and Questions," *Woman Citizen* 11 (June 1926): 22.

2. Alice Beal Parsons, *Woman's Dilemma* (New York: Thomas Crowell, 1926), 34.

3. Review by Eyler Newton Simpson, *American Journal of Sociology* 32 (November 1926): 510.

4. Humphrey, "The Modern Woman's Home," 22.

5. Horace Bushnell, *Women's Suffrage: The Reform against Nature* (New York: Charles Scribner and Co., 1869), 67.

6. Cited in Christine Stansell, *American Moderns: Bohemian New York and the Creation of a New Century* (New York: Metropolitan Books/Henry Holt and Co., 2000), 247.

7. Kenneth Rose, *American Women and the Repeal of Prohibition* (New York: New York University Press, 1996), 9, 75.

8. Zephine Humphrey, *God and Company* (New York: Harper and Brothers, 1953), 5.

9. Zephine Humphrey, *The Sword of the Spirit* (New York: E.P. Dutton, 1920); 294, 295.

10. The literature is vast and impossible to summarize, but for a representative sample, see Steven Bruce, *Secularization: In Defence of an Unfashionable Theory* (New York: Oxford University Press, 2011); Brad Gregory, *The Unintended Revolution: How a Religious Revolution Secularized Society* (Cambridge, MA: Harvard University Press, 2012); Christian Smith, ed. *The Secular Revolution: Power, Interest, Conflicts in the Secularization of American Life* (Berkeley: University of California Press, 2003); Charles Taylor, *A Secular Age* (Cambridge, MA: Harvard University Press, 2007); David Martin, *On Secularization: Towards a Revised General Theory* (London: Ashgate Publishing, 2005); Talal Asad, *Formations of the Secular: Christianity, Islam, Modernity* (Stanford, CA: Stanford University Press, 2003).

11. Ann Braude, "Women's History *Is* American Religious History," in *Re-Telling U.S. Religious History*, ed. Thomas Tweed (Berkeley: University of California Press, 1997), 87–107; Rita Felski, *The Gender of Modernity* (Cambridge, MA: Harvard University Press, 1995), 2, 15, 18. See also Virginia Brereton and Margaret Bendroth, "Secularization and Gender: An Historical Approach to Women and Religion in the Twentieth Century," *Method and Theory in the Study of Religion* 13 (2001): 209–223; Harry S. Stout and Catherine Brekus, "Declension, Gender, and the 'New Religious History,'" in *Belief and Behavior: Essays in the New Religious History*, ed. P. Vandemeer and R. Swierenga (New Brunswick, NJ: Rutgers University Press, 1991), 15–37; Linda Woodhead, "Gendering Secularization Theory," *Social Compass* 55 (1982): 187–192; Anne Phillips, "Gender and Modernity," *Political Theory* (2018), https://doi.org/10.1177/009059171875747, accessed November 13, 2020.

12. "What Shall Be Done with the Women?" *Christian Century* April 1, 1920, 6.

13. Lester Ward, *Dynamic Sociology* (New York: D. Appleton and Company, 1883), 2:23, cited in James Turner, *Without God, without Creed: The Origins of Unbelief in America* (Baltimore: Johns Hopkins University Press, 1985), 235.

14. Joint Committee of the Council of Women for Home Missions, Federation of Woman's Boards for Foreign Missions of North America, and the Federal Council of the Churches of Christ in America, *The Relative Place of Women in the Church* (New York: Federal Council of Churches, 1927); Elizabeth Wilson, "Is There a Last Analysis?" *Christian Century* May 1, 1929, 580–582.

15. Ella A. Boole, "May Women Speak?" *Federal Council Bulletin* October 1929, 11.

16. "Women and the Church," *Federal Council Bulletin* April 1929, 2.

17. Mila Frances Tupper, "Present Status of Women in the Church," and Kate Tannatt Woods, "Women in the Pulpit," both in *Transactions of the National Council of Women of the United States, Assembled in Washington, D.C., February 22 to 25, 1891*, ed. Rachel Foster Avery (Philadelphia: J.B. Lippincott, 1891), 105, 287.

18. Carolyn Walker Bynum, *Fragmentation and Redemption: Essays on Gender and the Human Body in Medieval Religion* (New York: Zone Books, 1991), 206.

19. Thomas Laquer, *Making Sex: Body and Gender from the Greeks to Freud* (Cambridge, MA: Harvard University Press, 1990), 62.

20. Denise Riley, *"Am I That Name?" Feminism and the Category of "Women" in History* (Minneapolis: University of Minnesota Press, 1988), 43.

21. Marilyn Chapin Massey, *Feminine Soul: The Fate of an Ideal* (Boston: Beacon Press, 1985), 39f.

22. Karen Halttunen, *Confidence Men and Painted Women: A Study of Middle-Class Culture, 1830–1870* (New Haven, CT: Yale University Press, 1982); John F. Kasson, *Rudeness and Civility: Manners in Nineteenth-Century Urban America* (New York: Hill and Wang, 1990).

23. Justin Dewey Fulton, *Woman as God Made Her; The True Woman* (Boston: Lee and Shepherd, 1869), 226.

24. Bushnell, *Women's Suffrage, the Reform against Nature* (New York: Charles Scribner and Co., 1869), 57.

25. *"Because They Are Women" and Other Editorials from "The Christian Advocate" on the Admission of Women to the General Conference* (New York: Hunt and Eaton, 1891), 26.

26. Bushnell, *Women's Suffrage*, 51.

27. Fulton, *Woman as God Made Her*, 99.

28. Quoted in Evelyn Kirkley, *Rational Mothers and Infidel Gentlemen: Gender and American Atheism, 1865–1915* (Syracuse, NY: University of Syracuse Press, 2000), 33.

29. Maureen Fitzgerald, "Losing Their Religion: Women, the State, and the Ascension of Secular Discourse," in *Women and Twentieth-Century Protestantism*, ed. Margaret Bendroth and Virginia Brereton (Urbana: University of Illinois Press, 2005), 281.

30. Karen Cox, *Dixie's Daughters: The United Daughters of the Confederacy and the Preservation of Confederate Culture* (Tallahassee: University of Florida Press, 2019); Gail Bederman, *Manliness and Civilization: A Cultural History of Gender and Race in the United States, 1880–1917* (Chicago: University of Chicago Press, 1995).

31. George A. Coe, *The Spiritual Life: Studies in the Science of Religion* (New York: Eaton and Mains, 1900), 239, 237, 238.

32. Edwin Starbuck, *The Psychology of Religion: An Empirical Study of the Growth of Religious Consciousness* (New York: Charles Scribner's Sons, 1899), 53; James Leuba, *The Belief in God and Immortality: A Psychological, Anthropological, and Statistical Study* (Chicago: Open Court, 1916), 186, 201, 283–284.

33. William T. Ellis, *"Billy" Sunday: The Man and His Message* (Philadelphia: John C. Winston, Co., 1914), 28. On fundamentalism, see Margaret Bendroth, *Fundamentalism and Gender, 1875 to the Present* (New Haven, CT: Yale University Press, 1993).

34. Arno C. Gaebelein, "The March of Emancipation," *Our Hope* 28 (November 1921): 304; "God's Word on Femininity," *Moody Bible Institute Monthly* 31 (June 1931): 486; E. Myers Knoth, "Women's Rebellion and Its Consequences," *Moody Bible Institute Monthly* 34 (October 1933): 55.

35. "Woman Suffrage," *Watchman* 7 (March 1895): 2.

36. Bendroth, *Fundamentalism and Gender*, 54–72; William Bell Riley, "She-Men, or How Some Become Sissies," Sermon preached at First Baptist Church, Minneapolis, MN, September 30, 1934, William Bell Riley Papers, Northwestern College, Minneapolis.

37. Kirchwey, "Introduction," to *Our Changing Morality: A Symposium*, ed. Freda Kirchwey (New York: Albert and Charles Boni Inc., 1924), v, viii–ix.

38. Winifred Starr Dobyns, quoted in Rose, *American Women and the Repeal of Prohibition*, 36. See also Barbara Burrell, *Women and Political Participation: A Reference Handbook* (Santa Barbara, CA: ABC-CLIO, 2004); Sandra Baxter and Marjorie Lansing, eds., *Women and Politics: The Visible Majority*, rev. ed. (Ann Arbor: University of Michigan Press, 1983).

39. Marguerite M. Wells, "Some Effects of Woman Suffrage," *Annals of the Academy of Political and Social Science* 143 (May 1929): 208.

40. Elizabeth Cady Stanton, "The Solitude of Self," in *Elizabeth Cady Stanton/ Susan B. Anthony: Correspondence, Writings, Speeches*, ed. Ellen Carol DuBois (New York: Schocken Books, 1981), 248.

41. Virginia Woolf, *A Room of One's Own* (London: Harcourt, Inc., 1929), 35, 111.

42. Elaine Showalter, ed. *These Modern Women: Autobiographical Essays from the Twenties* (New York: Feminist Press, 1970, 1989), 107, 44, 62.

43. Scotford, "The Church and the Feminine Emotions," *Congregationalist* April 16, 1922, 504.

44. "Woman Shakes Fist in Bishop's Face," *New York Times* May 9, 1924.

45. Rhoda McCulloch, *The War and the Woman Point of View* (New York: Association Press, 1920), 12, 15, 27, 30.

46. To name a few, M. M. Underhill, "Women's Work for Missions: Three Home Base Studies," *International Review of Missions* 14 (July 1925): 379–399; *The Place of Women in the Church on the Mission Field* (New York: International Missionary Council, 1927); "Report on the Official Relation of Women in the Church" (1920), and "Women's Service in the Church" (1930) RG 125-702, PHS; "Women in the Ministry" (1938), which included questionnaires to 20 denominations (NCC RG 27 Box 11-2, PHS); "Women's Status in Protestant Churches," *Information Service* November 16, 1940, 1–12; Inez Cavert, *Women in American Church Life: A Study Prepared under the Guidance of a Counseling Committee of Women Representing National Interdenominational Agencies* (New York: Friendship Press for the FCC, 1948); "Status of Women in the American Baptist Convention," 1953–54 American Baptist Women's Ministries RG 25 Box 21, ABHS.

Portrait: Helen Barrett Montgomery's Bittersweet Missionary Jubilee

1. See Kendal Mobley, *Helen Barrett Montgomery: The Global Mission of Domestic Feminism* (Waco, TX: Baylor University Press, 2009); Louise Armstrong Cattan, *Lamps Are for Lighting: The Story of Helen Barrett Montgomery and Lucy Waterbury Peabody* (Grand Rapids, MI: William B. Eerdmans, 1972); *Helen Barrett Montgomery,*

From Campus to World Citizenship (New York: Fleming H. Revell, 1940); William H. Brackney, "The Legacy of Helen B. Montgomery and Lucy W. Peabody," *International Bulletin of Missionary Research* (October 1991): 174–178; Conda Delite Hitch Abbott, *Envoy of Grace: The Life of Helen Barrett Montgomery* (Valley Forge, PA: American Baptist Historical Society, 1997).

2. "The Great Ecumenical Conference on Foreign Missions in New York City," *Missionary Review of the World* 13 (June 1900), 403.

3. Waterbury quoted in Alice M. Kyle, "Woman's Day at the Ecumenical Conference," *Light and Life for Woman* 30 (June 1900): 268. Married to Norman Waterbury in 1881 and widowed in 1886, she married Henry Peabody in 1906, and was widowed again in 1908.

4. Kyle, "Woman's Day," 269.

5. *Ecumenical Missionary Conference, New York, 1900, Vol. 1* (New York: American Tract Society, 1900), 215–217.

6. *Ecumenical Missionary Conference*, 216; *Foreign Missions Conference of North America, Being the Report of the Twenty-Seventh Conference of Foreign Mission Boards in the United States and Canada* (New York: Foreign Missions Conference, 1920), 128–129.

7. The Council of Women for Home Missions united the work of twenty women's boards, and the Federation of Women's Boards for Foreign Missions twenty-seven women's boards and four interdenominational agencies. See "All That Is Past Is Prologue: The Emergence of Interdenominational Organizations among Protestant Church Women," ed. Mrs. Fred S. Bennett, Florence G. Tyler, Mrs. E. H. Goedeke (New York: United Council of Church Women, 1944), Church Women United Collection RG 1244-3-2:09 UMCA.

8. Dana Robert, "Introduction," in *Gospel Bearers, Gender Barriers: Missionary Women in the Twentieth Century*, ed. Dana Robert (Maryknoll, NY: Orbis Books, 2002), 5–6, 8.

9. Gale Kenny, "The World Day of Prayer: Ecumenical Churchwomen and Christian Cosmopolitanism, 1920–1946," *Religion and American Culture* 27 (2017): 129–158.

10. Mrs. Franklin Warner, "About Face—Women!" (Boston: Woman's Board of Missions, n.d.), 2, 3.

11. R. Pierce Beaver, *All Loves Excelling: American Protestant Women in Mission* (Grand Rapids, MI: William B. Eerdmans Publishing, 1968), 179, 180.

12. Cattan, *Lamps Are for Lighting*, 56–61; Mobley, *Helen Barrett Montgomery*, 212–213.

13. Cited in Cattan, *Lamps Are for Lighting*, 60.

14. Mobley, *Helen Barrett Montgomery*, 212–3; Helen Barrett Montgomery, *Western Women in Eastern Lands: An Outline Study of Fifty Years of Woman's Work in Foreign Missions* (New York: Macmillan Co., 1910), 243–244.

15. See account in *Helen Barrett Montgomery: From Campus to World Citizenship*, 95, 96.

16. Montgomery, *Western Women in Eastern Lands*, 268, 271.

17. Andrew F. Walls, *The Cross-Cultural Process in Christian History* (Maryknoll, NY: Orbis Books), 53. See https://fullerstudio.fuller.edu/the-edinburgh-missionary-conference-of-1910/, accessed August 14, 2021.

18. Brian Stanley, *The World Missionary Conference, Edinburgh 1910* (Grand Rapids, MI: Eerdmans 2009), 313.

19. "Problems of Administration: Relation of Women's Boards to General Church Societies," in *Report of Commission VI: The Home Base* (New York: Fleming H. Revell, 1910), 233, 234.

20. Minna Gollock, "The Share of Women in the Administration of Missions," *International Review of Missions* 1 (October 1912): 674.

21. Stanley, *The World Missionary Conference, Edinburgh 1910*, 315.

Chapter 2

1. Dana Robert, *American Women in Mission: A Social History of Their Thought and Practice* (Macon, GA: Mercer University Press, 1996), 302, 303.

2. Grant Wacker, "Second Thoughts on the Great Commission: Liberal Protestants and Foreign Missions," in *Earthen Vessels: American Evangelicals and Foreign Missions*, ed. Joel Carpenter and Wilbert Shenk (Grand Rapids, MI: Eerdmans, 1990), 292.

3. David Hollinger, *Protestants Abroad: How Missionaries Tried to Change the World but Changed America* (Princeton, NJ: Princeton University Press, 2017). The primary financial squeeze on missions came from debt service on building programs conducted in the early 1920s. See Charles Fahs, *Trends in Protestant Giving: A Study of Church Finance in the United States* (New York: Institute of Social and Religious Research, 1929), 64–67; James Hudnut-Beumler, *In Pursuit of the Almighty's Dollar: A History of Money and American Protestantism* (Chapel Hill: University of North Carolina Press, 2007), 98–99.

4. Hollinger, *Protestants Abroad*, 293.

5. Robert, *American Women in Mission*, 272.

6. "Status of Women in Churches on the Mission Field, Prepared by Mrs. Thomas Nicholson, as Chairman of an American Group," 10, Presbyterian Church in the U.S.A. Office of the Stated Clerk RG 125 6-21 PHS.

7. *The Place of Women in the Church on the Mission Field: Statements Prepared by Groups in North America, Great Britain, Germany, Netherlands, France, Switzerland, Denmark, Norway, Sweden, and Finland* (New York: International Missionary Council, 1927), 55.

8. *Re-Thinking Missions: A Laymen's Inquiry after One Hundred Years* (New York: Harper and Brothers, 1932), 263, 280, 281.

9. Maitland Alexander, "Lectures on Preaching," *Presbyterian* February 10, 1927, 7.

10. Grant Wacker, "Pearl S. Buck and the Waning of the Missionary Impulse," *Church History* 72 (December 2003): 852–874; Hollinger, *Protestants Abroad*, 33.

11. Dana Robert, "Introduction," to *Gospel Bearers, Gender Barriers*, ed. Dana Robert (Maryknoll, NY: Orbis Books, 2002), 10. Mergers and amalgamations proceeded differently across denominations. Northern Baptist women did not reorganize until the 1940s, for example. (See, for example Jewel M. Asbury, "A History of the Integration of the Woman's American Baptist Missionary Society and the American Baptist Home Missionary Society: A Case Study of the Oppression of Women" [MA Thesis: Colgate Rochester Divinity School, 1983]). Other women's groups were largely fundraising

auxiliaries, as in the Protestant Episcopal Church, and were largely unaffected. The name changes and institutional status of women's missionary and ecumenical organizations are byzantine. One of the best summaries is still Virginia Brereton and Christa Klein, "American Women in Ministry: A History of Protestant Beginning Points," in *Women of Spirit: Female Leadership in the Jewish and Christian Traditions*, ed. Rosemary Ruether and Eleanor McLaughlin (New York: Simon and Schuster, 1979), 302–332.

12. Bettye Collier-Thomas, *Jesus, Jobs, and Justice: African-American Women and Religion* (Philadelphia: Temple University Press, 2014), 165–168.

13. Angela Hornsby-Gutting, "'Women's Work': Foreign Missions, and Respectability in the National Training School for Women and Girls," *Journal of Women's History* 31 (Spring 2019): 41; "Statement Made by Miss Burroughs at the Close of her Annual Report to the Woman's Convention at St. Louis," 3, Nannie Helen Burroughs Papers Container 46 Speeches and Writings File, Manuscript Division, Library of Congress. See also Evelyn Brooks Higginbotham, *Righteous Discontent: The Woman's Movement in the Black Church, 1880–1920* (Cambridge, MA: Harvard University Press, 1994).

14. Paul Harvey, "Saints but Not Subordinates: The Woman's Missionary Union of the Southern Baptist Convention," in *Women and Twentieth-Century Protestantism*, 12, 13. The tendency in smaller evangelical and fundamentalist denominations was to eliminate or fail to organize separate women's groups. See Margaret Bendroth, "The Search for 'Women's Role' in American Evangelicalism, 1930–1980," in *Evangelicalism and Modern America*, ed. George Marsden (Grand Rapids: Eerdmans Publishing, 1984), 122–134.

15. Alfred D. Chandler, *The Visible Hand: The Managerial Revolution in American Business* (Cambridge, MA: Harvard University Press, 1977), 347, 348.

16. James H. Moorhead, "Presbyterians and the Mystique of Organizational Efficiency, 1870–1936," in *Reimagining Denominationalism*, ed. Robert Bruce Mullin and Russell E. Richey (New York: Oxford University Press, 1994), 266, 267.

17. See, for example, Conrad Wright, "The Growth of Denominational Bureaucracies: A Neglected Aspect of American Church History," *Harvard Theological Review* 77 (1984): 177–194.

18. Amanda Porterfield, *Corporate Spirit: Religion and the Rise of the Modern Corporation* (New York: Oxford University Press, 2018), 133.

19. "The Efficient Christian," *The Baptist* June 12, 1928, 662; Richard Jensen, "Democracy, Republicanism, and Efficiency: The Values of American Politics, 1885–1930," in *Contesting Democracy: Substance and Structure in American Political History, 1775–2000*, ed. Byron E. Shafer and Anthony J. Badger (Lawrence: University Press of Kansas, 2001), 159.

20. "The Proposed Merger," *Congregationalist* October 15, 1925, 5289.

21. *Proceedings of the 17th Annual Convention of the New York State Sunday School Teachers' Association Held at Norwich, June 19, 20, and 21, 1872* (Syracuse, 1872), 75; J. W. M'Lean, "Woman's Work in the Sunday School," *National Sunday School Teacher* 17 (1872): 14.

22. Helen Barrett Montgomery, *Western Women in Eastern Lands: An Outline Study of Fifty Years of Woman's Work in Foreign Missions* (New York: Macmillan, 1911),

269. See also Stephen Schmidt, *History of the Religious Education Association* (Birmingham, AL: Religious Education Association, 1983).

23. Lucy Peabody, "Woman's Place in Missions Fifty Years Ago and Now," *Missionary Review of the World* (December 1927), 909. Northern Baptist women remained primarily focused on missions until a reorganization in 1953, itself the result of a gradual process that begin in 1902. See Asbury, "A History of the Integration of the WABHMS and the ABHMS."

24. "Moving toward Mergers: The National Council Approves Reorganization," *Congregationalist* November 5, 1925, 626.

25. Quoted in Priscilla Stuckey-Kauffman, "Women's Mission Structures and the American Board," https://www.ucc.org/who-we-are/about/history/about-us_hidden-histories-2_womens_mission_structures_and_the_american_board/, accessed October 1, 2021.

26. *Journal of the Thirty-First Delegated General Conference of the Methodist Episcopal Church Held in Atlantic City, New Jersey, May 2–25, 1932* (New York: Methodist Book Concern, 1932), 1627. No numbers were recorded before that, however.

27. Christopher Schlect, "Onward Christian Administrators" (PhD diss.: Washington State University, 2015).

28. J. W. G. Ward, "Minister, Wife and Secretary," *Church Management* 14 (January 1938), 206, 207. The article was an anonymous letter sent to *Church Management*, and opened with the editor's explanation that it was a "puzzling ministerial problem," and also a "real one." "Seldom has a question of this kind been discussed in serious ministerial literature. We are glad to present it."

29. "As the Secretary Sees Them," *Church Management* 14 (April 1938), 382.

30. "The Minister's Wife," *Church Management* 13 (October 1936): 19.

31. James Moorhead, "Presbyterians and the Mystique of Organizational Efficiency, 1870–1936," in *Reimagining Denominationalism: Interpretive Essays* (New York: Oxford University Press, 1994), 264–287; Louis Weeks, "The Incorporation of American Religion: The Case of the Presbyterians," *Religion and American Culture: A Journal of Interpretation* 1 (Winter 1991): 101–118.

32. Katherine Bennett and Margaret Hodge, *Causes of Unrest among the Women of the Church: Report of a Special Committee to the General Council of the Presbyterian Church in the U.S.A.* (Philadelphia: Presbyterian Board of Publication, 1927), 11.

33. Notably, in 1928–29, the women contributed over $2.5M to the missionary budget, and only $2,230.11 to Christian education. See "Women's Service in the Church," 5, 3, 15, Presbyterian Church in the U.S.A. Office of the Stated Clerk RG 125 7–2 PHS. See Janet Harbison Penfield, "Women in the Presbyterian Church—A Historical Overview," *Journal of Presbyterian History* 55 (March 1976): 114; Elizabeth Howell Verdesi, *In But Still Out: Women in the Presbyterian Church* (Philadelphia: Westminster Press, 1976), Boyd and Brackenridge, *Presbyterian Women in America*, 59–63.

34. "The Special Committee on the Official Relation of Women in the Church," Presbyterian Church in the U.S.A. Office of the Stated Clerk RG 125 box 6-2, PHS; Daniel Williams, "Three Articles on Women Speaking in Church," *Presbyterian*

August 5, 1920, 7. See also B. B. Warfield, "Paul on Women Speaking in the Church," *Presbyterian* July 15, 1920, 8–9; Blanche Dickens-Lewis, "The Ordination of Women," *Presbyterian* October 7, 1920, 10.

35. Mrs. Max (Nellie) Aszman to Lucy H. Dawson August 10, 1922, Eugene Carson Blake Papers RG 121 box 7, PHS.

36. *Causes of Unrest*, 3.

37. *Causes of Unrest*, 26.

38. *Causes of Unrest*, 11.

39. *Causes of Unrest*, 4, 27

40. *Causes of Unrest*, 21.

41. "Conference of the General Council with Fifteen Representative Women, at the Fourth Presbyterian Church, Chicago, Ill., November 22, 1928," 13, 15, 29, Presbyterian Church in the U.S.A. Office of the Stated Clerk RG 125 7–2 PHS.

42. "Conference of the General Council with Fifteen Representative Women," 12.

43. Katherine Bennett, *The Status of Women in the Presbyterian Church in the United States of America, with Reference to Other Denominations* (Philadelphia, 1929), 14.

44. George William Brown, "Fears on the Woman Question," *Presbyterian Banner* February 20, 1930, 11, 12.

45. "Women's Organizations Auxiliary to the Mission Boards—the Vote," 3, 6, 7, 9, Presbyterian Church in the U.S.A. Office of the Stated Clerk RG 125 7–2 PHS.

46. "Women's Organizations Auxiliary to the Mission Boards," 21, 5, 8, 9.

47. Robert, "Introduction," 10.

Chapter 3

1. Alma Newell Atkins, "A Great Women's Organization," *Church Management* 16 (November 1939): 73.

2. "A Woman Views Her Church, by an Iowa Laywoman," *Advance* April 1, 1937, 148.

3. Atkins, "A Great Women's Organization," 74, 77; Joan Gunderson, "Women and the Parallel Church: A View from Congregations," in *Episcopal Women: Gender, Spirituality, and Commitment in an American Mainline Denomination*, ed. Catherine Prelinger (New York: Oxford University Press, 1996), 113, 114.

4. William Rest, "This Selling Racket," *Church Management* 12 (May 1936): 423–424; Paul Sturges, "Church Quits the Selling Racket," *Church Management* 12 (September 1935): 565–566; William H. Leach, "Parish Organization for a New Day," *Church Management* 10 (July 1936): 523, 524.

5. "The Churchwoman," *Christian Century* March 10, 1930, 362.

6. "Church Work for Churchwomen," *Christian Century* July 2, 1930, 837, 838.

7. Lewis Mudge to Katherine Bennett, January 6, 1928, Presbyterian Church in the U.S.A. Office of the Stated Clerk RG 125 Folder 6-2 PHS.

8. Mae Speight, "The Ministerial Reformation: A History of Women and the Mainline, 1920–1980" (PhD diss.: University of Virginia, 2020), 21–59.

9. Mark Chaves, "The International Association of Women Ministers," in *Women and Twentieth Century Protestantism*, ed. Margaret Bendroth and Virginia Brereton (Champaign-Urbana: University of Illinois Press, 2005), 264–265.

10. Margaret Blair Johnston, *When God Says "No": Faith's Starting Point* (New York: Simon and Schuster, 1954), 37, cited in Speight, "The Ministerial Reformation," 49.

11. Christopher Coble, "The Role of Young People's Societies in the Training of Christian Womanhood and Manhood, 1880–1910," in *Women and Twentieth-Century Protestantism*, 74–92.

12. Mary Ann Glendon, *A World Made New: Eleanor Roosevelt and the Universal Declaration of Human Rights* (New York: Random House, 2001), 90, 91.

13. Kristin A. Goss, "The Swells between the 'Waves': American Women's Activism, 1920–1965," in *The Oxford Handbook of U.S. Women's Social Movement Activism*, ed. Holly J. McCammon et al., https://doi.org/10.1093/oxfordhb/9780190204204.013.2 accessed November 20, 2020.

14. Quoted in Susan Ware, *Partner and I: Molly Dewson, Feminism, and New Deal Politics* (New Haven, CT: Yale University Press, 1987), xii, 224.

15. "Will Women Launch Their Own Church?" *Christian Century* December 1, 1948, 1291–1292.

16. "A Spiritual Challenge from the Women," *The Baptist* February 11, 1922, 41.

17. "Loyalty Luncheons," American Baptist Women's Ministries RG 25 Box 4 ABHS.

18. "The Proposed Merger," *Congregationalist* October 15, 1925, 528; "Shall the Woman's Boards Be Merged? Thoughts Called Out by 'Enquiring Layman's Articles on Report of Committee of Twelve,'" *Congregationalist* October 15, 1925, 526.

19. "Shall the Woman's Boards Be Merged?" 526.

20. "Shall the Woman's Boards Be Merged?" 526; Mary Preston to the Committee of Nine for the Study of Women's Work, January 27, 1933, CLA Pamphlet Collection (AC12 Z9); The Committee of Nine for the Study of Women's Work, March 16, 1933, CLA Pamphlet Collection (AC12 Z9).

21. "Quotation from a letter written by Dean J.E. Taylor on March 16, 1933," CLA Pamphlet Collection (AC12 Z9); Stuckey-Kauffman, "Women's Mission Structures," https://www.ucc.org/who-we-are/about/history/about-us_hidden-histories-2_ womens_mission_structures_and_the_american_board/, accessed October 1, 2021. *Journal of the Thirty-First Delegated General Conference of the Methodist Episcopal Church Held in Atlantic City, New Jersey, May 2–25, 1932* (New York: Methodist Book Concern (1932), 1627.

22. Mary E. Stearns, "The Place of Women in Our Church Today," *Advance* July 1945, 34. On the Woman's Gift, see Bertha McClintock to Dr. Stauffacher, September 10, 1943, Lillian Gregory papers, S-G IV, Series B, Folder 1 CLA.

23. Gunderson, "Women and the Parallel Church," 111, 114–118.

24. The Women's Committee (later Commission) began within the Conference of Foreign Missions of North America, to address the future of one of its constituent bodies, the Federation of Women's Boards for Foreign Mission. That body was dissolved in 1942.

25. Mrs. Coffin quoted in Ann Pyott to Twila Cavert, January 8, 1946, Presbyterian Church in the U.S.A. General Assembly Permanent Judicial Commission Records RG 18 68-3 PHS.

26. "Findings of Discussion Periods, Annual Meeting of the Committee on Women's Work of the Foreign Mission Conference, Riverside Church, January 7, 1936," 1, 2 Foreign Missions Conference of North America NCC RG 27 Box 11-2, PHS.

27. Mrs. Rawlins Cadwallader to Anna E. Caldwell, March 23, 1940, Presbyterian Church in the U.S.A. General Assembly Permanent Judicial Commission Records RG 18 Box 68–3, PHS.

28. The survey garnered responses from 1,134 local "women leaders." See "Women in the Ministry," Committee on Women's Work Foreign Missions Council of North America, 1938 Foreign Missions Conference of North America NCC RG 27 Box 11-2; Mudge to Gertrude Schultz, July 28, 1938, Foreign Missions Conference of North America NCC RG 27 Box 11-2. Someone put two exclamation points in the margin of Mudge's letter next to this remark.

29. "Women's Status in Protestant Churches," *Information Service* November 16, 1940, 3.

30. See, for example, Samuel McCrea Cavert, *The American Churches in the Ecumenical Movement, 1900–1968* (New York: Association Press, 1968). On Congregationalists and Episcopalians, Margaret Bendroth, *The Last Puritans: Mainline Protestants and the Power of the Past* (Chapel Hill: University of North Carolina Press, 2015), 216 n41.

31. H. Paul Douglass, *Protestant Cooperation in American Cities* (New York: Institute of Social and Religious Research, 1930), 105; David Mislin, *Saving Faith: Making Religious Pluralism an American Value at the Dawn of the Secular Age* (Ithaca, NY: Cornell University Press, 2016), 90–95; Ross W. Sanderson, *Church Cooperation in the United States: The Nation-Wide Backgrounds and Ecumenical Significance of State and Local Councils of Churches in Their Historical Perspective* (Association of Council Secretaries, 1960), 125.

32. Douglass, *Protestant Cooperation*, 147, 146, 311. Full-time male secretaries received from $3,000 to $7,000 annually, women $2,000.

33. Douglass, *Protestant Cooperation*, 117, 170, 437, 445.

34. Quinlan quoted in Janine Denomme, "'To End the Day of Strife': Churchwomen and the Campaign for Integration, 1920–1970" (PhD diss.: University of Pennsylvania, 2001), 72–75.

35. "Report of Committee on Findings, Conference of Association of Federation Secretaries, May 29–June 2, 1922" Association of Council Secretaries NCC RG 24 Box 2-12; "Annual Meeting of Executive Secretaries, May 31-June 2, 1928 Association of Council Secretaries NCC RG 24 Box 2-12 PHS.

36. Cooperation Needed by Churches Today," *Boston Globe* June 17, 1929, 5; "Church Women Organizations Federate," clipping in Association of Council Secretaries RG 24, Box 2-12 PHS. The start was rockier than it might have appeared. Two groups had actually met in Boston in 1928, with confusingly similar names and agendas: the National Commission of Protestant Church Women and the National Council of Federated Church Women. The first was somewhat under the auspices of the two major women's interdenominational organizations, the Council of Women for Home

Missions (CWHM) and the Federation of Women's Boards of the National Conference of Foreign Missions (FWBNCFM). The other appeared to be a loosely organized coalition of local New England groups, with its own slate of officers. Eventually these two groups merged, taking the name of the second.

37. "Administrative Committee Federation of Woman's Boards of Foreign Missions of North America and Council of Women for Home Missions, June 13, 1929," 2, Foreign Missions Conference of North America Records NCC RG 27 Box 4-14 PHS.

38. "Joint Session of the Executive Committee of the Federation of Woman's Boards of Foreign Missions of North America and Council of Women for Home Missions, November 7, 1929," 4, 7, Foreign Missions Conference of North America NCC RG 27 Box 4-21. PHS. FCC president Samuel Cavert described the old guard as "hens whose broods were annually augmented by a few hundred ducklings." Samuel McCrea Cavert, *Church Cooperation and Unity in America*, 246. For more background on origins, see Conference of Executive Secretaries, Minutes and Memoranda, September 15, 1919, Association of Council Secretaries NCC RG 24 Box 2-12, PHS. The origins of the Massachusetts federation is described in "United Church Women of Massachusetts: A Historical Sketch," Mass. Council of Churches Collection, Series 1, subseries 4, Box 4, CLA.

39. Joint Session, Administrative Committees of the Council of Women for Home Missions, the Federation of Women's Boards of Foreign Missions, and the National Council of Federated Church Women," March 10–11, 1930, Foreign Missions Conference of North America NCC RG 27 Box 4-14 PHS.

40. "National Commission of Protestant Church Women and National Council of Federated Church Women," 2 [1929?], Foreign Missions Conference of North America NCC RG 27 4–14 PHS.

41. "A Proposed Plan for a National Organization of Church Women Uniting the National Council of Church Women, the Committee on Women's Work of the Foreign Missions Conference and the Council of Women for Home Missions, January 18, 1940, Foreign Missions Conference of North America NCC RG 27 11-16 PHS.

42. Margaret Shannon, *Just Because: The Story of the National Movement of Church Women United, 1941 through 1975* (Corte Madera, CA: Omega, 1977), 25.

43. "Women Join National Council of Churches," *Christian Century* October 26, 1949, 1253–1254. The UCW finally relented in 1949, but only for a time, leaving the NCC in 1966 and taking on the new name, Church Women United.

44. "A Plan for Organizing Councils of Church Women," pamphlet published by UCW, n.d. Church Women United collection 1224-3-2:06 UMCA.

45. "Regarding the Proposed National Council of Churches," pamphlet in CWU collection, 1224-3-2:16, UMCA.

46. Gladys Gilkey Calkins, *Follow These Women: Church Women in the Ecumenical Movement* (New York: National Council of Churches, 1961), 82f; "Women Join National Council of Churches," 1253–1254.

47. On UCW, see Virginia Brereton, "United and Slighted: Women as Subordinated Insiders," in *Between the Times: The Travail of the Protestant Establishment in America, 1900–1960*, ed. William R. Hutchison (Cambridge: Cambridge University Press,

1989), 143–167; Caryn E. Neumann, "Status Seekers: Long-Established Women's Organizations and the Women's Movement in the United States, 1945–1970s," (PhD diss.: Ohio State University, 2006); Shannon, *Just Because.*

48. "The Methodist Church," *Christian Century* May 24, 1939, 663. The denomination would dismantle the Central Jurisdiction at the same time it granted women full ordination rights, at the 1956 General Conference. Note that racial segregation was also a product of the 1931 merger of liberal-minded Congregationalists with the much smaller and more southern-based Christian Connection. The Southern Conference separated out the African American members of both groups.

49. See Clarence G. Newsome, "Mary McLeod Bethune and the Methodist Episcopal Church North: In but Out," in *This Far by Faith: Readings in African-American Women's Religious Biography*, ed. Judith Weisenfeld and Richard Newman (New York: Routledge, 1996), 125–139.

50. In 1880, Methodist Protestants ordained Anna Howard Shaw when the northern body refused to do so; they seated women as delegates to the General Conference in 1892, thirty years before northern Methodists acted in 1922.

51. Barbara B. Troxell, "Ordination of Women in the United Methodist Tradition," *Methodist History* 37 (January 1999): 124. Northern Methodists debated ordination fiercely in the 1920s. See William T. Noll, "A Welcome in the Ministry: The 1920 and 1924 General Conferences Debate Clergy Rights for Women," *Methodist History* 30 (January 1992): 91–99.

52. "The Uniting Conference," *Christian Advocate* March 30, 1939, 290; "A Man's Church," *Zion's Herald* August 10, 1938, 1020. In perhaps guilty awareness, the Conference issued an apology to Frances Willard, for failing to seat her in 1888, and called on Methodist schools, colleges, and universities to recognize her on the Sunday nearest September 28. There was also talk of asking the US Postmaster to issue a stamp in her honor." Orien W. Fifer, "Strange Rejections and Belated Honors," *Christian Advocate* September 14, 1939, 878.

53. Roy L. Smith, "A Fixed Faith and Stubborn Facts: Woman's Crusade for a Christian America," *The Methodist Woman* 1 (September 1940): 5.

54. F. F. Lindsay to Mrs. James Oldshue, January 19, 1939, Women's Division Unification Files 2594-2 3:1 UMCA.

55. "Findings of Joint Meeting of Methodist Women, Chicago, Illinois, June 3 and 4, 1938," 4; "Joint Meeting of Methodist Women, Chicago, Illinois June 3 and 4, 1938," 2, 6, Women's Division Unification Files, 2594:09 Folder 1 UMCA.

56. Thelma Stevens, *Legacy for the Future: The History of Christian Social Relations in the Women's Division of Christian Service, 1940–1968* (Women's Division, Board of Global Ministries, 1978), 11–14, 18; Task Force on the History of the Central Jurisdiction, *To a Higher Glory: The Growth and Development of Black Women Organized for Mission in the Methodist Church, 1940–1968* (Nashville: United Methodist Church, 1968), 24; *Annual Report of the Woman's Division of Christian Service of the Board of Missions and Church Extension of the Methodist Church* (New York, 1941), 117–131,

57. "Appropriations: Woman's Division of Christian Service of the Board of Missions and Church, *Annual Report for 1941* (pp. 117–131); Linda Gesling, *Mirror and Beacon: The*

History of Mission of the Methodist Church, 1939–1968 (New York: General Board of Global Ministries, 2005), 14.

58. Braude, "Women's History *Is* American Religious History," in *Re-Telling U.S. Religious History*, ed. Thomas Tweed (Berkeley: University of California Press, 1997), 93.

59. Calkins, *Follow Those Women*, 19.

60. Calkins, *Follow Those Women*, 65; Inez Cavert, *Women in American Church Life: A Study Prepared under the Guidance of a Counseling Committee of Women Representing National Interdenominational Agencies* (New York: Friendship Press, 1948), 52.

Chapter 4

1. Nancy Marie Robertson, *Christian Sisterhood, Race Relations, and the YWCA, 1906–1946* (Champaign-Urbana: University of Illinois Press, 2007), 106; Elsie Thomas Culver, *Women in the World of Religion* (Garden City, NY: Doubleday, 1967), 196.

2. Robertson, *Christian Sisterhood*, 103, 104. See also Clifford Putney, *Muscular Christianity: Manhood and Sports in Protestant America, 1880–1920* (Cambridge, MA: Harvard University Press, 2003).

3. "Shall We Drift or Steer?" *Missionary Review of the World* 43 (November 1920): 958; "The Young Women's Christian Association Quits Fellowship," *Christian Fundamentals in School and Church* 2 (July–September 1920): 395–396. See also Paul Holsinger, "Has the Y.W.C.A. Adopted a Modernistic Program?" *Bible Champion* 34 (September 1928): 493–495.

4. Robertson, *Christian Sisterhood*, 133.

5. James Findlay, *Church People in the Struggle: The National Council of Churches and the Black Freedom Movement, 1950–1970* (New York: Oxford University Press, 1993), 17, 18–19.

6. Findlay, *Church People in the Struggle*, 20, 22.

7. Quoted in Bettye Collier-Thomas, *Jesus, Jobs, and Justice: African-American Women and Religion* (Philadelphia: Temple University Press, 2014), 322.

8. Collier-Thomas, *Jesus, Jobs, and Justice*, 323–324; Betty Livingston Adams, *Black Women's Christian Activism: Seeking Social Justice in a Northern Suburb* (New York: NYU Press, 2016), 92; Brown quoted in Melinda Marie Johnson, "Building Bridges: Church Women United and Social Reform Work across the Mid-Twentieth Century" (PhD diss.: University of Kentucky, 2015), 42; Caryn E. Neumann, "Status Seekers: Long-Established Women's Organizations and the Women's Movement in the United States, 1945–1970s," (PhD diss.: Ohio State University, 2006), 174.

9. "Church Women in Interracial Conference," *Federal Council Bulletin* 11 (October 1928): 13–14. The Interracial Conference eventually became the Church Women's Committee under the FCC Commission on the Church and Race Relations.

10. Judith Weisenfeld, *African American Women and Christian Activism: New York's Black YWCA, 1905–1945* (Cambridge, MA: Harvard University Press, 1997), 5.

11. Gloria Hull, ed., *The Works of Alice Dunbar-Nelson*, vol. 2 (New York: Oxford University Press, 1988), 230–231, quoted in Adams, *Black Women's Christian Activism*, 96. Her husband was the poet Laurence Dunbar.

12. "United Council of Church Women," *Federal Council Bulletin* (January 1942): 11; "A Statement Prepared for Those Who are Asked to Accept Special Responsibilities in Connection with the 'United Council of Church Women' Meeting in Constituting Convention, Hotel Dennis, Atlantic City, New Jersey, December 11–13, 1941, Church Women United Collection 1224-3-2-:06 UMCA.

13. *To a Higher Glory: The Growth and Development of Black Women Organized for Mission in the Methodist Church, 1940–1968* (Women's Division of the Board of Global Ministries, n.p., n.d.), 24.

14. Jacqueline Jones, Interview with Thelma Stevens, February 13, 1972, Interview G-0058 Southern Oral History Program Collection (#4007), https://docsouth.unc.edu/sohp/html_use/G-0058.html, accessed October 2 2020.

15. Alice Knotts, "Race Relations in the 1920s: A Challenge to Southern Methodist Women," *Methodist History* 26 (July 1988): 199–212; Alice Knotts, "Methodist Women and Interracial Fairness in the 1930s," *Methodist History* 27 (July 1989): 230–240.

16. Rosalind Rosenberg, *Jane Crow: The Life of Pauli Murray* (New York: Oxford University Press, 2017), 185–187.

17. Cherisse Jones, "'How Shall I Sing the Lord's Song?': United Church Women Confront Racial Issues in South Carolina, 1940s–1960s," in *Throwing Off the Cloak of Privilege: White Southern Women Activists in the Civil Rights Era*, ed. Gail S. Murray (Tallahassee: University Press of Florida, 2004), 141, 146–147. Also Collier-Thomas, *Jesus, Jobs, and Justice*, 404–410.

18. Adams, *Black Women's Christian Activism*, 45.

19. Isabel Brown Ross, *Working Together: The Story of the United Church Women of Southern California-Southern Nevada, 1934–1959*, n.p., 6.

20. Christopher Evans, *The Social Gospel in American Religion* (New York: NYU Press, 2017); Samuel Moyn, *The Last Utopia: Human Rights in History* (Cambridge, MA: Harvard University Press, 2010), 64, 65.

21. Irene Ann Jones, "A Recommended Program of Training for Northern Baptist Women Lay Leaders" (PhD diss.: University of Pennsylvania, 1949), 23, 31.

22. Robert Griswold, *Fatherhood in America: A History* (New York: Basic Books, 1993), 93; Ronald Howard, *A Social History of American Family Sociology 1854–1940* (Westport, CT: Greenwood Press, 1981) 63, 73. See also Margaret Bendroth, *Growing Up Protestant: Parents, Children, and Mainline Churches* (New Brunswick, NJ: Rutgers University Press, 2002), 76–80.

23. Bertha Condé, *The New Day and Its Possibilities for Church Women: An Address Delivered at the Biennial Meeting of the Woman's Missionary Organizations, St. Paul, Minnesota, May 16, 1929* (Philadelphia: Board of Foreign Missions and Board of Home Missions of the PCUSA, 1929), 8, 10, 14.

24. Ruth Finwall to Mrs. John C. Killiam, May 13, 1947, American Baptist Women's Ministries RG 25 Box 7 ABHS.

25. "The Women's Collect," *Methodist Women's Association Bulletin* 17 (November 1939): 7–8.

26. Mrs. A. E. Caldwell, "Women's Meetings in Cleveland," *Missions* (June 1942): 388; "The Unbroken Line," Program suggested by the Commission of Conference to the Districts for the close of the District Meetings, 1937, American Baptist Women's Ministries RG 25 Box 4 ABHS; "Through the Years with the Love Gift," American Baptist Women's Ministries RG 25 Box 8 ABHS; Mrs. J. K. Romeyn, "Repairers of the Breach: A Program to be Used at the Opening of Gift-Boxes," n.d., American Baptist Women's Ministries RG 25 Box 4 ABHS.

27. The agencies included the FCC, the International Council on Religious Education, the Home Missions Council, the Foreign Missions Conference, the Missionary Education Movement, the Council of Church Boards of Education, and the United Stewardship Council. See Samuel Cavert, The *American Churches in the Ecumenical Movement, 1900–1968* (New York: Association Press, 1968), 203–212.

28. "Council of Church Women Meets in Biennial Assembly," *Federal Council Bulletin* (December 1946), 1117; Elsie Penfield, "Who We Are," *The Church Woman* (August–September 1951), 11.

29. Margaret Frakes, "Church Women Anticipate Wide Opportunity in National Council," *Christian Century* November 29, 1950, 1428.

30. Margaret Shannon, *Just Because: The Story of the National Movement of Church Women United in the U.S.A. 1941 through 1975* (Corte Madera, CA: Omega Books, 1977), 56, 57; Mrs. William Sale Terrell, "Historical Summary of UCW Relationships with the National Council of Churches, May 15, 1952," Church Women United collection 1224-3-2:22, UMCA.

31. Beata Mueller, "The United Council of Church Women," *Federal Council Bulletin* May 1950, 23.

32. "Qualifications to be considered in selecting a woman Associate Secretary, Tentative undated memo January 31, 1952," Mildred Horton papers 1DD7 folder 5-12, Wellesley College Archives.

Portrait: Anna Swain and the Fundamentalists

1. ACS to Leslie Swain, n.d., Swain Papers RG 1076 Box 7, ABHS.

2. Pearl Jeffrey to ACS October 9, 1944, Swain Papers RG 1076 Box 5 ABHS.

3. ACS to Leslie Swain, October 22, 1944, Swain Papers RG 1076 Box 5, ABHS; ACS to Leslie Swain, n.d. [previously cited]; ACS to Mrs. Earl V. Pierce October 22, 1944, Swain Papers RG 1076 Box 5 ABHS.

4. Biographical information on Swain is limited to Margaret Frakes, "Baptist—and Ecumenical," *Christian Century* July 30, 1952, 872–875. Swain wrote numerous pageants for Baptist missionary groups, and several books, including *My Book of Missionary Heroines* (New York: Baptist Board of Education, 1930); *Pioneer Missionary Heroines in America* (New York: Baptist Board of Education, 1932); *Youth Unafraid: A Century of Christian Adventure in South China, Assam, Bengal-Orissa, South China* (New York: Baptist Board of Education, 1935).

5. The anonymous critic is quoted in William Vance Trollinger, *God's Empire: William Bell Riley and Midwestern Fundamentalism* (Madison: University of Wisconsin Press, 1990), 138–139.

6. Trollinger, *God's Empire*, 154; Rick Shrader, "Richard Clearwaters," *Baptist Bible Tribune* 52 (October 15, 2001), https://printfriendly.com/p/g/KpHwpX, accessed April 4, 2020. See also Chester E. Tulga, *The Foreign Mission Controversy in the Northern Baptist Convention, 1919–1949* (Chicago: Conservative Baptist Fellowship, 1950).

7. John W. Bradbury to ACS June 2, 1944, Swain Papers RG 1076 Box 2 ABHS;

8. "Mrs. Swain Convention President," *The Baptist News* 31 (June 1944): 1.

9. Walter O. Lewis (General Secretary of Baptist World Alliance) to ACS June 7, 1944, Swain Papers RG 1076 Box 2 ABHS.

10. Roy Epps to ACS October 25, 1944, Swain Papers RG 1076 Box 2 ABHS.

11. Ruth Mougey Worrell to ACS June 5, 1944, Swain Papers RG 1076 Box 2 ABHS.

12. "Editorial Comment," *Northern Baptist World-Times* February 27, 1944, 5; "What the Women Believe," *Watchman-Examiner* March 9, 1944, 231; "Baptists and Theology," *Watchman-Examiner* March 23, 1944, 271; "The Word of God," *Watchman-Examiner* May 18, 1944, 486; Clarence Roddy, "The Need for Theology," *Watchman-Examiner* September 7, 1944, 876–877.

13. Frakes, "Baptist—and Ecumenical," 872.

14. "Mrs. Swain Convention President," 1.

15. "The State of the Family," President's Keynote Address delivered at the Northern Baptist Convention, Grand Rapids, MI, May 21, 1946, 3, 11, Swain Papers RG 1076 Box 3 ABHS.

16. Margaret Frakes, "Baptist—and Ecumenical," 875.

17. May Strood to ACS, June 3, 1944, Swain Papers RG 1076 Box 2; Lorraine Spoerri to ACS June 4, 1944, Swain Papers RG 1076 Box 2.

18. Grace Y. Elliott to ACS May 3, 1944, Swain Papers RG 1076 Box 2 ABHS.

Chapter 5

1. On "muscular Christianity," Clifford Putney, *Muscular Christianity: Manhood and Sports in Protestant America, 1880–1920* (Cambridge, MA: Harvard University Press, 2001); Donald E. Hall, ed. *Muscular Christianity: Embodying the Victorian Age* (Cambridge: Cambridge University Press, 2010).

2. There no current scholarly treatment of Protestant laymen's movements, unfortunately, nor a full-length, interdenominational treatment of American laity rights.

3. "Our Readers' Forum: Men for Moderators" [Lillian M. Knight, LaJolla, CA] *Congregationalist* June 11, 1925, 748; "Women's Status in Protestant Churches," *Information Service* 19 (November 16, 1940): 1–12.

4. George Punchard, *A View of Congregationalism* (New York: J.P. Jewett, 1840), 194–195.

5. "Editorial," *The Pacific* June 20, 1870.

6. Karen Heetderks Strong, "Ecclesiastical Suffrage: The First Women Participants at General Conference in the Antecedents of the United Methodist Church,"

Methodist History 25 (October 1986): 29–33; Frances Willard, *Woman in the Pulpit* (Chicago: WCTU Publication Association, 1889).

7. *"Because They Are Women" and Other Editorials from "The Christian Advocate" on the Admission of Women to the General Conference* (New York: Hunt and Eaton, 1891), 26. See also A. J. Kynett, *Our Laity: And Their Equal Rights without Distinction of Sex* (Cincinnati, OH: Cranston and Curtis, 1896).

8. *Because They Are Women,"* 8, 27.

9. Carolyn DeSwarte Gifford, ed. *The Debate in the Methodist Episcopal Church over Laity Rights for Women* (New York: Garland Publishing, 1987).

10. "Young Men and Religion," *Watchman* December 26, 1901, 7.

11. Bureau of the Census, *Religious Bodies, 1906,* 2 vols. (Washington, DC, 1906) and H. K. Carroll, *The Religious Forces of the United States* (New York, 1912), lvii–lix.

12. *Presbyterian Brotherhood: Report of the First Convention Held at Indianapolis, November Thirteenth through Fifteenth, 1906* (Philadelphia: Presbyterian Board of Publication, 1907), 116.

13. George Barton Cutten, *The Psychological Phenomena of Christianity* (New York: Charles Scribner's Sons, 1908), 295, 297, 300.

14. Carl Delos Case, *The Masculine in Religion* (Philadelphia: American Baptist Publication Society, 1906), 29, Wheeler quoted, 24.

15. Coe, *The Spiritual Life: Studies in the Science of Religion* (New York: Eaton and Mains, 1900), 236, 238, 239.

16. Edwin Diller Starbuck, *The Psychology of Religion: An Empirical Study in the Growth of Religious Consciousness* (New York: Charles Scribner's Sons, 1899), 95.

17. Case, *The Masculine in Religion*, 89.

18. John R. Rice, "The Lonely Christ," *Sword of the Lord* August 14, 1936, 4; William Bell Riley, "The Church and Men: Its Hold on Them Considered," March 3, 1910, unid. Clipping, Riley papers, Billy Graham Center Archives.

19. Margaret Bendroth, "Men, Masculinity and Urban Revivalism: J. Wilbur Chapman's Boston Crusade, 1909," *Journal of Presbyterian History* 75 (Winter 1997): 235–246. By 1910, according to one estimate, there were over 12,000 men in Bible and Sunday school classes in Chicago alone. See Henry F. Cope, *The Efficient Layman or the Religious Training of Men* (Boston: Pilgrim Press, 1911), 101. Fundamentalists did not abandon men's organizations, of course, but maintained a primarily evangelistic intent, as in the Christian Men's Businessmen Association. See, for example, "The Ministry of Laymen," *King's Business* 27 (March 1936): 82.

20. Gail Bederman, "'The Women Have Had Charge of the Church Work Long Enough': The Men and Religion Forward Movement of 1911–1912 and the Masculinization of Middle Class Protestantism," *American Quarterly* 41 (September 1989): 432–465.

21. My own survey of membership statistics for two revivalist churches in Boston during this time found no significant increase after a visit from Billy Sunday or Wilbur Chapman. If anything, the campaigns only brought in more female members. See Margaret Bendroth, *Fundamentalists in the City: Conflict and Division in Boston's Churches, 1885–1950* (New York: Oxford University Press,

2005), 114, 166. The US census kept statistics on male and female church membership until 1936, at which time it calculated five women for every four men—though this differed considerably by denomination and faith tradition. Mainline church bodies (Presbyterian U.S.A. [northern], Protestant Episcopal, Methodist Episcopal, Northern Baptist, and Congregational Christian reported 60–70 percent female. US Department of Commerce, US Bureau of the Census, *Religious Bodies: 1936*, vol. 1, *Summary and Detailed Tables* (Washington, DC: US Government Printing Office, 1941), 23, 410. Comparisons are difficult, given regional differences and methods of reporting, but the Pew Research Center's recent tracking of religiosity by gender finds similar patterns. See "Christian Women in the U.S. Are More Religious Than Their Male Counterparts," https://www.pewr esearch.org/fact-tank/2018/04/06/christian-women-in-the-u-s-are-more-religi ous-than-their-male-counterparts/, accessed April 4, 2018.

22. Margaret Bendroth, "Why Women Loved Billy Sunday: Urban Revivalism and Popular Entertainment in Early-Twentieth-Century American Culture," *Religion and American Culture* 14 (Summer 2004): 251–271.

23. John R. Scotford, "The Church and the Feminine Emotions," *Congregationalist* April 16, 1922, 504.

24. Case, *The Masculine in Religion*, 84.

25. Case, *The Masculine in Religion*, 114–115, 83.

26. "The 'Men and Religion' Social Programme," *Record of Christian Work* 31 (September 1912): 611.

27. "Practical Methods of Reaching and Holding Men," *Congregationalist* August 19, 1897, 266. On fundamentalists and lodges, see Bendroth, *Fundamentalists in the City*, 72–75.

28. Charles S. Holt, "The Church and the Men," in *Presbyterian Brotherhood: Report of the First Convention, Held at Indianapolis, 1906* (Philadelphia: Presbyterian Board of Publication 1907), 70–71.

29. *Presbyterian Brotherhood*, Report of the Second Convention, Held at Cincinnati, 1907 (Philadelphia: Presbyterian Board of Publication, 1908), 347.

30. Charles Macfarland, *Christian Unity in the Making: The First Twenty-Five Years of the Federal Council of the Churches of Christ in America 1905–1930* (New York: FCC, 1949), 67–68.

31. Committee on the War and the Religious Outlook, *Religion among Men, As Revealed by a Study of Conditions in the Army* (New York: Association Press, 1920), 9, 13, 14, 25.

32. Charles Stafford Brown, "Why Men *Do* Go to Church," *Christian Century* July 31, 1929, 965.

33. Lloyd Harter, *The Chicago Congregational Men's Movement: An Adequate Work by Men in Every Congregational Church in Chicago* (n.p., 1907), 14, 15.

34. David K. Sloatman, "Ritual for a Men's Club," *Church Management* 13 (October 1936), 20.

35. Chauncy Hawkins, *Samuel Billings Capen: His Life and Work* (Boston: Pilgrim Press, 1914), 165.

36. Hawkins, *Samuel Billings Capen*, 166, 171, 173, 177–178.

37. John A. Hutchinson, *We Are Not Divided: A Critical and Historical Study of the Federal Council of the Churches of Christ in America* (New York: Round Table Press, 1941), 64; "Vital Questions for Congregationalists to Come Before the National Council," *Congregationalist* July 9, 1925, 47.

38. Elsie McCormick, "From the Beginning," *Laymen's Movement Review* 4 (July–August 1961): 3–8; "Ralph W. Gwinn (1884–1961)," *Laymen's Movement Review* 5 (May–June 1962): 9–10.

39. Ozora Davis, *Preaching by Laymen: A Study of the Elementary Principles of Presenting the Gospel* (New York: Fleming H. Revell, 1923), 19–20.

40. Bayard Hendrick, "Protestant Laymen's Organization Needed," *Church Management* 15 (September 1938), 654.

41. *Laymen Speaking*, ed. Wallace Speers (New York: Association Press, 1947).

42. "Lay Leadership Emerging," *Federal Council Bulletin* October 1946, 3–4.

43. LaRoe, "The Whole Armor of God," *National Council Outlook* January 1954, 8.

44. Alex G. Highton, "Advertising to Conserve Character," *Church Management* 13 (November 1936), 71.

45. Mark May, William Adams Brown, and Frank Shuttlesworth, *The Education of American Ministers*, 4 vols. (New York: Institute of Social and Religious Research, 1934).

46. "I Want a Pastor, By a Disappointed Layman," *Advance* (June 1945), 22.

47. *The Layman Looks at the Minister* (Nashville: Abingdon-Cokesbury Press, 1947). The information came from a survey of male lay leaders with a "supplemental sample" of women's opinions from a "representative group."

48. "Play Ball," *Andover Newton Bulletin* (1943), n.p. See Bendroth *A School of the Church: Andover Newton across Two Centuries* (Grand Rapids, MI: Eerdmans, 2008), 151.

49. Richard S. Bond, "A Layman's Creed," *Church Management* 13 (December 1936), 127, 128.

50. Kevin Kruse, *One Nation under God: How Corporate America Invented Christian America* (New York: Basic Books, 2015).

51. "Methodist Laymen March On," *Church Management* 12 (January 1936): 206; Robert Moats Miller, *American Protestantism and Social Issues, 1919–1939* (Chapel Hill: University of North Carolina Press, 1958), 68.

52. Margaret Bendroth, *The Last Puritans: Mainline Protestants and the Power of the Past* (Chapel Hill: University of North Carolina Press, 2015), 139–144.

53. Ethelbert V. Graybill, "Laymen and the General Council," *Advance* November 15, 1934, 657.

54. "Babson Discusses Beloit," *Advance* June 1, 1938, 270.

55. "An Open Letter," *Truth in Action* January 15, 1953, n.p.; James Fifield, *The Tall Preacher: Autobiography of Dr. James W. Fifield, Jr. with Bill Youngs* (Los Angeles, CA: Pepperdine University Press, 1977).

56. Deborah Rhinesmith, "The League to Uphold Congregational Principles," *International Congregational Journal* 92 (Winter 2010): 39–52.

57. To my knowledge, no formal study of the ACCL exists. The main body of its papers are at the University of Wisconsin: http://digicoll.library.wisc.edu/cgi/f/findaid/findaid-idx?c=wiarchives;view=reslist;subview=standard;didno=uw-whs-mss00700;focus rgn=bioghist;cc=wiarchives;byte=231087176.

58. "Women in the Ordained Ministry: Reflections for the Boston Task Force, Community of Women and Men Study, December 14, 1975, Constance Parvey papers Box 37 Folder 15 Schlesinger Library; Theressa Hoover, *With Unveiled Face: Centennial Reflections on Women and Men in the Community of the Church* (New York: Women's Division, General Board of Global Ministers of The Methodist Church, 1983), 16.

Chapter 6

1. William Schmidt, *Architect of Unity: A Biography of Samuel McCrea Cavert* (New York: Friendship Press, 1978).

2. Diarmond MacCulloch, *Christianity: The First Three Thousand Years* (New York: Penguin, 2009), 955–6.

3. On the Tokyo school see Rui Kohiyama, "'No Nation Can Rise Higher Than Its Women'" The Women's Ecumenical Missionary Movement and Tokyo Woman's Christian College, in *Competing Kingdoms: Women, Mission, Nation, and the American Protestant Empire, 1812-1960* (Durham, NC: Duke University Press, 2009): 218–239.

4. Susannah Herzel, *A Voice for Women: The Women's Department of the World Council of Churches* (Geneva: WCC, 1981), 110–115.

5. Margaret Shannon, *Just Because: The Story of the National Movement of Church Women United in the U.S.A., 1941 Through 1975* (Corte Madera, CA: Omega Books, 1977), 60. The literature on women in the WCC is significant and growing. See Herzel, *Voice for Women*; Janet Estridge Crawford, "Rocking the Boat: Women's Participation in the World Council of Churches, 1948-1991 (Ph.D. diss: Victoria University of Wellington, 1995); Gail Allen, "We Intend to Move Together," *International Review of Missions* 2015; 3–17; Melanie May, *Bonds of Unity: Women, Theology, and the Worldwide Church* (Atlanta: Scholars Press, 1989); Natalie Maxson, *Journey for Justice: The Story of Women In the WCC* (Geneva, Switz.: WCC Publications, 2013).

6. Rhoda McCulloch, "The Role of Women in the Life of the Church," *The Woman's Press* February 1947, 21.

7. David Cornick, "'So Practical a Mystic' – Olive Wyon (1881-1966)," *Journal of the United Reformed Church History Society* 8 (December 2010), 407.

8. Quoted in Herzel, *A Voice for Women*, 6–7.

9. Herzel, *Voice for Women*, 7. See also Lesslie Newbigin, "The Legacy of W.A. Visser 't Hooft," *International Bulletin of Missionary Research* 16 (April 1992): 78–82.

10. On Barot see Andre Jacques, *Madeleine Barot* (Geneva: WCC Publications, 1991); Judith Greenberg, "Paths of Resistance: French Women Working from the Inside," in

Experience and Expression Women, the Nazis, and the Holocaust, ed. Eliza Baer and Myrna Goldberg (Detroit: Wayne State University Press, 2003), 155.

11. Hans Ruedi Weber, *The Courage to Live: A Biography of Suzanne de Dietrich* (Geneva: WCC Publications, 1995).

12. Jürgen Moltmann, "Henriette Visser 't Hooft and Karl Barth," *Theology Today* 55 (January 1999): 524–531. See "Eva, wo bist Du?" *Student World* 27 (1934): 12–15.

13. Bertil E. Gaartner and Carl Strandberg, "The Experience of the Church of Sweden," in *Man, Woman, and Priesthood*, ed. Peter Moore (London: SPCK, 1978), 123–133; "Preliminary and Unofficial Report on the Study of the Life and Work of Women in the Church" [confidential]" Home Missions Council of North America RG 26 19-23 PHS; "Women Win Out in Denmark," *Presbyterian Life* April 24, 1948, 7.

14. Ultimately gender issues were not part of the series, however, which was to include "Preaching in War-Time," "The Church and its Youth," and "The Church Speaks to the World."

15. Fritz Zerbst, *Office of Women in the Church: A Study in Practical Theology.* Trans. Albert G. Merkens (St Louis: Concordia Publishing House, 1955; rpt Omaha: Mercinator Press, 2017), 2–3.

16. Elisabeth Schmidt, *When God Calls a Woman: The Struggle of a Woman Pastor in France and Algeria*, trans. Allen Hackett (New York: Pilgrim Press, 1981), 102.

17. Royden came to the United States in 1928, but was disinvited by Methodists when she was caught smoking, and rumors circulated about her liberal views on marriage. "Maude Royden in America," *Congregationalist* January 12, 1928, 36, 37.

18. Susan White, "'The Church Militant': A. Maude Royden and the Quest for Women's Equality in the Inter-War Years," in *The Theologically Informed Heart: Essays in Honor of David J. Gouwens*, ed. Warner M. Bailey, Lee C. Barrett, and James O. Duke (Eugene, OR: Pickwick Publications, 2014), 47–71; V. Nelle Bellamy, "Participation of Women in the Public Life of the Church from Lambeth Conference," *Historical Magazine of the Protestant Episcopal Church* 51 (1982): 81–98.

19. Twila Cavert to Miss Ann Pyott, November 14, 1945 Presbyterian Church in the U.S.A. General Assembly Stated Clerk Lewis Seymour Mudge Correspondence RG 17 68-3 PHS

20. Herzel, *A Voice for Women*, 8–9.

21. Herzel, *Voice for Women*, 7.

22. Questionnaire: Life and Work of Women in the Church," History of the Department and the Commission RG4321.06 WCC archives.

23. Twila Cavert to Sarah Chakko April 30, 1950 History of the Department and the Commission RG4321.068 WCC Archives.

24. Inez M. Cavert, "Extensive Study Being Made of Women in the Church," *Federal Council Bulletin* May 1947, 10; "Preliminary and Unofficial Report," 3, 4.; *Revised Interim Report of a Study on the Life and Work of Women in the Church* (Geneva: WCC, 1948), 11; Herzel, *Voice for Women*, 8–9.

25. Inez Cavert, *Women in American Church Life: A Study Prepared Under the Guidance of a Counseling Committee of Women Representing National Interdenominational Agencies* (New York: Friendship Press, 1948), 20. See also "Women in American

Church Life: Study Reveals Trend Towards Greater Participation," *Federal Council Bulletin* March 1949, 10–11. The survey is discussed in the following chapter.

26. Rhoda McCulloch to Sue Wedell, June 21, 1948 Foreign Missions Council of North America Records RG 27 11–1, PHS. Inez Cavert had done the majority of research and writing for the FCC's *Information Service,* a four-page weekly bulletin. Notes from the Meeting of the Advisory Committee on the Study of Women in the Church," May 22, 1946 Foreign Missions Council of North America Records RG 27 Box 1-11. The Committee included Marion Norris, Florence Gordon, Edith Lowry, Rhoda McCulloch, Twila Cavert, and Anne Pyott, as well as Inez Cavert.

27. Charles S. MacFarland, *Christian Unity in the Making: The First Twenty-Five Years of the Federal Council of the Churches of Christ in America, 1905-1930* (New York: FCC, 1948), 261–2.

28. Thelma Stevens, *Legacy for the Future: The History of Christian Social Relations in the Women's Division of Social Service, 1940-1968*(Women's Division, Board of Global Ministries, United Methodist Church, 1978), 51. Eileen Lindner describes it as a "complex and troubled history" in her essay, "Still In But Out," in *Women and Church: The Challenge of Ecumenical Solidarity in an Age of Alienation* ed. Melanie A. May (Grand Rapids: Eerdmans 1991), 103.

29. F.A. Iremonger, *William Temple: Archbishop of Canterbury: His Life and Letters* (London: Oxford University Press, 1948), 452. Iremonger asserts that Temple retained his opposition "to the end."

30. H.N. Bate, ed., *Faith and Order; Proceedings of the World Conference, Lausanne, August 3-21, 1927* (London: Student Christian Movement, 1927), 372–3.

31. Bate, *Faith and Order,* 372–3. The signatories were Eliza Kendrick (an American Congregationalist), Elizabeth Hill Lyman, H.S. Sanford, Lucy Gardner, Mary A. Bagnall, and Elizabeth Budd. The Conference did not completely ignore the memorial, but misunderstood the women's request. The Call to Unity included a short salute to "youth" and to women, by "we men" who have carried the work of the church "too much alone through many years." The women "henceforth should be accorded their share of responsibility. See *Reports of the World Conference on Faith and Order, Lausanne, Switzerland, August 3 to 21, 1927* (Boston: Published by the Secretariat, 1927), 6.

32. *The Jerusalem Meeting of the International Missionary Council, March 24-April 8, 1928,* vol. VIII, 171–174; "World Conference, 1937, 'Oxford' and 'Edinburgh,'" *The Church Woman* 4 (October 1937): 3–4.

33. "Minutes of the Meeting of Commission II of the Committee of Women's Work, May 14, 1936," Foreign Missions Council of North America Records RG 27 Box 11-2 PHS; "Minutes of the Meeting of the Commission II of the Committee on Women's Work, September 23, 1936," Foreign Missions Council of North America Records RG 27 Box 11-2 PHS.

34. "Minutes of the Meeting of the Commission II of the Committee on Women's Work of the Foreign Missions Conference, October 16, 1936," Foreign Missions Council of North America Records RG 27 Box 11-2 PHS.

35. May Curwen, "Una Sancta," *World's Y.W.C.A. Monthly* September 1937, 2. Two of the four plenary speakers were American women, Georgiana Sibley and Georgia Harkness.

36. "Remarks of Dr. Georgia Harkness at the Oxford Conference—Summer 1937," Harkness papers Box 10-38, GETS.

37. "Minutes of the Meeting of Commission II, October 7, 1937, 1 Foreign Missions Council of North America Records RG 27 Box 11–2 PHS.

38. *The Life of the Church: "The Madras Series," Presenting Papers Based upon the Meeting of the International Missionary Council, at Tambaram, Madras, India December 12th to 29th, 1938, Volume IV* (New York: IMC, 1939), 22–50. Yet at the same time, Baptist Anna Canada Swain wrote to friends on the IMC board that "the women have been a wonderful group" and "have been allowed to make their contributions as full members of the Conference" with "poise and good sense." True, there was a "woman's sub-section" and "a little excitement regarding ordination of women," for the most part, they had been "taken for granted as fully authorized members of the group. Swain to Friends of Our Board (IMC) December 28, 1938, ABHS Anna Swain Papers RG 1076 Box 5.

39. "Commission II Annual Report, January 1938, Foreign Missions Council of North America Records RG 27 Box 11-2 PHS.

40. H. Richard Niebuhr, *The Social Sources of Denominationalism* (New York: Henry Holt and Co, 1929; rpt. ed New York: Meridian Books, 1957), 6.

41. Michael G. Thompson, *For God and Globe: Christian Internationalism in the United States Between the Great War and the Cold War* (Ithaca, NY: Cornell University Press, 2015), 14.

42. Twila Cavert to Miss Olive Wyon, July 25, 1947, History of the Commission and of the Department RG 4321.016 WCC archives.

43. "I believe you are very interested in the work of the World's Y.W.C.A.," Cavert wrote to a Frenchwoman involved in UNESCO, "and consequently will be interested to know that Miss Helen Roberts, Miss Winifred Galbraith, Miss van Asch van Wijk, Miss Sarah Chakko and others will be attending the Conference." Twila Cavert to Mrs. P.W. Martin, July 15, 1948, History of the Commission and of the Department RG4321.06 WCC Archives.

44. Cornick, "'So Practical a Mystic'"; on Evelyn Underhill, see for example, *The Evelyn Underhill Reader*, comp. Thomas S. Kepler (New York: Abingdon Press, 1962).

45. Twila Cavert to Olive Wyon, July 25, 1947.

46. Twila Cavert to Helen Roberts, June 25, 1948 History of the Commission and of the Department RG 4321.06 WCC Archives.

47. Twila Cavert to Sue Weddell, June 19, 1948 History of the Commission and of the Department RG 4321.06 WCC Archives. The list of attendees is found in The History of the Commission, 4321.016 WCC Archives.

48. Of the 39 Europeans, 12 were from the United Kingdom, and another 5 from Canada and New Zealand. Twelve of the attendees were from the United States. Some of the women at Baarn were already delegates to the Amsterdam meeting; those who attended were given Accredited Visitor status so that they could attend if they wished.

49. *Remembering Reinhold Niebuhr: Letters of Reinhold and Ursula M. Niebuhr*, ed. Ursula M. Niebuhr (San Francisco: HarperSanFrancisco, 1991), 257–258.

50. Swain to "Dear Folks," August 15, 1948, Anna Swain Papers RG 1076 Box 7 ABHS.

51. Visser 't Hooft, "Karl Barth and the Ecumenical Movement," *Ecumenical Review* 32 (April 1980): 145; *The First Assembly of the World Council of Churches, Held at Amsterdam, August 22nd to September 4th, 1948*, ed. W.A. Visser 't Hooft (New York: Harper and Brothers, 1948), 146–147, 148.

52. Mildred Horton, "Women in the Light of Amsterdam" [c1949] 5, 6 Horton papers 1DD7 Box 9–33, Wellesley College archives.

53. "Report of a Conference," 71.

Chapter 7

1. John Oliver Nelson, "The Amsterdam Assembly in Review," *Federal Council Bulletin* (October 1948): 5–7; Harold E. Fey, "The Amsterdam World Assembly of Churches," *Christian Century* October 4, 1948, 1030–1034.

2. Mildred Horton, "Women in the Light of Amsterdam" [c1949] 5, 6, Horton papers 1DD7 Box 9–33, Wellesley College archives; Swain to "Dear Folks," August 15, 1948, Anna Swain papers RG 1076 Box 7, ABHS.

3. Visser 't Hooft, "Karl Barth and the Ecumenical Movement," *Ecumenical Review* 32 (April 1980): 129–151; Harold Ehrensperger, "Churchwoman of India," *Christian Century* March 11, 1953, 283–287. See also Sarah Chakko, "The Indian S.C.M.: A Witnessing Fellowship," in Correspondence of Members of the Commission, RG 4321.068 WCC Archives.

4. "WCC Assembly at Amsterdam, Plenary Session Minutes," 4, WCC Assembly at Amsterdam RG31.001/12 WCC Archives. The Baarn report was one of four "concerns of the churches" selected for consideration in special afternoon sessions— the others were Christian Approach to the Jews, Training of Laymen, and Christian Reconstruction and Inter-Church Aid.

5. "Plenary Session Minutes," 4–5. Not without reason did Harold Fey complain that "nobody else wanted to talk as much as did the Anglicans." "The Amsterdam World Assembly of Churches," 1030.

6. "Plenary Session Minutes," 7.

7. On Barth's presence, see Visser 't Hooft, "Karl Barth and the Ecumenical Movement"; Karl Barth, "No Christian Marshall Plan," *Christian Century* December 8, 1948, 1330–1333.

8. Horton, "Women in the Light of Amsterdam," 2. Barth's discussion is found in *Church Dogmatics, Volume III, Part Four* (Edinburgh: T&T Clark, 1960), 116–239. Olive Wyon, who came down with appendicitis and was unable to attend the Baarn meeting, had actually translated this section. On Wyon and Barth, see Sarah Chakko to Olive Wyon, June 21, 1950, History of the Commission and of the Department, RG4321.068 WCC Archives. See also Karl Barth, *On Marriage* (Philadelphia: Fortress Press, 1968);

George Tavard, *Woman in Christian Tradition* (Notre Dame, IN: University of Notre Dame Press, 1973), 179–181.

9. Visser 't Hooft, "Karl Barth and the Ecumenical Movement," 145. "Autobiography of Dr. Georgia Harkness written for the Pacific Coast Theological group," 28, Harkness Papers Box 1 Folder 1, GETS. Galatians 3:28 is often cited as the fundamental argument for gender equality: "There is no longer Jew nor Greek, there is neither slave nor free, there is no longer male and female; for all of you are one in Christ Jesus" (NRSV).

10. Visser 't Hooft, "Karl Barth and the Ecumenical Movement," 145.

11. "Autobiography of Dr. Georgia Harkness written for the Pacific Coast Theological group," 28; Visser 't Hooft, "Karl Barth and the Ecumenical Movement," 145.

12. The full list included nineteen members, six of whom were men—and four of whom were absent at the initial meeting in 1950. The "consultants" included two more Americans, Cynthia Wedel and Twila Cavert. See Sarah Chakko to Members of the Commission on the Life and Work of Women in the Church, May 3, 1950, History of the Department and of the Commission RG 4321.09 WCC.

13. Twila Cavert to Sarah Chakko April 30, 1950, History of the Commission and of the Department RG4321.068 WCC Archives.

14. "Minutes of the Meeting of the Commission on the Life and Work of Women in the Church held at Bossey, 6th March—10th March, 1950, History of the Commission and of the Department RG4321.09 WCC Archives.

15. Kathleen Bliss to Sarah Chakko, [n.d. 1950?], History of the Department and of the Commission 4321.067 WCC Archives.

16. "The Commission on the Life and Work of Women in the Church, The Second draft for the study and discussion brochure" [confidential] n.d., History of the Commission and of the Department 4321.09 M1.

17. W. A. Visser 't Hooft to Members of the Commission on the Life and Work of Women in the Church, April 14, 1951, Women's Commission, 4321.09 M1, WCC Archives. Mark Hulsether notes the almost complete absence of articles by women or about gender in crisis theology, 8 out of 158 between 1952 and 1956. See Hulsether, *Building a Protestant Left: Christianity and Crisis Magazine, 1941–1993* (Knoxville: University of Tennessee Press, 1999), 55.

18. The original German is closer to "rank" or the "arrangement of things in order."

19. Fritz Zerbst, *The Office of Women in the Church: A Study in Practical Theology*, trans. Albert G. Merkens (St. Louis: Concordia Publishing House, 1955; rpt. ed. Omaha: Mercinator Press, 2017), 64, 102, 108. Zerbst's book was translated into English in 1955 and became a major influence on Missouri Synod Lutheran conservatism in the 1950s and 1960s. See Mary Todd, *Authority Vested: A Story of Identity and Change in the Lutheran Church—Missouri Synod* (Grand Rapids, MI: Eerdmans, 2000), 154–156.

20. Zerbst, *Office of Women in the Church*, 100, 101.

21. Barth, *Church Dogmatics*, 149, 119, 120.

22. Sarah Chakko, "The Place and Work of Women in Our Protestant Churches," *Advance* February 1951, 17.

23. Joan Arnold Romero, "The Protestant Principle: A Woman's-Eye View of Barth and Tillich," in *Religion and Sexism: Images of Woman in the Jewish and Christian Traditions*, ed. Rosemary Radford Ruether (New York: Simon and Schuster, 1974) 324. Barth's legacy is certainly debated. Katherine Sonderegger, "Barth and Feminism," in *The Cambridge Companion to Karl Barth*, ed. John Webster (Cambridge: Cambridge University Press, 2000), 267–268, 269. Barth's complementarianism did not necessarily preclude ordination: American church historian Cyril Richardson suggested that they could be ordained as "priestesses" with an appropriate set of duties, though he emphasized *"priestesses are not the same thing as priests."* Cyril Richardson, "Women in the Ministry," *Christianity and Crisis* December 10, 1951, 166.

24. Mrs. W. A. Visser 't Hooft, *Vom Wesen der Geschlecter*, February 2, 1951, History of the Department and of the Commission RG4321.068 WCC Archives.

25. Bliss to Chakko, July 22, 1950, Correspondence Members Old Commission, 1949–1954, 4321.067 WCC Archives.

26. Nancy Cott, *The Grounding of Modern Feminism* (New Haven, CT: Yale University Press, 1987), 142.

27. Minutes of the Meeting of the Commission on the Life and Work of Women in the Church held at Bossey, 6th March–10th March, 1950, 2, History of the Commission and of the Department RG 4321.09 WCC Archives.

28. "Men and Women in Church and Society: The Davos Statement," October 13, 1956, 1. Headquarters Staff RG 42.5.029 WCC Archives; "Report of the Division of Ecumenical Action to the Central Committee, 1959," 14, History of the Commission and of the Department RG 4321.016 WCC archives.

29. "Men and Women in Church and Society," 2.

30. "Men and Women in Church and Society," 2. It is worth pointing out some of the general similarities with contemporary evangelical Protestant "complementarianism," which posits the spiritual equality of the sexes and, paradoxically, the necessity of female subordination in the home and church. Critics have rightly identified the potential for abuse in this power imbalance, not to mention the fallacy of assuming that gender issues only concern the role of women. More problematic, however, is that complementarianism makes any consideration of sex and gender differences exceedingly difficult ground for evangelical feminists.

31. "Report of the Consultation Held by the Department on the Cooperation of Men and Women in Church and Society at Herrenhalb, Germany, July 15–19," 1956, History of the Commission ad of the Department RG 4321.016 WCC Archives.

32. Maude Royden, "American Women and Religion," *Forum* (September 1928): 352, 356.

33. Sarah Chakko to Members of the Commission on the Life and Work of Women in the Church, January 25, 1951, History of the Commission and of the Department RG4321.09, WCC archives.

34. Mary Ely Lyman, "From an American Point of View," in "Report of the Meeting of the Commission in the Life and Work of Women in the Church, held at St. Anne's College, Oxford, September 8–13, 1952," 1, History of the Commission and of the Department RG 4321.09 WCC; Lyman, "Women in the Church," *Church Woman* (December 1951), 16.

35. Kathleen Bliss, *The Service and Status of Women in the Churches* (London: SCM Press, 1952), 137, 133.
36. Bliss, *Service and Status*, 183.

Portrait: Georgia Harkness and the Spirit of Heaviness

1. Georgia Harkness to President H. G. Smith, April 17, 1943, Harkness papers Box 1 Series II-23 GETS.
2. On Harkness's career, see Rosemary Skinner Keller, *Georgia Harkness: For Such a Time as This* (Nashville, TN: Abingdon Press, 1992); Margaret Frakes, "Theology Is Her Province," *Christian Century* September 24, 1952, 1088–1091.
3. Frakes, "Theology Is Her Province," 1090.
4. See, for example, Brett Silverstein and Deborah Perlick, *The Cost of Competence: Why Inequality Causes Depression, Eating Disorders, and Illness in Women* (New York: Oxford University Press, 1995). The prototypical female sufferer, living through a time of transition in gender roles, greatly admired her father and was alienated from her mother. Helen Barrett Montgomery, for example, professed "hatred" for her mother, and identified deeply with her father. *Helen Barrett Montgomery: From Campus to World Citizenship* (New York: Fleming H. Revell, 1940), 22, 23. The most famous case of supposed neurasthenia was feminist author Charlotte Perkins Gilman, who chronicled her supposed cure in a short story, "The Yellow Wallpaper."
5. R. Marie Griffith, "Female Suffering and Religious Devotion in American Pentecostalism," in *Women and Twentieth-Century Protestantism*, ed. Margaret Bendroth and Virginia Brereton (Urbana: University of Illinois Press, 2002), 184–208.
6. Harkness, "The Spirit of Heaviness," 4, Harkness Papers Box 11 Folder 10 GETS.
7. "Spirit of Heaviness," 6, 8.
8. Joan Chamberlain Englesman, "The Legacy of Georgia Harkness," in *Women in New Worlds: Historical Perspectives on the Wesleyan Tradition*, ed. Rosemary Skinner Keller et al. (Nashville: Abingdon Press, 1981), 345.
9. Harkness, "Women and the Church," *Christian Century* June 2, 1937, 707, 708.
10. Bill Rose, "Berkeleyan Wins Battle for Women in Ministry," *Oakland Tribune* May 5, 1956, 16D Harkness Papers Box 13 Folder 82, GETS.

Chapter 8

1. Margaret Shannon, *Just Because: The Story of the National Movement of Church Women United in the U.S.A., 1941 through 1975* (Corte Madera, CA: Omega Books, 1977) 62.
2. James Hudnut-Beumler, *Looking for God in the Suburbs: The Religion of the American Dream and Its Critics, 1945–1965* (New Brunswick, NJ: Rutgers University Press, 1994), 1; Stephen J. Whitfield, *The Culture of the Cold War*, 2nd ed. (Baltimore: Johns Hopkins University Press, 1996), 83.

3. Report quoted in Melanie May, *Bonds of Unity: Women, Theology and the Worldwide Church* (Atlanta: Scholars Press, 1989), 26.

4. André Jacques, *Madeleine Barot* (Geneva: WCC Publications, 1991), 65.

5. "Report to the Assembly on the Commission on the Life and Work of Women in the Church," History of the Commission and of the Department RG4321.09 M1, 1, 2, 5 WCC Archives.

6. "Report to the Assembly," 3.

7. Margaret Shannon to Mrs. Douglas Horton July 26, 1954, Mildred Horton Papers 1DD7 folder 5-25 Wellesley College Archives.

8. Margaret Shannon to Madeleine Barot July 17, 1954, Mildred Horton Papers 1DD7 Folder 5-25 Wellesley College Archives.

9. From Chair of Finance Committee to Eugene Carson Blake, July 31, 1957, History of the Commission and the Department RG4321.016 WCC Archives.

10. Susannah Herzel, *A Voice for Women: The Women's Department of the World Council of Churches* (Geneva, Switzerland: WCC, 1981), 13–14.

11. Cynthia Wedel, "Don't Talk—Listen," typescript, March 1955, History of the Commission and of the Department RG 4321.016 WCC Archives.

12. Anticipating criticisms of a "feminist uprising," the women made sure to include influential men: Liston Pope, the dean of Yale Divinity School; Reuben Nelson, General Secretary of the American Baptist Convention; and Ansley Moore, a Presbyterian minister from Pittsburgh.

13. Mildred Horton, "The Status of Women in the Protestant Churches," *Advance* November 30, 1953, 19–20.

14. "Status of Women of the American Baptist Convention," ABWM RG 25 Box 21 ABHS; "Report of New Hampshire Baptist Convention," ABWM RG 25 Box 21 ABHS.

15. Oddly, her husband has received far more attention for his role as dean of Harvard Divinity School and architect of the ecumenical merger that created the United Church of Christ. See Theodore Trost, *Douglas Horton and the Ecumenical Impulse in American Religion* (Cambridge, MA: Harvard Divinity School, Theological Studies, 2003). On Mildred Horton, see Elizabeth Hendricks, "Mildred McAfee Horton (1900–1994): Portrait of a Pathbreaking Christian Leader," *Journal of Presbyterian History* 76 (Summer 1998): 159–174; Margaret Frakes, "Counselor to Councils," *Christian Century* June 25, 1952, 745–748.

16. Horton, "Status of Women," 20.

17. Wyker, *Church Women in the Scheme of Things* (St. Louis: Bethany Press, 1953), 91–92, 95, 96

18. Mrs. James D. Wyker, "The President's Message," *Church Woman* 20 (January 1954): 20; Wyker, *Church Women in the Scheme of Things*, 41.

19. Wyker, *Church Women in the Scheme of Things*, 61, 62.

20. Walter Muelder, "The Christian Message on the Cooperation between Men and Women in Church and Society," held at Lake Forest, Illinois, 11–14 August 1954, ABWM RG 10 Box 5-17 ABHS.

21. Ursula Niebuhr, "Women and the Church and the Fact of Sex," *Christianity and Crisis* August 6, 1951, 106–110; Betty Rice, "Report of Meeting on 'Women and Church,'" *Christianity and Crisis* August 6, 1951, 110–112.

22. Cavert is quoted in John P. Marcum, "Family, Birth Control, and Sexuality in the Christian Church (Disciples of Christ), 1880–1980," *Encounter* 52 (1991): 120; John Charles Wynn, "Where the Churches Speak and Where They Are Silent," in *Foundations for Christian Family Policy*, ed. Elizabeth Steel Genné and William Henry Genné (New York: National Council of Churches of Christ in the U.S.A., 1961), 35–40; "The Task before Us," in *Foundations for Christian Family Policy*, 254–258. See also Margaret Bendroth, *Growing Up Protestant: Parents, Children, and Mainline Churches* (New Brunswick, NJ: Rutgers University Press, 2002), 129–134.

23. "Report of the Consultation on Theological and Scientific Perspectives on the Role of Men and Women and Its Implications for the Cooperation of Men and Women in Church and Society," 3, History of the Commission and of the Department RG 4321.016 WCC Archives.

24. Wedel, "Conclusions," in "Report of the Consultation on Obstacles to the Cooperation of Men and Women—in Working Life—in Public Service—Implications for the Work of the Department, Held at Odense, Denmark, August 8–12, 1958," 27, History of the Commission and of the Department RG 4321.016 WCC Archives.

25. John Patrick Diggins, *The Proud Decades: America in War and Peace, 1941–1960* (New York: W.W. Norton, 1988), 214.

26. Robert Putnam, *The Upswing: How America Came Together a Century Ago and How We Can Do It Again* (New York: Simon and Schuster, 2020).

27. Stephen Whitfield, *The Culture of the Cold War* 2nd ed. (Baltimore, MD: Johns Hopkins University Press, 1996), 12.

28. Chandler, *The Visible Hand: The Managerial Revolution in American Business* (Cambridge, MA: Harvard University Press, 1977), 476–483.

29. Godfrey Hodgson, *America in Our Time: From World War II to Nixon, What Happened and Why* (New York: Vintage Books, 1976), 12.

30. Bendroth, *Growing Up Protestant*, 94, 95.

31. Robert Wuthnow, *After Heaven: Spirituality since the 1950s* (Berkeley: University of California Press, 1998), 30.

32. Horace Bushnell, *Christian Nurture* (1861; rpt. ed. Cleveland, OH: Pilgrim Press, 1994), 245, 293.

33. Jackson Wilcox, "The Marks of a Christian Home," *Hearthstone* 2 (January 1950): 31–32, 44; Hazel Lewis, "Your Child *Is* Learning the Christian Way," *Hearthstone* 2 (June 1950): 17.

34. Robert Wuthnow, *The Restructuring of American Religion: Society and Faith since World War II* (Princeton, NJ: Princeton University Press, 1988), 49.

35. James Findlay, *Church People in the Struggle: The National Council of Churches and the Black Freedom Movement, 1950–1970* (New York: Oxford University Press, 1997), 20, 22.

36. Inez Cavert, *Women in American Church Life; A Study Presented under the Guidance of a Counseling Committee of Women Representing National Interdenominational Agencies* (New York: Friendship Press, 1948), 87–91; Mildred Horton, "The Status of Women in the Protestant Churches," *Advance* November 30, 1953, 19.

37. Interview with Thelma Stevens, RG 1224-3-2:1. A reminiscence about the early history of UCW, notes a problem with one of the early presidents, when she "didn't come across with the cash they hoped to get." "Early History about the Church Woman Magazine," CWU Records 1224-3-2-03 UMCA.

38. "Council Personalities," *National Council Outlook* 4 (April 1951): 18.

39. Nancy Cott, *The Grounding of Modern Feminism* (New Haven, CT: Yale University Press, 1987), 237.

40. Margaret Mead, *Male and Female: A Study of the Sexes in a Changing World* (New York: William Morrow, 1949), 322.

41. Mildred Horton to Roswell Barnes, February 28, 1962, Horton Papers 1DD7 folder 5-23 Wellesley College Archives.

42. Margaret Frakes, "She Heads United Church Women," *Christian Century* May 14, 1952, 587. "Mrs. Douglas Horton Elected Vice President," *Federal Council Bulletin* January 1949, 10.

43. "News-Free Press Forum: Womanpower: Drue Smith Upholds Woman's Place in Defense Day," news clipping in Horton papers, 1DD7 5-26 Wellesley College Archives.

44. Mary Beth Fulton, "So You've Been Elected," *Missions* May 1951, 305.

45. Louise Bondie, "Are You a Self-Confident Church Woman? A Talk with Ruth Graham," *Methodist Woman* 15 (September 1954): 5.

46. Leonard Brummett, "Mrs. Housewife, Meet the Master," *Hearthstone* 3 (January 1951): 19–21.

47. *Meet Mrs. Jones, Typical American Baptist* (New York: American Baptist Home Mission Societies, 1961), 14–21.

48. Ruth Rosen, *The World Split Open: How the Women's Movement Changed America* (New York: Penguin Books, 2000), 19, 20, 25.

49. Thelma Stevens to Mrs. Martha Harvey, February 20, 1959, Women's Division Records 2597-3-6:5 UMCA; Woman's Society of Christian Service, The Methodist Church Southwest Texas Conference circular letter, August 20, 1959, Women's Division Records 2597-3-6:5 UMCA. See also "Changing Patterns for Women," Women's Division of Christian Service, 1957, Women's Division Records 2597-3-6:03, Folder 1, UMCA.

50. Cynthia Wedel, "Womanpower," *Church Woman* (March 1958): 8; "Why Women Work," *Church Woman* (August–September 1958): 10–12, 30. See also Helen E. Baker, "Employed Women and the Church," *Church Woman* 24 (June–July 1958): 10–13, and study guide prepared by Cynthia Wedel, "Employed Women and the Church," [pamphlet] United Church Women, 1959.

51. Helen Smith, "Only Potential Cookie Bakers?" *Church Woman* 25 (August–September 1959), 12–15; Committee Report of the Pilot Study on Employed Women in Church and Community," draft copy, n.d. Women's Division 2597-3-6:5 UMCA.

52. "Conference on Women in the Church," March 28–April 1, 1955, 19, Lillian Gregory Papers S-GIV Series M Folder 5, CLA.

53. Elsie Thomas Culver, *Women in the World of Religion* (Garden City, NY: Doubleday, 1967), 199–200.

54. The text of the overture from the Rochester Presbytery and the committee report are found in *Minutes of the General Assembly of the Presbyterian Church in the United States of America, Part I. Journal and Supplement* (Philadelphia: Office of the General Assembly, 1955), 95–98.

55. "Presbyterian Church U.S.A. Ordains First Woman Minister," *Presbyterian Life* October 27, 1956, 18.

56. Burkhart, "Should Women Be Ordained to the Ministry? Yes," *Presbyterian Life* November 26, 1955, 20.

57. John D. Craig, "Should Women Be Ordained to the Ministry? No," *Presbyterian Life* November 26, 1955, 36.

58. "'Should Women Be Ordained to the Ministry?' Debate Continues," *Presbyterian Life* January 7, 1956, 4.

59. Burkhart, "Should Women Be Ordained?," 38.

60. Craig, "Should Women Be Ordained?," 36.

61. Craig, "Should Women Be Ordained to the Ministry?," 36; "Breakthrough for the Woman Minister," *Christian Century* 23 (January 1957): 100.

62. *Daily Christian Advocate* May 4, 1956, n.p.

63. Emory Stevens Bucke, "Should Women Be Granted Full Ministerial Status?" *The Pastor* 19 (November 1955), 11.

64. "Favors Women Ministers," *The Pastor* 19 (January 1956); "Not That Bad," *The Pastor* 19 (January 1956).

65. Harkness, "A Matter of Justice," *The Pastor* 19 (February 1956), 2–3.

66. The verbatim account is found in the *Daily Christian Advocate*, May 4, 1956. See also Barbara B. Troxell, "Ordination of Women in the United Methodist Tradition," *Methodist History* 37, no. 2 (January 1999): 119–130; Connor S. Kenaston, "From Rib to Robe: Women's Ordination in the United Methodist Church," *Methodist History* 53, no. 3 (April 2015): 162–172.

67. *Daily Christian Advocate*, May 4, 1956, n.p.

Chapter 9

1. "Great Day for Women on the March," *New York Times* August 30, 1970, 125, 128; Maggie Doherty, "Feminist Factions United and Filled the Streets for this Historic March," *New York Times* August 26, 1970, https://www.nytimes.com/2020/08/26/us/womens-strike-for-equality.html?smid=em-share, accessed September 16, 2020.

2. Nelle Morton, *The Journey Is Home* (Boston: Beacon Press, 1985), 2, 4.

3. Mark Toulouse, "Feminist Gains," *Christian Century* December 20, 2000, 1341–1343.

4. Mark Chaves, *American Religion: Contemporary Trends* (Princeton, NJ: Princeton University Press, 2011), 73–75; Wade Clark Roof and William McKinney, *American Mainline Religion: Its Changing Shape and Future*, 4th ed. (New Brunswick, NJ: Rutgers University Press, 1992), 204–209; Robert Putnam and David Campbell,

American Grace: How Religion Divides and Unites Us (New York: Simon and Schuster, 2010), 242–246.

5. https://www.theaquilareport.com/pca-general-assembly-should-not-approve-cmcs-recommendation-to-form-a-study-committee-on-women-serving-in-ministry/, accessed October 8, 2020

6. See, for example, Mark Chaves, *Ordaining Women: Conflict and Culture in Religious Institutions* (Cambridge, MA: Harvard University Press, 1999); Jackson Carroll, Barbara Hargrove, and Adair Lummis, *Women of the Cloth: A New Opportunity for Churches* (San Francisco: Harper and Row, 1983); E. C. Lehman, *Women Clergy Breaking through Gender Barriers* (New Brunswick, NJ: Transaction, 1985); Barbara Brown Zikmund, Adair Lummis, and Patricia Change, *An Uphill Calling: Ordained Women in Contemporary Protestantism* (Louisville, KY: Westminster/John Knox Press, 1997).

7. Doris Leenhouts Hunter, "'The Monstrous Regiment of Women': Their Search for Vocation in the Church," *Nexus* 7 (November 1963): 2, 42.

8. Norma Ramsey Jones, "Women in the Ministry," in *Women's Liberation and the Church: The New Demand for Freedom in the Life of the Christian Church*, ed. Sarah Bentley Doely (New York: Association Press, 1970), 63, 65.

9. Earl Main, "Are Women More Active Church Members Than Men?" *Renewal* 4 (October 1964): 17–18.

10. Elton Trueblood and Pauline Trueblood, *The Recovery of Family Life* (New York: Harper and Row, 1953), 113. Also Margaret Bendroth, *Growing Up Protestant: Parents, Children, and Mainline Churches* (New Brunswick: Rutgers University Press, 2002), 99–118.

11. Elizabeth Achtemeier, *The Feminine Crisis in Christian Faith* (Nashville, TN: Abingdon Press, 1965), 14, 19, 34–35.

12. Peggy Way, "Women in the Church," *Renewal* 4 (October 1964): 4.

13. Eileen Lindner, "Still In but Out," in *Women and Church: The Challenge of Ecumenical Solidarity in an Age of Alienation*, ed. Melanie May (Grand Rapids, MI: Eerdmans, 1991), 103.

14. "History of the Council for Lay Life and Work," Lillian Gregory Papers, S-G III, Series A, Folder 2, CLA; J. Martin Bailey, "Consultation on Lay Life and Work," *United Church Herald* March 22, 1962, 2.

15. "Opening Devotions," Executive Board, National Women's Fellowship, February 1963, Lillian Gregory Papers, S-G IV Series D Folder 2 CLA; "From the Editor's Uneasy Chair," *Guide Posts* 20 (February–March 1963), 1. In 1956, the Evangelical and Reformed Women's Guide had 4 professional staff members, and 13 support staff (for 350,000 members), and the Congregational Christian Women's Fellowship one full-time professional staff person and one secretary for some 700,000 members. "Minutes of the Women's Work Committee of the Women's Council," June 20, 1956, Lillian Gregory Papers, S-G IV Series B, Folder 3, CLA.

16. "From the Editor's Uneasy Chair," *Guide Posts* 20 (April 1962), 1. The dissolution also hindered the relationship with United Church Women.

17. "Helen Huntington Smith Heads Council for Lay Life and Work," *United Church Herald* September 6, 1962, 2.

18. Mildred Horton, Church Women—Yesterday, Today, and Tomorrow," 4 Mildred Horton Papers, Box 9 Folder 36, Wellesley College Archives.

19. "Women's Role in the United Church," *United Church Herald* April 19, 1962, 7.

20. Mary Sudman Donovan, "Beyond the Parallel Church: Strategies of Separatism and Integration in the Governing Councils of the Episcopal Church," in *Gender, Spirituality, and Commitment in an American Mainline Denomination*, ed. Catherine M. Prelinger (New York: Oxford University Press, 1996), 146.

21. Donovan, "Beyond the Parallel Church," 150, 157.

22. "Editor's Preface: Women: What Do We Want?" *Church Woman* (October–June 1969), 2.

23. Margaret Shannon, *Just Because: The Story of the National Movement of Church Women United in the U.S.A. 1941 through 1975* (Corte Madera, CA: Omega Books, 1977), 278, 282.

24. Shannon, *Just Because*, 276; "Comment and Commentary," *Church Woman* (February 1968): 33, 34.

25. Doug Rossinow, *The Politics of Authenticity: Liberalism, Christianity, and the New Left in America* (New York: Columbia University Press, 1998), 314; Ruth Rosen, *The World Split Open: How the Modern Women's Movement Changed America* (New York: Penguin Books 2000), esp. 63–93; Estelle Friedman, *No Turning Back: The History of Feminism and the Future of Women* (New York: Ballantine Books, 2002), 84–94. Neither Rosen nor Friedman devote more than a few pages to considerations of religion and feminism.

26. Rebecca Klatch, "The Formation of Feminist Consciousness among Left- and Right-Wing Activists of the 1960s," *Gender and Society* 15 (December 2001): 795–797.

27. Virginia Lieson Brereton, *From Sin to Salvation: Stories of Women's Conversions, 1800 to the Present* (Bloomington: Indiana University Press, 1991), 106–121.

28. Mary Henold, *Catholic and Feminist: The Surprising History of the American Catholic Feminist Movement* (Chapel Hill: University of North Carolina Press, 2008), 5.

29. Harold Lindsell, "Egalitarianism and Scriptural Integrity," *Christianity Today* March 26, 1976, 693–694.

30. Rev. Albert C. Thomas to Mrs. Leslie Swain, May 31, 1944, Anna Swain Papers RG 1076 Box 2 ABHS.

31. The list included Catholic authors Mary Daly and Sidney Callahan, author of *The Illusion of Eve: The Modern Woman's Search for Identity* (New York: Sheed and Ward, 1965), as well as the work of French ecumenists Andre Dumas and Francine Dumas, author of *Man and Woman, Similarity and Difference* (Geneva, Switzerland: WCC, 1966) and also D. S. Bailey, *The Man–Woman Relationship in Christian Thought* (London: Longmans, 1959). The sole Protestant author was Lutheran Krister Stendahl, and his work *The Bible and the Role of Women* (Philadelphia: Fortress Press, 1966). See "Guidelines: Operation Grass Roots," 15, NOW papers MC 496 Carton 210 #57, Schlesinger Library. The two compilers were Arlene Swidler, a Roman Catholic

laywoman and scholar, and Elizabeth Farians, a professor of theology at Sacred Heart University in Bridgeport, Connecticut.

32. "Report of the Consultation held at 'Uplands', Hy Wycombe, Bucks, England July 27–August 2, 1960, on "Towards Responsible Cooperation between Men and Women, Our Christian Responsibility," 12, 14, History of the Commission and of the Department 4321.016 WCC Archives.

33. "Consultation on "Relationship of Men and Women at Work," Geneva, June 29–July 4, 1964, 26, History of the Commission and of the Department 4321.018 WCC Archives.

34. Andrè Jacques, *Madeleine Barot* (Geneva: WCC Publications, 1991), 68.

35. Barot, *Cooperation of Men and Women in Church, Family and Society* (Geneva, Switzerland: WCC Publications, 1964), 10, 38, 39.

36. "The Ordination of Women: An Ecumenical Problem: Report of a Consultation organized by the Department on Cooperation of Men and Women in Church, Family and Society and the Department on Faith and Order, in Geneva 10th–12th May 1963," in *Concerning the Ordination of Women* (Lausanne, Switzerland: WCC, 1963), 5. See also Elise Gibson, "Ecumenism and the Ordination of Women," *CrossCurrents* 28 (Fall 1976): 299–305.

37. Gail Allan, "We Intend to Move Together: The Story of Ecumenical Women on a Pilgrimage of Gender Justice," *International Review of Missions* (2015), 6; Melanie May, *Bonds of Unity: Women, Theology, and the Worldwide Church* (Atlanta, GA: Scholars Press, 1989); 36; "Amended Report, Submitted to Central Committee, August 1968," 4, 5, History of the Commission and of the Department 4321.018 WCC Archives.

38. May, *Bonds of Unity*, 35; Betty Johns, "Uppsala": The New in the Midst of the Old," *Church Woman* (October 1968): 27–31.

39. Pauline Webb, *She Flies Beyond: Memories and Hopes of Women in the Ecumenical Movement* (Geneva, Switzerland: WCC Publications, 1993), 18–19; Marga Buhrig, "Discrimination against Women," in *Technology and Social Justice; an International Symposium on the Social and Economic Teaching of the World Council of Churches from Geneva 1966 to Uppsala 1968*, ed. Ronald Preston (Valley Forge, PA: Judson Press, 1971), 299.

40. "Discrimination against Women," by Rev. Dr. Philip Potter, General Secretary of the WCC at the Consultation on "Sexism in the 1970s: Discrimination against Women, West Berlin, June 1974," 5, Constance Parvey papers Box 38 Folder 7, Schlesinger Library; "On Behalf of the Women: A Tribute to Philip A. Potter," *Ecumenical Review* 67 (July 2015): 167.

41. "The Journey of an Idea," n.d., 1, 2, Parvey papers Box 44, Folder 9, Schlesinger Library.

42. "Churches," November 7, 1975, Parvey papers 3, Box 37, Folder 13, Schlesinger Library; "Introduction: Experiences of Women in the Institutional Church" [draft], Parvey papers, Box 44, Folder 9, Schlesinger Library. The group included theologian Letty Russell, biblical scholar Sharon Rindge, and Elizabeth Verdesi, who published *In*

but Still Out: Women in the Church, one of the first histories of Presbyterian women, in 1973.

43. "Notes for the Report of the Boston Area World Council Task Force on the Community of Women and Men in the Church; Letty Russell, "Theological Aspects of Partnership of Women and Men in Christian Communities," 7, Parvey papers Box 38, F7, Schlesinger Library.

44. "Women in the Ordained Ministry: Reflections for the Boston Task Force, Community of Women and Men Study, December 14, 1974," 1–2, Parvey papers Box 37, F13, Schlesinger Library.

45. John McGreevey, *Catholicism and American Freedom: A History* (New York: W.W. Norton, 2004).

46. Henold, *Catholic and Feminist*, 22, 49.

47. Henold, *Catholic and Feminist*, 60, 22. See Sidney Callahan, *The Illusion of Eve: Modern Woman's Quest for Identity* (New York: Sheed and Ward, 1965); Sally Cunneen, *Sex: Female, Religion: Catholic* (New York: Holt Rhinehart Winston, 1968).

48. Henold, *Catholic and Feminist*, 20–21, 86.

49. Henold, 19; Eva Fleischer and Donna Myers Ambrogi, "Grailville in the Sixties: Catechetics and Ecumenism," *U.S. Catholic Historian* 11 (Fall 1993): 42.

50. Sarah Cunningham, "The Grail as a Movement," *Church Woman* (November 1965): 9,10; Janet Kalven, *Women Breaking Boundaries: A Grail Journey 1940–1972* (Albany: SUNY Press, 1999). The session leaders were Dr. Alice Wonders, chair of the philosophy department at Texas Western College, and Sister Maria McDermott of the Sisters of St. Joseph. Henold, *Catholic and Feminist*, 74, 77.

51. "A Theological Experience," *Church Woman* (December 1968): 34, 35.

52. Farians "How NOW Got Religion," NOW MC496, Carton 49, #8, Schlesinger Library; Henold, *Catholic and Feminist*, 72–81. On religion and feminism, see Ann Braude, "A Religious Feminist—Who Can Find Her? Historiographical Challenges from the National Organization for Women," *Journal of Religion* (2004): 555–572.

53. Henold, *Catholic and Feminist*, 62–63,76, 77.

54. Henold, *Catholic and Feminist*, 74, 77; "National NOW Conference Resolutions Relating to Religion," NOW Records MC 496, Carton 49, Folder 8, Schlesinger Library.

55. "Ecumenical Sister Celebration Marks All-Out Assault on the Male Image of God and Patriarchal Religions," *Sisterhood for Personhood* 1 (December 1972), in NOW Records, MC 496, Carton 201, Folder 55, Schlesinger Library; "Women + Religion = Action," 45, 48 NOW records MC 496, Carton 201, Folder 60, Schlesinger Library.

56. Jill Gill, *Embattled Ecumenism: The National Council of Churches, the Vietnam War, and the Trials of the Protestant Left* (DeKalb: Northern Illinois University Press, 2011), 6.

57. Elsie Gibson, "Ecumenism and the Ordination of Women," *CrossCurrents* 28 (Fall 1978): 305.

58. Margaret O'Gara, "Ecumenism and Feminism in Dialogue on Authority," in *Women and Church: The Challenge of Ecumenical Solidarity in an Age of Alienation*, ed. Melanie May (Grand Rapids, MI: Eerdmans, 1991), 118.

59. Rossinow, *The Politics of Authenticity*.

60. Sara Evans, *Journeys That Opened Up the World: Women, Student Christian Movements, and Social Justice, 1955–1975* (New Brunswick, NJ: Rutgers University Press, 2004), 3, 4–5, 9.

61. Ethel Brooks and Dorothy Hodgson, "'An Activist Temperament': An Interview with Charlotte Bunch," *Women's Studies Quarterly* 35 (Fall–Winter 2007): 60–74. For an earlier perspective, see the interview "Church Women, Politics, and Change: A Conversation with Charlotte Bunch Weeks," *Church Woman* (June–July 1968): 14–20.

62. "Women Exploring Theology at Grailville, Loveland, Ohio, June 18–25, 1972," Unpaginated mimeograph in author's possession.

63. Davida Foy Crabtree, "Ordination Paper," 2 [1972], Davida Crabtree Papers, MS 5324, B1, F27, CLA.

64. Speight, "The Ministerial Reformation," 136.

65. "Autobiographical Typescript," Parvey Papers Box 49, Folder 10, Schlesinger Library; "Autobiography," Parvey Papers Box 49, Folder 7, Schlesinger Library.

66. Catherine Brekus, *Strangers and Pilgrims: Female Preaching in America, 1740–1845* (Chapel Hill: University of North Carolina Press, 1998), 181–186; Maren Hansen and Debby Streeter, "GTU Women's Chapels." *Newsletter* (GTU Center for Women and Religion) 4 (Fall 1977): n.p.

67. Morton, *The Journey Is Home* (Boston: Beacon Press, 1985), 49. The quotation is from an article included in this collection, from 1971, "The Rise of Woman Consciousness in a Male Language Structure."

68. Edith Platz, "My Story, Our Story," in *Lutheran Women in Ordained Ministry*, ed. Gloria Bengston (Minneapolis, MN: Augsburg Press, 1995), 49–50, cited in Speight, "Ministerial Revolution."

69. "A Conversation with Valerie Saiving," *Journal of Feminist Studies in Religion* 4 (Fall 1988): 102.

70. Valerie Saiving Goldstein, "The Human Situation: A Feminine View," *Journal of Religion* 40 (April 1960): 109.

71. Lilian Calles Barger, *The World Come of Age: An Intellectual History of Liberation Theology* (New York: Oxford University Press, 2018), 179–181.

72. Ruth Peale, *The Adventure of Being a Wife* (Carmel, NY: Guideposts Association, Inc., 1971), 35.

73. Carol V. R. George, *God's Salesman: Norman Vincent Peale and the Power of Positive Thinking* (New York: Oxford, 1993), 239.

74. Peale, *Adventure of Being a Wife*, 102, 236, 238.

75. Harkness, "Women Confront a New Age," *The Methodist Woman* (June 1964): 17–18; Harkness Papers Box 12-145 GETS; Harkness quoted in Rosemary Skinner Keller, *Georgia Harkness: For Such a Time as This* (Nashville, TN: Abingdon Press, 1992), 292.

76. Horton, "There Ought to Be a Woman," 2, Horton Papers 1DD1 9-31, Wellesley College. According to Davida Crabtree, Horton was adamantly opposed to a proposal, brought to her by Crabtree and Mary Daly, for a Boston Theological Institute. Author interview with Davida Crabtree, December 2, 2019.

77. Horton, "Church Women—Yesterday, Today and Tomorrow, 5.

78. Davida Foy Crabtree, "Women's Liberation and the Church," in *Women's Liberation and the Church: The New Demand for Freedom in the Life of the Christian Church* (New York: Association Press, 1970), 19–20.

79. Peggy Way, "Women in the Church," *Renewal* 4 (October 1964), 5, 8.

80. Beverly Wildung Harrison, "Sexism and the Contemporary Church: When Evasion Becomes Complicity," in *Sexist Religion and Women in the Church*, ed. Alice Hageman (New York: Association Press 1974), 209.

81. Patricia Hundley, "No Touchstone from the Past: A Woman Theology Student's Views," *Comment* 8 (Winter 1974):

82. Jackson Carroll, Barbara Hargrove, and Adair Lummis, *Women of the Cloth: A New Opportunity for the Churches* (San Francisco: Harper and Row, 1983), 76–77; Speight, "Ministerial Revolution," 220. For a tracking of church conflicts regarding ordination, see Mark Chaves and James Cavendish, "Recent Changes in Women's Ordination Conflicts: The Effects of a Social Movement on Intraorganizational Controversy," *Journal for the Scientific Study of Religion* 36 (December 1997), 582.

83. Jill Lepore, *The Secret History of Wonder Woman* (New York: Alfred A. Knopf, 2014), 293.

84. Peggy Way, "Contemporary Women and the Contemporary Church: Challenges to Commitment," 2, in Personal Files of Madeline Barot RG 4321.115 WCC Archives.

Portrait: Cynthia Wedel and the Limits of Cooperation

1. "Church Council Victor," *New York Times* December 5, 1969, 32.

2. Alan Geyer, "Joy Box with No Joy: The N.C.C. at Detroit," *Christian Century* December 17, 1969, 1601–1605.

3. Cynthia Wedel, "Recollections of History," August 10, 1985, CWU 1223-7-3:25 UMCA. See also Jill Gill, *Embattled Ecumenism: The National Council of Churches, the Vietnam War, and the Trials of the Protestant Left* (DeKalb: Northern Illinois University Press, 2011), 273, 274.

4. Geyer, "Joy Box with No Joy," 1601–1605.

5. Geyer, "Joy Box with No Joy," 1601.

6. Geyer, "Joy Box with No Joy," 1601.

7. "Church Council Victor," *New York Times* December 5, 1969, 32; "Cynthia Wedel—UCW President: A Woman of Convictions," *National Council Outlook* 6 (May 1956): 7.

8. Wedel, "Recollections," 1; Bettye Collier-Thomas, *Jesus, Jobs, and Justice: African American Women and Religion* (Philadelphia: Temple University Press, 2014), 410–420; Susan Hartmann, "Expanding Feminism's Field and Focus: Activism in the National Council of Churches in the 1960s and 1970s," in *Women and Twentieth Century Protestantism*, 51, 52; Dorothy Rensenbrink, "Introductions, Please: NCC's Gracious New President," *Tempo* (December 1969—January 1970), 11.

9. "Cynthia Wedel, Past National President of Church Women United, Dies at 77," Press release, CWU 1223-7-3:25 UMCA.

10. Wedel, "Women in the Church," [pamphlet, n.d.]; "The Place of Women in the Churches' Work," *Church Woman* 23 (April 1957): 14–17, 37.

11. "Cynthia Wedel: UCW President: A Woman of Convictions," 7; "Cynthia Wedel: President and Friend," *Church Woman* 24 (December 1958): 17–19.

12. Cynthia Wedel, "Cooperation," *Church Woman* 22 (November 1956): 19–21; Wedel, "Co-operation of Men and Women," *Church Woman* 24 (October 1958): 12–13, 39; "Women in the News," *Church Woman* 24 (April 1958): 18; Wedel "Recollections," 3.

13. Dorothy Rensenbrink, "Introductions, Please: NCC's Gracious New President," *Tempo* (December 1969—January 1970), 11.

14. "Statement of the Women's Caucus of the National Council of the Churches of Christ in the U.S.A., December 1969, Detroit, Michigan," Davida Crabtree Papers MS 5324 B1/F13 CLA.

15. "Report of Women's Caucus," Crabtree Papers MS5324 B1/F27 CLA. See also Hartmann, "Expanding Feminism's Field and Focus."

16. Resenbrink, "Introductions, Please," 1.

Afterword

1. John Demos, *The Enemy Within: 2,000 Years of Witch-Hunting in the Western World* (New York: Viking Penguin, 2008), 57, 58, 108.

2. Sondra Chemaly, *Rage Becomes Her: The Power of Women's Anger* (New York: Atria Books 2018), 5.

3. "Stubborn Unlaid Ghosts," *Advance* November 30, 1953, 4.

4. Carol Osiek, *Anger: On Being a Feminist in the Church* (New York: Paulist Press, 1986), 16.

5. Osiek, *Anger*, 2.

6. Florence Hooper, "A Woman Speaks Out: Warning against Bachelor Suggestions," *Zion's Herald* April 17, 1946, 362.

7. Leslie Jamison, "Lungs Full of Burning," in *Burn It Down: Women Writing about Anger*, ed. Lilly Dancyger (New York: Seal Press, 2019), 20.

8. Gunnar Myrdal, *An American Dilemma: The Negro Problem and Modern Democracy*, vol. 2 (New York: Harper and Brothers, 1944), 1979; Helen Mayer Hacker, "Women as a Minority Group," *Social Forces* 30 (October 1951): 67.

Selected Bibliography

Manuscript Collections

American Baptist Historical Society, Macon, Georgia
- Anna Canada Swain Papers
- American Baptist Women's Ministries Collection

Congregational Library and Archives, Boston, Massachusetts
- Lillian Gregory Papers
- Davida Crabtree Papers
- Massachusetts Council of Churches

Garrett-Evangelical Theological School Library, Evanston, Illinois
- Georgia Harkness Papers

Presbyterian Historical Society, Philadelphia, Pennsylvania
- Home Missions Council of North America
- Presbyterian Church in the U.S.A. General Assembly Stated Clerk Lewis Seymour Mudge Correspondence
- Presbyterian Church in the U.S.A. Office of the Stated Clerk
- Presbyterian Church in the U.S.A. General Assembly Permanent Judicial Commission Records
- National Council of Churches
  - Association of Council Secretaries (24)
  - Foreign Missions Council of North America
  - Christian Unity Records

Schlesinger Library, Cambridge, Massachusetts
- National Organization for Women Collection
- Constance Parvey Papers

United Methodist Church General Commission on Archives and History, Madison, New Jersey

Women's Division of the General Board of Global Ministries
- Church Women United Records

United States Library of Congress, Washington, D.C.
- Nannie Helen Burroughs Papers

Wellesley College Archives, Wellesley, Massachusetts
- Mildred Horton Papers

World Council of Churches Archives
- History of the Commission (1946–1943) and of the Department (1954–1958)
- Headquarters Staff Papers
- Madeleine Barot Papers

Periodicals
Advance
The Baptist
Baptist News

Christian Century
Church Woman
Congregationalist
Church Management
Daily Christian Advocate
Ecumenical Review
Federal Council Bulletin
Guideposts
Hearthstone
Layman's Movement Review
Methodist Woman
Methodist Woman's Association Bulletin
Mission
Missionary Review of the World
Motive
National Council Outlook
Nexus
The Pastor
The Presbyterian
Presbyterian Banner
Renewal
Tempo
World's YWCA Monthly
Watchman-Examiner
Zion's Herald

Books and Articles

"A Conversation with Valerie Saiving." *Journal of Feminist Studies in Religion* 4 (Fall 1988): 99–115.

Achtemeier, Elizabeth. *The Feminine Crisis in Christian Faith*. Nashville, TN: Abingdon Press, 1965.

Adams, Betty Livingston. *Black Women's Christian Activism: Seeking Social Justice in a Northern Suburb*. New York: New York University Press, 2016.

Allen, Gail. "We Intend to Move Together: The Story of Ecumenical Women on a Pilgrimage of Gender Justice." *International Review of Missions* 104, no. 1 (2015): 3–17.

Annual Report of the Woman's Division of Christian Service of the Board of Missions and Church Extension of the Methodist Church. New York, Methodist Board of Publication, 1941.

Asbury, Jewel M. "A History of the Integration of the WABHMS and the ABHMS: A Case Study of the Oppression of Women." Master's thesis: Colgate Rochester Divinity School, 1983.

Barger, Lilian Calles. *The World Come of Age: An Intellectual History of Liberation Theology*. New York: Oxford, 2018.

Barot, Madeleine. *Cooperation of Men and Women in Church, Family and Society*. Geneva, Switzerland: WCC Publications, 1964.

Barth, Karl. *Church Dogmatics, Volume III, Part Four*. Edinburgh: T&T Clark, 1960.

Bate, H. N., ed. *Faith and Order; Proceedings of the World Conference, Lausanne, August 3–21, 1927*. London: Student Christian Movement, 1927.

"Because They Are Women" and Other Editorials from "The Christian Advocate" on the Admission of Women to the General Conference. New York: Hunt and Eaton, 1891.

Bederman, Gail. "'The Women Have Had Charge of the Church Work Long Enough': The Men and Religion Forward Movement of 1911–1912 and the Remasculinization of Middle-Class Protestantism." *American Quarterly* 41 (September 1989): 432–465.

Bellamy, V. Nelle. "Participation of Women in the Public Life of the Church from Lambeth Conference." *Historical Magazine of the Protestant Episcopal Church* 51 (1982): 81–98.

Bendroth, Margaret. *Fundamentalism and Gender, 1875 to the Present*. New Haven, CT: Yale University Press, 1993.

Bendroth, Margaret. *Growing Up Protestant: Parents, Children, and Mainline Churches*. New Brunswick, NJ: Rutgers University Press, 2002.

Bendroth, Margaret, and Virginia Brereton, eds. *Women and Twentieth-Century Protestantism*. Champaign-Urbana: University of Illinois Press, 2002.

Bengston, Gloria, ed. *Lutheran Women in Ordained Ministry*. Minneapolis, MN: Augsburg Press, 1995.

Bennett, Katherine. *The Status of Women in the Presbyterian Church in the United States of America, with Reference to Other Denominations*. Philadelphia: Presbyterian Board of Publication, 1929.

Bennett, Katherine, and Margaret Hodge. *Causes of Unrest among the Women of the Church: Report of a Special Committee to the General Council of the Presbyterian Church in the U.S.A.* Philadelphia: Presbyterian Board of Publication, 1927.

Bennett, Mrs. Fred (Mary Katherine), Florence G. Tyler, and Mrs. E. H. Goedeke, eds. "All That Is Past Is Prologue: The Emergence of Interdenominational Organizations among Protestant Church Women." New York: United Council of Church Women, 1944.

Boyd, Lois A., and R. Douglas Brackenridge. *Presbyterian Women in America: Two Centuries of a Quest for Status*. Westport, CT: Greenwood Press, 1983.

Bradley, Mark. *The World Reimagined: Americans and Human Rights in the Twentieth Century*. Cambridge: Cambridge University Press, 2016.

Braude, Ann. "Women's History *Is* American Religious History," in *Re-Telling U.S. Religious History*, ed. Thomas Tweed, 87–107. Berkeley: University of California Press, 1997.

Braude, Ann. "A Religious Feminist—Who Can Find Her? Historiographical Challenges from the National Organization for Women." *Journal of Religion* 84, no. 4 (2004): 555–572.

Brekus, Catherine. *Strangers and Pilgrims: Female Preaching in America, 1740–1845*. Chapel Hill: University of North Carolina Press, 1998.

Brereton, Virginia. "United and Slighted: Women as Subordinated Insiders." In *Between the Times: The Travail of the Protestant Establishment in America, 1900–1960*, ed. William R. Hutchison, 143–167. Cambridge: Cambridge University Press, 1989.

Brereton, Virginia, and Margaret Bendroth. "Secularization and Gender: An Historical Approach to Women and Religion in the Twentieth Century." *Method and Theory in the Study of Religion* 13 (2001): 209–223.

Brereton, Virginia, and Christa Klein, "American Women in Ministry: A History of Protestant Beginning Points." In *Women of Spirit: Female Leadership in the Jewish and Christian Traditions*, ed. Rosemary Ruether and Eleanor McLaughlin, 302–332. New York: Simon and Schuster, 1979.

Brown, Callum. *The Death of Christian Britain: Understanding Secularisation, 1800–2000.* London: Routledge, 2001.

Bruce, Steven. *Secularization: In Defence of an Unfashionable Theory.* New York: Oxford University Press, 2011.

Buhrig, Marga. "Discrimination against Women." In *Technology and Social Justice: An International Symposium on the Social and Economic Teaching of the World Council of Churches from Geneva 1966 to Uppsala 1968,* ed. Ronald Preston, 295–321. Valley Forge, PA: Judson Press, 1971.

Bushnell, Horace. *Christian Nurture.* New York, 1861; rpt. ed. Cleveland, OH: Pilgrim Press, 1994.

Bushnell, Horace. *Women's Suffrage; The Reform against Nature.* New York: Charles Scribner and Co., 1869.

Butler, Jon. "Jack-in-the-Box Faith: The Religion Problem in Modern American History." *Journal of American History* 90 (March 2004): 1357–1378.

Bynum, Carolyn Walker. *Fragmentation and Redemption: Essays on Gender and the Human Body in Medieval Religion.* New York: Zone Books, 1991.

Calkins, Gladys Gilkey. *Follow Those Women: Church Women in the Ecumenical Movement.* New York: National Council of Churches, 1961.

Carroll, H. K. *The Religious Forces of the United States.* New York: 1912.

Carroll, Jackson W., Barbara Hargrove, and Adair Lummis. *Women of the Cloth: A New Opportunity for Churches.* San Francisco: Harper and Row, 1983.

Case, Carl Delos. *The Masculine in Religion.* Philadelphia: American Baptist Publication Society, 1906.

Cavert, Inez. *Women in American Church Life: A Study Prepared under the Guidance of a Counseling Committee of Women Representing National Interdenominational Agencies.* New York: Friendship Press, 1948.

Cavert, Samuel McCrea. *The American Churches in the Ecumenical Movement, 1900–1968.* New York: Association Press, 1968.

Chandler, Alfred D. *The Visible Hand: The Managerial Revolution in American Business.* Cambridge, MA: Harvard University Press, 1977.

Chaves, Mark. *American Religion: Contemporary Trends.* Princeton, NJ: Princeton University Press, 2011.

Chaves, Mark. *Ordaining Women: Conflict and Culture in Religious Institutions.* Cambridge, MA: Harvard University Press, 1999.

Chaves, Mark, and James Cavendish. "Recent Changes in Women's Ordination Conflicts: The Effects of a Social Movement on Intraorganizational Controversy." *Journal for the Scientific Study of Religion* 36 (December 1997): 574–584.

Chemaly, Sondra. *Rage Becomes Her: The Power of Women's Anger.* New York: Atria Books, 2018.

Coe, George A. *The Spiritual Life: Studies in the Science of Religion.* New York: Eaton and Mains, 1900.

Coffman, Elesha. *The Christian Century and the Rise of the Protestant Mainline.* New York: Oxford University Press, 2013.

Collier-Thomas, Bettye. *Jesus, Jobs, and Justice: African-American Women and Religion.* Philadelphia: Temple University Press, 2014.

Committee on the War and the Religious Outlook. *Religion among Men, As Revealed by a Study of Conditions in the Army.* New York: Association Press, 1920.

Concerning the Ordination of Women. Lausanne, Switzerland: WCC, 1963.

Condé, Bertha. *The New Day and Its Possibilities for Church Women: An Address Delivered at the Biennial Meeting of the Woman's Missionary Organizations, St. Paul, Minnesota, May 16, 1929.* Philadelphia: Board of Foreign Missions and Board of Home Missions of the PCUSA, 1929.

Cope, Henry F. *The Efficient Layman or the Religious Training of Men.* Boston: Pilgrim Press, 1911.

Cornick, David. "'So Practical a Mystic'—Olive Wyon (1881–1966)." *Journal of the United Reformed Church History Society* 8 (December 2010): 400–417.

Cott, Nancy. *The Grounding of Modern Feminism.* New Haven, CT: Yale University Press, 1987.

Crawford, Janet Estridge. "Rocking the Boat: Women's Participation in the World Council of Churches, 1948–1991." PhD diss. New Zealand: Victoria University of Wellington, 1995.

Culver, Elsie Thomas. *Women in the World of Religion.* Garden City, NY: Doubleday, 1967.

Cutten, George Barton. *The Psychological Phenomena of Christianity.* New York: Charles Scribner's Sons, 1908.

Dancyger, Lilly, ed. *Burn It Down: Women Writing about Anger.* New York: Seal Press, 2019.

Davis, Ozora. *Preaching by Laymen: A Study of the Elementary Principles of Presenting the Gospel.* New York: Fleming H. Revell, 1923.

De Maeyer, Jan, Leen Van Molle, Tine Van Osselaer, and Vincent Viaene, eds. *Gender and Christianity in Modern Europe: Beyond the Feminization Thesis.* Leuven, Belgium: Leuven University Press, 2012.

Demos, John. *The Enemy Within: 2,000 Years of Witch-Hunting in the Western World.* New York: Viking Penguin, 2008.

Denomme, Janine. "'To End the Day of Strife': Churchwomen and the Campaign for Integration, 1920–1970." PhD diss.: University of Pennsylvania, 2001.

Doely, Sarah Bentley, ed. *Women's Liberation and the Church: The New Demand for Freedom in the Life of the Christian Church.* New York: Association Press, 1970.

Douglas, Ann. *The Feminization of American Culture.* New York: Avon Books, 1977.

Douglass, H. Paul. *Protestant Cooperation in American Cities.* New York: Institute of Social and Religious Research, 1930.

Dreher, Rod. "The Feminization (and Decline) of Religion." *American Conservative* April 2, 2018, https://theamericanconservative.com/dreher/the-feminization-and-decline-of-religion/, accessed January 3, 2021.

Ecumenical Missionary Conference, New York, 1900, Vol. 1. New York: American Tract Society, 1900.

Englesman, Joan Chamberlain. "The Legacy of Georgia Harkness." In *Women in New Worlds: Historical Perspectives on the Wesleyan Tradition*, ed. Rosemary Skinner Keller, Louise Queen, and Hila Thomas, 338–358. Nashville, TN: Abingdon Press, 1981.

Evans, Sara. *Journeys That Opened Up the World: Women, Student Christian Movements, and Social Justice, 1955–1975.* New Brunswick, NJ: Rutgers University Press, 2004.

Fahs, Charles. *Trends in Protestant Giving: A Study of Church Finance in the United States.* New York: Institute of Social and Religious Research, 1929.

Felski, Rita. *The Gender of Modernity.* Cambridge, MA: Harvard University Press, 1995.

Fifield, James. *The Tall Preacher: Autobiography of Dr. James W. Fifield, Jr. with Bill Youngs.* Los Angeles, CA: Pepperdine University Press, 1977.

Findlay, James. *Church People in the Struggle: The National Council of Churches and the Black Freedom Movement, 1950–1970*. New York: Oxford University Press, 1993.

The First Assembly of the World Council of Churches, Held at Amsterdam, August 22nd to September 4th, 1948, ed. W. A. Visser 't Hooft. New York: Harper and Brothers, 1948.

Fleischer, Eva, and Donna Myers Ambrogi. "Grailville in the Sixties: Catechetics and Ecumenism," *U.S. Catholic Historian* 11 (Fall 1993): 37–44.

Foreign Missions Conference of North America, Being the Report of the Twenty-Seventh Conference of Foreign Mission Boards in the United States and Canada. New York: Foreign Missions Conference, 1920.

Friedman, Estelle. *No Turning Back: The History of Feminism and the Future of Women*. New York: Ballantine Books, 2002.

Fry, Luther. *The United States Looks at Its Churches*. New York: Institute of Social and Religious Research, 1930.

Fulton, Justin Dewey. *Woman as God Made Her; The True Woman*. Boston: Lee and Shepherd, 1869.

Gaartner, Bertil E., and Carl Strandberg. "The Experience of the Church of Sweden." In *Man, Woman, and Priesthood*, ed. Peter Moore, 123–133. London: SPCK, 1978.

George, Carol V. R. *God's Salesman: Norman Vincent Peale and the Power of Positive Thinking*. New York: Oxford University Press, 1993.

Gesling, Linda. *Mirror and Beacon: The History of Mission of the Methodist Church, 1939–1968*. New York: General Board of Global Ministries, 2005.

Gibson, Elise. "Ecumenism and the Ordination of Women." *CrossCurrents* 28 (Fall 1976): 299–305.

Gifford, Carolyn DeSwarte, ed., *The Debate in the Methodist Episcopal Church over Laity Rights for Women*. New York: Garland Publishing, 1987.

Gill, Jill. *Embattled Ecumenism: The National Council of Churches, the Vietnam War, and the Trials of the Protestant Left*. DeKalb: Northern Illinois University Press, 2011.

Glendon, Mary Ann. *A World Made New: Eleanor Roosevelt and the Universal Declaration of Human Rights*. New York: Random House, 2001.

Goldstein, Valerie Saiving. "The Human Situation: A Feminine View." *Journal of Religion* 40 (April 1960): 100–112.

Goss, Kristin A. "The Swells between the 'Waves': American Women's Activism, 1920–1965," in *The Oxford Handbook of U.S. Women's Social Movement Activism*, ed. Holly J. McCammon et. al. New York: Oxford University Press, 2017. 202010.1093/oxfordhb/9780190204204.013.2, accessed November 20.

Greenberg, Judith. "Paths of Resistance: French Women Working from the Inside." In *Experience and Expression Women, the Nazis, and the Holocaust*, ed. Eliza Baer and Myrna Goldberg, 131–160. Detroit: Wayne State University Press, 2003.

Hacker. Helen Mayer. "Women as a Minority Group," *Social Forces* 30 (October 1951): 60–69.

Hageman, Alice, ed. *Sexist Religion and Women in the Church*. New York: Association Press, 1974.

Hall, Peter Dobkin. "The Rise of the Civic Engagement Tradition." In *Taking Faith Seriously*, ed. Mary Jo Bane, Brent Coffin, and Richard Higgins, 21–59. Cambridge, MA: Harvard University Press, 2005.

Harter, Lloyd. *The Chicago Congregational Men's Movement: An Adequate Work by Men in Every Congregational Church in Chicago*. Chicago Young Men's Congregational Union, 1907.

Hendricks, Elizabeth. "Mildred McAfee Horton (1900–1994): Portrait of a Pathbreaking Christian Leader." *Journal of Presbyterian History* 76 (Summer 1998): 159–174.

Henold, Mary. *Catholic and Feminist: The Surprising History of the American Catholic Feminist Movement.* Chapel Hill: University of North Carolina Press, 2008.

Herzel, Susannah. *A Voice for Women: The Women's Department of the World Council of Churches.* Geneva, Switzerland: WCC, 1981.

Higginbotham, Evelyn Brooks. *Righteous Discontent: The Woman's Movement in the Black Church, 1880–1920.* Cambridge, MA: Harvard University Press, 1994.

Hocking, William Ernest. *Re-Thinking Missions: A Laymen's Inquiry after One Hundred Years.* New York: Harper and Brothers, 1932.

Hodgson, Godfrey. *America in Our Time: From World War II to Nixon, What Happened and Why.* New York: Vintage Books, 1976.

Hollinger, David. *After Cloven Tongue of Fire: Protestant Liberalism in Modern American History.* Princeton, NJ: Princeton University Press, 2012.

Hollinger, David. *Protestants Abroad: How Missionaries Tried to Change the World but Changed America.* Princeton NJ: Princeton University Press, 2017.

Hoover, Theressa. *With Unveiled Face: Centennial Reflections on Women and Men in the Community of the Church.* New York: Women's Division, General Board of Global Ministers of the Methodist Church, 1983.

Hornsby-Gutting, Angela. "'Women's Work': Foreign Missions, and Respectability in the National Training School for Women and Girls." *Journal of Women's History* 31 (Spring 2019): 37–61.

Horowitz, Daniel. *Betty Friedan and the Making of the Feminine Mystique: The American Left, the Cold War, and Modern Feminism.* Amherst: University of Massachusetts Press, 1998.

Howard, Ronald. *A Social History of American Family Sociology 1854–1940.* Westport, CT: Greenwood Press, 1981.

Hudnut-Beumler, James. *In Pursuit of the Almighty's Dollar: A History of Money and American Protestantism.* Chapel Hill: University of North Carolina Press, 2007.

Hulsether, Mark. *Building a Protestant Left: Christianity and Crisis Magazine, 1941–1993.* Knoxville: University of Tennessee Press, 1999.

Humphrey, Zephine. *God and Company.* New York: Harper and Brothers, 1953.

Humphrey Zephine. *The Sword of the Spirit.* New York: E. P Dutton, 1920.

Hutchinson, John A. *We Are Not Divided: A Critical and Historical Study of the Federal Council of the Churches of Christ in America.* New York: Round Table Press, 1941.

Hutchison, William, ed. *Between the Times: The Travail of the Protestant Establishment, 1900–1960.* Cambridge: Cambridge University Press, 1989.

Imhoff, Sarah. "The Myth of Jewish Feminization," *Jewish Social Studies: History, Culture, Society* n.s. 21 (Spring/Summer 2016): 126–152.

Iremonger, F. A. *William Temple: Archbishop of Canterbury: His Life and Letters.* London: Oxford University Press, 1948.

Jacques, Andre. *Madeleine Barot.* Geneva, Switzerland: WCC Publications, 1991.

Jensen, Richard. "Democracy, Republicanism, and Efficiency: The Values of American Politics, 1885–1930." In *Contesting Democracy: Substance and Structure in American Political History, 1775–2000.* ed. Byron E. Shafer and Anthony J. Badger, 149–180. Lawrence: University Press of Kansas, 2001.

Johnson, Melinda Marie. "Building Bridges: Church Women United and Social Reform Work across the Mid-Twentieth Century." PhD diss.: University of Kentucky, 2015.

Joint Committee of the Council of Women for Home Missions, Federation of Woman's Boards for Foreign Missions of North America, and the Federal Council of the Churches of Christ in America. *The Relative Place of Women in the Church*. New York: 1927.

Jones, Irene Ann. "A Recommended Program of Training for Northern Baptist Women Lay Leaders." PhD diss.: University of Pennsylvania, 1949.

Jones, Jacqueline. Interview with Thelma Stevens, February 13, 1972, Interview G-0058, Southern Oral History Program Collection (#4007), https://docsouth.unc.edu/sohp/html_use/G-0058.html, accessed October 2, 2020.

Jones, Robert. *White Too Long: The Legacy of White Supremacy in American Christianity*. New York: Simon and Schuster, 2020.

Kalven, Janet. *Women Breaking Boundaries: A Grail Journey 1940–1972*. Albany: SUNY Press, 1999.

Keller, Rosemary Skinner. *Georgia Harkness: For Such a Time as This*. Nashville, TN: Abingdon Press, 1992.

Kenaston, Connor S. "From Rib to Robe: Women's Ordination in the United Methodist Church." *Methodist History* 53, no. 3 (April 2015): 162–172.

Kenny, Gale. "The World Day of Prayer: Ecumenical Churchwomen and Christian Cosmopolitanism, 1920–1946." *Religion and American Culture* 27 (2017): 129–158.

Kirchwey, Freda, ed. *Our Changing Morality: A Symposium*. New York: Albert and Charles Boni Inc., 1924.

Klatch, Rebecca. "The Formation of Feminist Consciousness among Left- and Right-Wing Activists of the 1960s." *Gender and Society* 15 (December 2001): 795–797.

Kling, David. *The Bible in History: How the Texts Have Shaped the Times*. New York: Oxford University Press, 2004.

Knotts, Alice. "Methodist Women and Interracial Fairness in the 1930s." *Methodist History* 27 (July 1989): 230–240.

Knotts, Alice. "Race Relations in the 1920s: A Challenge to Southern Methodist Women." *Methodist History* 26 (July 1988): 199–212.

Kynett, A. J. *Our Laity: And Their Equal Rights without Distinction of Sex*. Cincinnati, OH: Cranston and Curtis, 1896.

Laquer, Thomas. *Making Sex: Body and Gender from the Greeks to Freud*. Cambridge, MA: Harvard University Press, 1990.

Lehman, E. C. *Women Clergy Breaking through Gender Barriers*. New Brunswick, NJ: Transaction, 1985.

Leiffer, Murray. *The Layman Looks at the Minister*. Nashville, TN: Abingdon-Cokesbury Press, 1947.

Leuba, James. *The Belief in God and Immortality: A Psychological, Anthropological, and Statistical Study*. Chicago: Open Court, 1916.

The Life of the Church: "The Madras Series," Presenting Papers Based upon the Meeting of the International Missionary Council, at Tambaram, Madras, India December 12th to 29th, *1938, Volume IV*. New York: International Missionary Council, 1939.

Lister, Ruth. *Citizenship: Feminist Perspectives*. New York: New York University Press, 1997.

Macfarland, Charles. *Christian Unity in the Making: The First Twenty-Five Years of the Federal Council of the Churches of Christ in America 1905–1930*. New York: Federal Council of Churches, 1949.

Marcum, John P. "Family, Birth Control, and Sexuality in the Christian Church (Disciples of Christ), 1880–1980." *Encounter* 52 (1991): 105–145.

Massey, Marilyn Chapin. *Feminine Soul: The Fate of an Ideal*. Boston: Beacon Press, 1985.

May, Mark, William Adams Brown, and Frank Shuttlesworth. *The Education of American Ministers*, 4 vols. New York: Institute of Social and Religious Research, 1934.

May, Melanie. *Bonds of Unity: Women, Theology, and the Worldwide Church*. Atlanta, GA: Scholars Press, 1989.

May, Melanie, ed. *Women and Church: The Challenge of Ecumenical Solidarity in an Age of Alienation*. Grand Rapids, MI: Eerdmans Publishing, 1991.

Maxson, Natalie. *Journey for Justice: The Story of Women in the WCC*. Geneva, Switzerland: World Council of Churches Publications, 2013.

McCulloch, Rhoda, *The War and the Woman Point of View*. New York: Association Press, 1920.

McGreevey, John. *Catholicism and American Freedom: A History*. New York: W.W. Norton, 2004.

Mead, Margaret. *Male and Female: A Study of the Sexes in a Changing World*. New York: William Morrow, 1949.

Meet Mrs. Jones, Typical American Baptist. New York: American Baptist Home Mission Societies, 1961.

Miller, Robert Moats. *American Protestantism and Social Issues, 1919–1939*. Chapel Hill: University of North Carolina Press, 1958.

Mislin, David. *Saving Faith: Making Religious Pluralism an American Value at the Dawn of the Secular Age*. Ithaca, NY: Cornell University Press, 2016.

Mobley, Kendal. *Helen Barrett Montgomery: The Global Mission of Domestic Feminism*. Waco, TX: Baylor University Press, 2009.

Moltmann, Jürgen. "Henriette Visser 't Hooft and Karl Barth." *Theology Today* 55 (January 1999): 524–531.

Montgomery, Helen Barrett. *Western Women in Eastern Lands: An Outline Study of Fifty Years of Woman's Work in Foreign Missions*. New York: Macmillan Co., 1910.

Moorhead, James H. "Presbyterians and the Mystique of Organizational Efficiency, 1870–1936," in *Reimagining Denominationalism*, ed. Robert Bruce Mullin and Russell E. Richey, 264–287. New York: Oxford University Press, 1994.

Morton, Nelle. *The Journey Is Home*. Boston: Beacon Press, 1985.

Murray, Gail S., ed. *Throwing Off the Cloak of Privilege: White Southern Women Activists in the Civil Rights Era*. Tallahassee: University Press of Florida, 2004.

Myrdal, Gunnar. *An American Dilemma: The Negro Problem and Modern Democracy*. Vol.2. New York: Harper and Brothers, 1944.

Nesbitt, Paula. *The Feminization of the Clergy in America*. New York: Oxford University Press, 1997.

Neumann, Caryn E. "Status Seekers: Long-Established Women's Organizations and the Women's Movement in the United States, 1945–1970s." PhD diss.: Ohio State University, 2006.

Newbigin, Lesslie. "The Legacy of W.A. Visser 't Hooft." *International Bulletin of Missionary Research* 16 (April 1992): 78–82.

Newsome, Clarence G. "Mary McLeod Bethune and the Methodist Episcopal Church North: In But Out," in *This Far by Faith: Readings in African-American Women's Religious Biography*, ed. Judith Weisenfeld and Richard Newman. New York: Routledge, 1996, 125–139.

Niebuhr, H. Richard. *The Social Sources of Denominationalism*. New York: Henry Holt and Co, 1929; rpt. ed. New York: Meridian Books, 1957.

Niebuhr, Ursula, ed. *Remembering Reinhold Niebuhr: Letters of Reinhold and Ursula M. Niebuhr*. San Francisco: HarperSanFrancisco, 1991.

Niebuhr, Ursula. "Women and the Church and the Fact of Sex." *Christianity and Crisis*. August 6, 1951, 106–110.

Noll, William T. "A Welcome in the Ministry: The 1920 and 1924 General Conferences Debate Clergy Rights for Women." *Methodist History* 30 (January 1992): 91–99.

Osiek, Carol. *Anger: On Being a Feminist in the Church*. New York: Paulist Press, 1986.

Parsons, Alice Beal. *Woman's Dilemma*. New York: Thomas Crowell, 1926.

Peabody, Lucy. "Woman's Place in Missions Fifty Years Ago and Now." *Missionary Review of the World* 50 (December 1927): 906–911.

Peale, Ruth. *The Adventure of Being a Wife*. Carmel, NY: Guideposts Association, Inc., 1971.

Penfield, Janet Harbison. "Women in the Presbyterian Church—A Historical Overview." *Journal of Presbyterian History* 55 (March 1976): 107–123.

Pew Research Center, "America's Changing Religious Landscape," May 12, 2015, https://www.pewforum.org/2015/05/12/americas-changing-religious-landscape/.

Phillips, Anne. "Gender and Modernity." *Political Theory* 46 (2018): 837–860. https://doi.org/10.1177/0090591171875747, accessed November 13, 2020.

The Place of Women in the Church on the Mission Field: Statements Prepared by Groups in North America, Great Britain, Germany, Netherlands, France, Switzerland, Denmark, Norway, Sweden, and Finland. New York: International Missionary Council, 1927.

Podles, Leon. *The Church Impotent: The Feminization of Christianity*. Dallas, TX: Spence Publications, 1999.

Porterfield, Amanda. *Corporate Spirit: Religion and the Rise of the Modern Corporation*. New York: Oxford University Press, 2018.

Prelinger, Catherine, ed. *Episcopal Women: Gender, Spirituality, and Commitment in an American Mainline Denomination*. New York: Oxford University Press, 1996.

Presbyterian Brotherhood: Report of the First Convention Held at Indianapolis, November Thirteenth through Fifteenth, 1906. Philadelphia: Presbyterian Board of Publication, 1907.

Presbyterian Brotherhood: Report of the Second Convention Held at Cincinnati, November Twelfth through Fourteenth. Philadelphia: Presbyterian Board of Publication, 1908.

Putnam, Robert, and David Campbell. *American Grace: How Religion Divides and Unites Us*. New York: Simon and Schuster, 2010.

Putnam, Robert, with Shaylyn Romey Garrett. *The Upswing: How America Came Together a Century Ago and How We Can Do It Again*. New York: Simon and Schuster, 2020.

Putney, Clifford. *Muscular Christianity: Manhood and Sports in Protestant America, 1880–1920*. Cambridge, MA: Harvard University Press, 2001.

Reports of the World Conference on Faith and Order, Lausanne, Switzerland, August 3 to 21, 1927. Boston: Published by the Secretariat, 1927.

Revised Interim Report of a Study on the Life and Work of Women in the Church. Geneva, Switzerland: World Council of Churches, 1948.

Reynolds, David S. "The Feminization Controversy: Sexual Stereotypes and the Paradoxes of Piety in Nineteenth-Century America." *New England Quarterly* 53 (March 1980): 96–106.

Rhinesmith, Deborah. "The League to Uphold Congregational Principles," *International Congregational Journal* 92 (Winter 2010): 39–52.

Richardson, Cyril. "Women in the Ministry," *Christianity and Crisis* (December 10, 1951) 11, 166–167.

Riley, Denise. *"Am I That Name?" Feminism and the Category of "Women" in History.* Minneapolis: University of Minnesota Press, 1988.

Robert, Dana. *American Women in Mission: The Modern Mission Era, 1792–1992.* Macon, GA: Mercer University Press, 1996.

Robert, Dana. *Gospel Bearers, Gender Barriers: Missionary Women in the Twentieth Century.* Maryknoll, NY: Orbis Books, 2002.

Robertson, Nancy Marie. *Christian Sisterhood, Race Relations, and the YWCA, 1906–1946.* Champaign-Urbana: University of Illinois Press, 2007.

Romero, Joan Arnold. "The Protestant Principle: A Woman's-Eye View of Barth and Tillich," in *Religion and Sexism: Images of Woman in the Jewish and Christian Traditions,* ed. Rosemary Radford Ruether, 319–341. New York: Simon and Schuster, 1974.

Roof, Wade Clark, and William McKinney. *American Mainline Religion: Its Changing Shape and Future.* 4th ed. New Brunswick, NJ: Rutgers University Press, 1992.

Rose, Kenneth. *American Women and the Repeal of Prohibition.* New York: New York University Press, 1996.

Rosen, Ruth. *The World Split Open: How the Modern Women's Movement Changed America.* New York: Penguin Books, 2001.

Rosenberg, Rosalind. *Divided Lives: American Women in the Twentieth Century.* New York: Hill and Wang, 1992.

Rosenberg, Rosalind. *Jane Crow: The Life of Pauli Murray.* New York: Oxford University Press, 2017.

Ross, Isabel Brown. *Working Together: The Story of the United Church Women of Southern California-Southern Nevada, 1934–1959.* n.p., n.d.

Rossinow, Doug. *The Politics of Authenticity: Liberalism, Christianity, and the New Left in America.* New York: Columbia University Press, 1998.

Royden, Maude. "American Women and Religion." *Forum* 80, no. 3 (September 1928): 348–357.

Sanderson, Ross W. *Church Cooperation in the United States: The Nation-Wide Backgrounds and Ecumenical Significance of State and Local Councils of Churches in Their Historical Perspective.* New York: Association of Council Secretaries, 1960.

Schlect, Christopher. "Onward Christian Administrators." PhD diss.: Washington State University, 2015.

Schmidt, Elisabeth. *When God Calls a Woman: The Struggle of a Woman Pastor in France and Algeria.* Trans. Allen Hackett. New York: Pilgrim Press, 1981.

Schmidt, William. *Architect of Unity: A Biography of Samuel McCrea Cavert.* New York: Friendship Press, 1978.

Shrader, Rick. "Richard Clearwaters," *Baptist Bible Tribune* 52 (October 15, 2001), https://printfriendly.com/p/g/KpHwpX, accessed April 4, 2020.

Schuyler, David. "Inventing a Feminine Past." *New England Quarterly* 51 (September 1978): 291–308.

Shannon, Margaret. *Just Because: The Story of the National Movement of Church Women United in the U.S.A. 1941 through 1975.* Corte Madera, CA: Omega Books, 1977.

Showalter, Elaine, ed. *These Modern Women: Autobiographical Essays from the Twenties.* New York: Feminist Press, 1970.

Silverstein, Brett, and Deborah Perlick. *The Cost of Competence: Why Inequality Causes Depression, Eating Disorders, and Illness in Women*. New York: Oxford University Press, 1995.

Sklar, Kathryn Kish, and Connie Shemo, eds. *Competing Kingdoms: Women, Mission, Nation, and the American Protestant Empire, 1812–1960*. Durham, NC: Duke University Press, 2010.

Sonderegger, Katherine. "Barth and Feminism," in *The Cambridge Companion to Karl Barth*, ed. John Webster, 258–273. Cambridge: Cambridge University Press, 2000.

Speers, Wallace, ed. *Laymen Speaking*. New York: Association Press, 1947.

Speight, Mae. "The Ministerial Reformation: A History of Women and the Mainline, 1920–1980." PhD diss.: University of Virginia, 2020.

Stanley, Brian. *The World Missionary Conference, Edinburgh 1910*. Grand Rapids, MI: Eerdmans, 2009.

Stanton, Elizabeth Cady. "The Solitude of Self," in *Elizabeth Cady Stanton/Susan B. Anthony: Correspondence, Writings, Speeches*, ed. Ellen Carol DuBois, 246–254. New York: Schocken Books, 1981.

Starbuck, Edwin. *The Psychology of Religion: An Empirical Study of the Growth of Religious Consciousness*. New York: Charles Scribner's Sons, 1899.

Stevens, Thelma. *Legacy for the Future: The History of Christian Social Relations in the Women's Division of Christian Service, 1940–1968*. Cincinnati, OH: Women's Division, Board of Global Ministries, 1978.

Stout, Harry S., and Catherine Brekus. "Declension, Gender, and the 'New Religious History,'" in *Belief and Behavior: Essays in the New Religious History*, ed. P. Vandemeer and R. Swierenga, 15–37. New Brunswick, NJ: Rutgers University Press, 1991.

Strong, Karen Heetderks. "Ecclesiastical Suffrage: The First Women Participants at General Conference in the Antecedents of the United Methodist Church. *Methodist History* 25 (October 1986): 29–33.

Task Group on the History of the Central Jurisdiction. *To a Higher Glory: The Growth and Development of Black Women Organized for Mission in the Methodist Church, 1940–1968, by the Task Group on the History of the Central Jurisdiction Women's Organization*. Nashville, TN: United Methodist Church, 1968.

Thompson, Michael G. *For God and Globe: Christian Internationalism in the United States between the Great War and the Cold War*. Ithaca, NY: Cornell University Press, 2015.

Todd, Mary. *Authority Vested: A Story of Identity and Change in the Lutheran Church— Missouri Synod*. Grand Rapids, MI: Eerdmans, 2000.

Trollinger, William Vance. *God's Empire: William Bell Riley and Midwestern Fundamentalism*. Madison: University of Wisconsin Press, 1990.

Troxell, Barbara B. "Ordination of Women in the United Methodist Tradition." *Methodist History* 37 (January 1999): 119–130.

Turner, James. *Without God, without Creed: The Origins of Unbelief in America*. Baltimore: Johns Hopkins University Press, 1985.

Underhill, M. M. "Women's Work for Missions: Three Home Base Studies." *International Review of Missions* 14 (July 1925): 379–399.

United States Bureau of the Census, *Religious Bodies, 1906*. 2 vols. Washington, DC, 1906.

United States Bureau of the Census. *Religious Bodies: 1916*. Washington, DC, 1919.

United States Bureau of the Census. *Religious Bodies: 1936*. Vol. 1. Washington, DC, 1941.

Verdesi, Elizabeth Howell. *In but Still Out: Women in the Presbyterian Church*. Philadelphia: Westminster Press, 1976.

Visser 't Hooft, Henriette. "Eva, wo bist Du?" *Student World* 27 (1934): 12–15.

Visser 't Hooft, W. A. "Karl Barth and the Ecumenical Movement." *Ecumenical Review* 32 (April 1980): 129–151.

Wacker, Grant. "Pearl S. Buck and the Waning of the Missionary Impulse." *Church History* 72 (December 2003): 852–874.

Wacker, Grant. "Second Thoughts on the Great Commission: Liberal Protestants and Foreign Missions," in *Earthen Vessels: American Evangelicals and Foreign Missions*, ed. Joel Carpenter and Wilbert Shenk, 281–300. Grand Rapids: Eerdmans, 1990.

Ware, Susan. *Partner and I: Molly Dewson, Feminism, and New Deal Politics*. New Haven, CT: Yale University Press, 1987.

Webb, Pauline. *She Flies Beyond: Memories and Hopes of Women in the Ecumenical Movement*. Geneva, Switzerland: WCC Publications, 1993.

Weber, Hans Ruedi. *The Courage to Live: A Biography of Suzanne de Dietrich*. Geneva, Switzerland: WCC Publications, 1995.

Weeks, Louis. "The Incorporation of American Religion: The Case of the Presbyterians." *Religion and American Culture: A Journal of Interpretation* 1 (Winter 1991): 101–118.

Weisenfeld, Judith. *African American Women and Christian Activism: New York's Black YWCA, 1905–1945*. Cambridge, MA: Harvard University Press, 1997.

Wells, Marguerite M. "Some Effects of Woman Suffrage." *Annals of the Academy of Political and Social Science* 143 (May 1929): 207–216.

Welter, Barbara. "The Feminization of American Religion, 1800–1860," in *Dimity Convictions*. Athens: Ohio University Press, 1976.

White, Susan. "'The Church Militant': A. Maude Royden and the Quest for Women's Equality in the Inter-War Years," in *The Theologically Informed Heart: Essays in Honor of David J. Gouwens*, ed. Warner M. Bailey, Lee C. Barrett, and James O. Duke, 47–71. Eugene, OR: Pickwick Publications, 2014.

Whitfield, Stephen. *The Culture of the Cold War*. 2nd ed. Baltimore: Johns Hopkins University Press, 1996.

Willard, Frances. *Woman in the Pulpit*. Boston: Woman's Christian Temperance Union, 1888.

"Women's Status in Protestant Churches." *Information Service* 19, no. 37 (November 16, 1940): 1–12.

Woodhead, Linda. "Gendering Secularization Theory." *Social Compass* 55 (1982): 187–192.

Woolf, Virginia. *A Room of One's Own*. London: Harcourt, 1929.

Wright, Conrad. "The Growth of Denominational Bureaucracies: A Neglected Aspect of American Church History." *Harvard Theological Review* 77 (1984): 177–194.

Wuthnow, Robert. *After Heaven: Spirituality since the 1950s*. Berkeley: University of California Press, 1998.

Wyker, Mossie. *Church Women in the Scheme of Things*. St. Louis, MO: Bethany Press, 1953.

Wynn, John Charles. "Where the Churches Speak and Where They Are Silent," in *Foundations for Christian Family Policy*, ed. Elizabeth Steel Genné and William Henry Genné, 35–40. New York: National Council of Churches of Christ in the U.S.A., 1961.

Zerbst, Fritz. *The Office of Women in the Church: A Study in Practical Theology*. Trans. Albert G. Merkens. St Louis: Concordia Publishing House, 1955; rpt. ed. Omaha: Mercinator Press, 2017.

Zikmund, Barbara, Adair Lummis, and Patricia Chang. *An Uphill Calling: Ordained Women in Contemporary Protestantism*. Louisville, KY: Westminster/John Knox Press, 1997.

Index

For the benefit of digital users, indexed terms that span two pages (e.g., 52–53) may, on occasion, appear on only one of those pages.